BENJ
DISRAELI

To Geraldine, Liam and Rosemary

BENJAMIN DISRAELI

THE NOVEL AS POLITICAL DISCOURSE

Michael Flavin

sussex
ACADEMIC
PRESS

BRIGHTON • PORTLAND

2 4 6 8 10 9 7 5 3 1

First published 2005 in Great Britain by
SUSSEX ACADEMIC PRESS
PO Box 2950
Brighton BN2 5SP

and in the United States of America by
SUSSEX ACADEMIC PRESS
920 NE 58th Ave   Suite 300
Portland, Oregon 97213–3786

British Library Cataloguing in Publication Data
A CIP catalogue record for this book is available from the British Library.

Library of Congress Cataloging-in-Publication Data
Flavin, Michael.
    Benjamin Disraeli : the novel as political discourse / Michael
Flavin.
        p. cm.
    Includes bibliographical references and index.
    ISBN 1-903900-30-1 (acid-free paper) —
    ISBN 1-903900-80-8 (pbk. : acid-free paper)
    1. Disraeli, Benjamin, Earl of Beaconsfield, 1804–1881—
Criticism and interpretation. 2. Politics and literature—
Great Britain—History—19th century. 3. Political fiction,
English—History and criticism. 4. Great Britain—Politics
and government—1837–1901. I. Title.
PR4087.F58   2004
823'.8—dc22   2004000510
                                                      CIP

Typeset and designed by G&G Editorial, Brighton
Printed by MPG Books, Ltd, Bodmin, Cornwall
This book is printed on acid-free paper.

Contents

Preface

Benjamin Disraeli emerged from the milieu of the British middle class to become Conservative Prime Minister. In an era in which social mobility was a very limited concept, his life was remarkable. However, even before Disraeli entered Parliament in 1837, he had already gained a significant reputation as a novelist. Disraeli's literary achievements were subsequently overshadowed by his political career, but it is in his novels that he first produced a coherent and consistent political philosophy based around material and equal prosperity and social reform. The same Disraeli who wrote *Vivian Grey* would later support the Corn Laws; the author of *Sybil* was the same anti-Whiggist who made Queen Victoria the Empress of India.

This book is primarily a literary study. It is not a biography, nor is it an analysis of Disraeli's contribution to politics. That said, an examination of how Disraeli's novels construct a political standpoint will inevitably encroach on his life both inside and outside Parliament. A handful of books have been published previously on Disraeli's career as a novelist. However, this book broadens the perspective on Disraeli the writer, taking into account his work within other literary genres and non-fiction. Consequently, this wide-ranging study of Disraeli's literary excursions investigates the connections between Disraeli's political and literary lives, showing how he gestated a distinct political creed through his artistic endeavours. The Disraeli that emerges from his literary works is both a traditionalist and a radical, advocating government by the upper classes alongside a far-reaching agenda of social and economic amelioration.

Acknowledgements

I am grateful to Rochester Independent College and the University of Kent at Medway for sponsoring my research. I am also indebted to staff at the Bodleian library, Oxford, for allowing me access to the Disraeli Papers. Louis James commented upon early drafts of the chapters, and Ron Knights provided technical support. In addition, I am glad to acknowledge a debt to previous scholars, whose work on Disraeli has substantially informed my own analysis. In particular, Robert Blake's biography of Disraeli was a constant source of reference, while Daniel Schwarz's *Disraeli's Fiction* (1979) influenced considerably my own critical appreciation of Disraeli as a novelist.

Jacket/cover illustration: Benjamin Disraeli, Earl of Beaconsfield, Prime Minister and novelist, by Sir John Everett Millais, 1st Baronet and President of the Royal Academy (1829–1896), 1276 mm × 931mm. Reproduced by permission of the National Portrait Gallery, London.

Frontispiece: Benjamin Disraeli, Earl of Beaconsfield, by Harry Furniss. Medium: pen and ink, 229 mm × 216 mm. Reproduced by permission of the National Portrait Gallery, London.

Introduction) 'I wish to act what I write'

'I wish to act what I write.' These words from an entry in a diary Benjamin Disraeli kept between September 1833 and 1836 (known as the 'mutiliated diary' because of its half-destroyed condition), express the close, even inextricable relationship between his writing and his life. Through his writings Disraeli postulated his personal investment in society and politics. Often, fictional heroes with strong autobiographical traits reach beyond their own milieu to attain both material and spiritual prosperity. The hero of Disraeli's first novel, Vivian Grey, wants to succeed in politics but is thwarted by the malign influence of others; the hero of his final novel, Endymion, enjoys sufficient patronage to guide him from office junior to Prime Minister. By the time of *Endymion's* publication Disraeli had twice led a Conservative government, an achievement that would have appeared unlikely when he began his literary career. Disraeli's wish to *act* what he *wrote* was eventually fulfilled, his early literary success translating into later political acclaim.

It is not the purpose of this book to recreate Disraeli's life through a study of his novels; such an endeavour would be superfluous in view of the fact that a large number of biographies of Disraeli have been published since his death in 1881, and there is no sign of the interest in Disraeli as a political and cultural figure coming to an end. Instead, this book examines Disraeli's published writings, with particular emphasis on his novels, in order to trace the development of his political ethos from his youth, encompassing his spell as an MP for Maidstone (1837–41) through to 1880–1, the period immediately after his second spell as Prime Minister.

Disraeli's novels are the site on which he produced and developed the ideas which informed his political creed. The series of dilemmas and challenges confronting his fictional heroes reveals how Disraeli constructed a set of principles around which his politics were rooted. From the exploratory adventures of his first published novel, *Vivian Grey*, through to the declamatory method of the Young England trilogy, and finally to the evaluative approach of *Endymion*, Disraeli used the novel to develop and present ideas connected with forms of government and the relations between social classes.

Chapter one, 'The Young Man', focuses on the 1820s and 1830s, the decades during which Disraeli was at his most productive as a writer. The chapter undertakes a wide-ranging examination of Disraeli's literary output of the 1820s and '30s, taking into account his short stories, poetry, drama and non-fiction as well as his novels. In this phase of his career, the experimental nature of much of his work reflected his own struggle for a cohesive identity which would allow him to realise his ambitions. Novels such as *Vivian Grey, The Young Duke* and *Venetia* feature characters seeking to achieve an accommodation with the world around them, their values and expectations shaped by experience, until they are able to come to terms with their environment. In contrast to these pragmatic existentialists, *Alroy* features a hero who wishes to subsume the world to his will and ends up being beheaded. The tension between character and environment is a central feature of Disraeli's early literary output. The author was recreating in art an inner dilemma – how much a politician should respond to the social environment, and how much they should seek to control that environment – which required resolution in order for him to have a coherent strategy with which to embark upon political life. The aim of chapter one is to present a comprehensive account of Disraeli's thoughts and principles as they developed, prior to his becoming a parliamentarian.

Chapter two, 'The Young Englander', argues for the coherence of the Young England trilogy. The final novel in the series, *Tancred*, can be seen as a departure from the concerns raised in *Coningsby* and *Sybil*, as it leaves political struggle in England behind, and follows the hero's journey to the East. However, *Tancred* builds upon the explicitly political issues debated in the earlier two novels, and thereafter launches an examination of the very basis on which government can exist. For Disraeli, the basis was faith, by which he meant not only religion, but also unswerving adherence to principles validated by history. Consequently, Catholicism, with its historical longevity, had appealed to the young Disraeli, but, by the 1840s, Judaism became Disraeli's faith of choice. However, for Disraeli this did not mean membership of a formal congregation, but a belief in the stoicism, potency and wisdom of the Jewish race, one to which he himself belonged, despite being converted to Christianity in his youth by his father. In the 1840s Disraeli was clearly 'using' the novel for political purposes. As he disassociated himself from his party leader, Sir Robert

Peel, his novels allowed the presentation of a clear political philosophy in which the twin platforms of aristocratic rule and social responsibility predominated. The final text of this phase of Disraeli's career, *Lord George Bentinck*, is nominally a biography of a parliamentary ally. However, *Lord George Bentinck* promotes unambiguously Disraeli's own agenda on a range of subjects, from his conflict with Peel over the Corn Laws to his theory of race.

In chapter three, 'The Elder Statesman', Disraeli's last two novels, *Lothair* and *Endymion* are examined, together with the unfinished work, *Falconet*. *Lothair* is arguably the most skilfully written of Disraeli's novels, the fruition of decades of literary composition across a multitude of genres. The chapter places Disraeli's final novels primarily in the context of his literary *oeuvre* as a whole. Consequently, *Lothair* is viewed in relation to the earlier *Tancred*. The chief difference between them is that Lothair returns to England, rather than remaining in the East, as Tancred does. Written at a time when Disraeli was formulating a party-politicised concept of patriotism, *Lothair* articulates faith in England and mistrust of the foreign, whether national, political or spiritual. In *Endymion* a sense of balance and reconciliation is more pronounced, as the hero rises from obscurity to become Prime Minister. There is a comparative absence of anxiety in *Endymion*, which implies a sort of evaluative reflection from Disraeli. Paradoxically, and with typical Disraelian energy, he then went on to commence a highly political and rebarbative work, *Falconet*, but died while the novel was still in its early stages.

The chapters that follow concentrate primarily on exploring the ways in which the novels contribute to the development of Benjamin Disraeli's distinct political philosophy. The textual analysis is supported by an assessment of Disraeli's non-fiction writings, along with biographical information and a consideration of the wider literary, political, social and economic contexts within which he worked. For Disraeli, writing satisfied an *intrinsic* purpose, as he played through and developed his ideas in an imaginative form. Moreover, it also fulfilled an *extrinsic* agenda, in the sense that it provided him with an effective platform from which he could reach a wider audience beyond the confines of Parliament. Crucially, this audience became increasingly important politically, as the electoral franchise was extended in stages throughout the nineteenth century. In an act of symbiosis between life and literature, Disraeli acted what he wrote, and his writing, by developing his thoughts and raising his public profile, enabled him to act on increasingly influential stages.

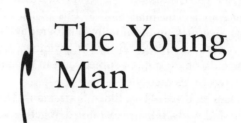

Chapter One | The Young Man

'Pity his fatal youth!'
The Young Duke

In his diary Disraeli identifies three key novels with regard to his personal development: 'in *Vivian Grey* I have pourtrayed [sic] my active and real ambition. In *Alroy* my ideal ambition. The P.R. (Disraeli's preferred title for *Contarini Fleming* was Psychological Romance) is a developm[en]t of my poetic character. This Trilogy is the secret history of my feelings. I shall write no more about myself.'[1] This chapter will focus on these three novels in order to construct a portrait of Disraeli's persona as it developed through the 1820s and '30s. The hero that dominated this phase of Disraeli's literary output was fundamentally a dreamer, a visionary. The context of Disraeli's imaginings took a variety of forms, some of which were unquestionably political: they demonstrate both a development and, paradoxically, a consistency of thought which refutes the accusation made against Disraeli, both in his lifetime and thereafter, that he was an unprincipled opportunist. As early as 1818, a thirteen-year-old Disraeli had written that, 'the reason why Republics so soon degenerate in Europe is that the members of them are men who have been governed by a monarchy, who have partaken of the advantages which monarchy dispenses and consequently become disappointed and dissatisfied with a republican form of government', and his pro-monarchy, anti-republican stance remained a feature of his thought and his political conduct.[2] Disraeli's other published works of the 1820s and '30s will also be analysed, in order to get a full sense of the development of his thought during this formative period, in which he explored issues of politics, faith and the individual.

According to Philip Guedella, editor of the Bradenham edition of Disraeli's works, Leigh Hunt's *Indicator* published a short story by Disraeli, 'A True Story' (about a woman with a broken heart) in July 1820, when Disraeli was just fifteen.[3] In 1823, Disraeli and his friend,

William George Meredith, produced two copies of a reworking of the fairy tale, *Rumpel Stiltskin*. Meredith also became engaged to Disraeli's sister, Sarah, but the marriage never took place as Meredith died in Cairo in 1831, where he and Disraeli had been travelling. According to Michael Sadleir, who wrote the preface for the published edition of *Rumpel Stiltskin* in 1952, 'tradition maintains that the arias, songs and choruses were the work of Disraeli', with Meredith supplying the rest.[4] The preface to the work shows the good humour with which it was composed, as Disraeli and Meredith attempt to persuade the reader that the work was 'writ at Oxforde in ye yere of our Lord 1596'. The manuscript copy of *Rumpel Stiltskin* (now held at the Bodleian library), features some elaborate capital letters and intricate small sketches (purportedly supplied by Meredith's sister). The book is an amusing distraction, light entertainment, rather than a serious foray into the world of literature.[5]

In 1824 Disraeli wrote his first novel, *Aylmer Papillon,* a political satire. It was rejected by the publisher John Murray, and most of it was subsequently destroyed. However, features of *Aylmer Papillon* resurfaced in Disraeli's satire of 1828, *The Voyages of Captain Popanilla,* as both texts are set in Vraibleusia (an imaginary island located in the middle of the Indian Ocean). *Aylmer Papillon* opens with the eponymous hero discovering that a man is to be transported for killing a hare, from which he assumes that the hare is a sacred animal, leading to a confrontation when he sees one being served at an inn. Disraeli satirises the harsh punishment meted out to the poacher, exhibiting sympathy for the common man, a theme which was to influence aspects of both his literary and political career. The inn characters' names, crudely satirical, reflect the triviality of the wealthy and powerful. Among those Aylmer meets are Sir Somebody Somebody, the Honourable Nobody Nobody, and Lord Knows Who.[6] In addition, the experience of writing a first novel and having it rejected by a publisher is narrated in his novel of 1832, *Contarini Fleming*; thus *Aylmer Papillon*, while not appearing in a published form, was not without its uses.

In 1825, a financier, John Diston Powles, hired Disraeli to write on the state of the financial markets in relation to South American mining companies. Powles was an interested party in these matters, being a director of a number of the companies involved. Subsequently, John Murray published *An Inquiry into the Plans, Progress and Policy of the American Mining Companies*. It was, in effect, an extended advertisement for the profitability of central and southern American mining companies, and it was the first of three such pamphlets written by Disraeli in 1825. *An Inquiry* was published anonymously and it is perhaps just as well: Disraeli himself had been buying shares in South American mining companies since November 1824, and at the end of January 1825 he bought some on behalf of John Murray. Therefore, he was clearly not a disinterested commentator on the subject. The then Chancellor of the Exchequer, Lord Eldon, had threatened to intervene in the rampant speculation on foreign mining companies, and *An Inquiry* is in part a presentation of the counter-argument. In the event Lord Eldon did not take action, though this was not due to the impact of Disraeli's pamphlet.

An Inquiry is notable for its sense of confidence. The writer appears to have a thorough grasp of his subject matter, and as early as page six informs us of the South American miners' 'utter deficiency of the principles of subterraneous geometry'. A similar sense of implicit nationalism is present when Disraeli states, 'by the introduction of English capital, skill, experience and machinery, the expenses of working these mines might be greatly reduced, and their produce much augmented' (pp. 15–16). However, Disraeli's vigorous promotion of companies in which he had a clear, vested interest destroys the integrity of the pamphlet: 'we have every reason to believe that they [the companies] are both desirous and enabled to fulfil the contracts which they have entered into with the public' (p. 41). Furthermore, far from acknowledging his own investments in the companies, he deliberately feigns neutrality. *An Inquiry* must therefore go down as an inglorious début in publishing; at its worst, it is downright disingenuous. Disraeli informs us that, 'unfortunately, there is a set of individuals in this world who are very desirous of gaining property without working for it. They have what they consider "enough to speculate on," but loss to them is annihilation' (p. 56). This is an apt statement of Disraeli's own position, and is further validated when we consider that his reckless speculation did result in considerable loss and debts that he was unable to discharge fully until 1849. He further criticises writers 'detailing false statements in a flippant style' (p. 69), but again the accusation would be better directed against Disraeli himself. At the end of the pamphlet Disraeli writes, 'we now close these observations: imperfect as they may be, they have been penned in the spirit of sincerity, and with no other view than that of enabling the public to form an opinion on a very important subject' (p. 88). The impression of the writer of this pamphlet as a fraudster is underlined in the preface to the third edition, which informs the reader that, 'these passages have been written for the information and benefit of the public'.

However, beneath the skilled rhetoric of the would-be confidence trickster lie one or two thoughts relevant to Disraeli's future political development. He declares himself hostile to economic competition, deriding 'the false business which is created by this system' (pp. 52–3). Conversely, he is supportive of the mining companies: 'by them no private interests are injured, but the interests and resources of great nations supported and extended; by them no unnatural demand for labour is created, but a people employed and enriched by an employment which is neither temporary nor unnecessary' (p. 53). By showing a large and powerful structure acting in the interests of its operatives whilst also pursuing its own, Disraeli presents a prefiguration of the system of benign feudalism which was to occupy a significant place in his later political creed. Industry becomes beneficial to country and individual, creating a mutual symbiotic, financial relationship. Disraeli went on to publish two further pamphlets in 1825 on similar themes: *Lawyers and Legislators, or Notes on the American Mining Companies* and *The Present State of Mexico.*[7]

Extensive Stock Exchange losses were bad enough for Disraeli, but a far worse calamity lay just around the corner. The fiasco of *The Representative*, a short-lived and financially ruinous newspaper project initially conceived as a rival to *The Times*, was more than just an unsuccessful enterprise. Knowledge of the débâcle is necessary in order to be able to fully understand the significance behind Disraeli's first published novel, *Vivian Grey*. In August 1825, an agreement was drawn up between Disraeli, Murray and Powles. A new daily paper was to be produced: Murray would put up half the capital, and Disraeli and Powles a quarter each. In September Disraeli travelled to Edinburgh hoping to get J. G. Lockhart, Sir Walter Scott's nephew, involved in the project. All of the available information suggests that Disraeli revelled in this escapade. He wrote encoded letters to Murray in London, referring to himself as The Political Puck, and he conceived schemes far more grand than merely a daily newspaper to challenge *The Times*. In his letters he stated that, if Lockhart could be found a seat in Parliament, 'I have no doubt that I shall be able to organise, in the interest, with which I am now engaged, a most IMMENSE PARTY, and MOST SERVICEABLE ONE.'[8] It is highly unlikely that this had ever been part of Murray's intention when he despatched Disraeli to Scotland, a point underlined by Thom Braun: 'his letters to Murray speak of organising a new political party, but there is no supporting evidence to suggest that this was anything other than a figment of Disraeli's active fantasy'.[9] Lockhart subsequently declined a central role in the new project, seeking and accepting instead the editorship of Murray's successful periodical, *Quarterly Review*, while agreeing to contribute to the new paper.

In December 1825, having come up with the name for the new paper, Disraeli vanished from the project. It is not known for certain what brought about his departure, but it seems likely that part of the reason lay in internal feuding within the Murray camp. In particular, J. W. Croker, an important writer at the *Quarterly*, was concerned at the extent to which Lockhart's arrival at the magazine would threaten his own position.[10] Disraeli was aware of the forces organised against him, and wrote to Murray on 23 November complaining of the 'junta of official scamps who have too long enslaved you'.[11] Lockhart himself, having gained the prestigious position at the *Quarterly Review*, was no longer interested in *The Representative*. A less intriguing, though obviously pertinent, reason for Disraeli's withdrawal from *The Representative* lay in the fact that a crash in the financial markets had wiped out the value of Disraeli's shares in the mining companies and he was therefore unable to provide his share of the capital. The paper itself came out in January 1826 and lasted for six months, during which time Murray lost £26,000. Later, in 1854, Disraeli was keen to distance himself from any involvement in the project, writing in a letter, 'I never was Editor of the Representative newspaper, or even a contributor, in an way or degree, to its columns.'[12] *The Representative* provided an outlet for Disraeli's rampant ambition but, at this early stage in his career, he was devoid of pragmatism; his unfettered imagination projected glory without taking heed of any of the obstacles lying in wait.

VIVIAN GREY

'But am I entitled – I, who can lose nothing; am I entitled to play with other men's fortunes?'

The Representative is relevant to *Vivian Grey* because the first two volumes of Disraeli's début novel replay the entire fiasco from Disraeli's perspective, with the episode transposed from the journalistic to the explicitly political realm, a gesture prefigured in reality by Disraeli's letters to Murray from Edinburgh in November 1825.[13] The internal dating of the novel spans the period from the summer of 1825 to the spring of 1826. However, *The Representative* is not the only influence on *Vivian Grey*. In the spring of 1825, *Tremaine, or the Man of Refinement* was published anonymously (it was later revealed that the writer was Robert Plumer Ward). According to Robert Blake, '*Tremaine* was perhaps the first so-called "society novel" to be published in England'.[14] *Tremaine* recorded fashionable life with detail and accuracy. Its success was achieved in part through its anonymous authorship, which suggested that the individual was himself a man of high society, obliged to protect his position and reputation through namelessness. Disraeli followed the same path (he is purported to have taken the idea of his novel from

Tremaine)[15] and it was as well in view of the fact that he was not part of high society. In the early part of *Vivian Grey*, Disraeli refers to *Tremaine*: Vivian states, 'I thought the third edition of *Tremaine* would be a very fair specimen of your ancient literature' (p. 52). In book seven, part of the final three volumes of *Vivian Grey* published in 1827, the fashionable novel is itself satirised through the person of von Chronicle, the writer: 'according to von Chronicle, we have all, for a long time, been under a mistake. We have ever considered that the first point to be studied in novel writing is character: miserable error! It is costume. Variety of incident, novelty, and nice discrimination of character; interest of story, and all those points which we have hitherto looked upon as necessary qualities of a fine novel, vanish before the superior attractions of variety of dresses, exquisite descriptions of the cloak of a signor, or the trunk hose of a serving man' (p. 426). Fiasco and accomplished literary satire serve to highlight the eclecticism, both in style and content, by which the work as a whole is characterised.

Within *Vivian Grey*, characters and incidents clearly relate to *The Representative*. Murray becomes the Marquis of Carabas, a politician in decline, temporarily galvanised by the dynamic Vivian but ultimately malleable, particularly in the hands of unscrupulous parties who undermine the faithful Vivian's position. Lockhart becomes Cleveland (with his home changed from Scotland to Wales), Powles is converted to Premium and Croker becomes Stapylton Toad, an unpleasant and transparent sycophant. Croker was also later to appear as the devious and ultimately vanquished Rigby in *Coningsby*.

While *Vivian Grey* provides Disraeli's perspective on *The Representative*, the narrative style is not always characterised by verisimilitude. This has been used by some critics to challenge the extent to which *Vivian Grey* is strictly autobiographical. Thom Braun notes that 'the similarities between Murray and Carabas as characters are virtually non-existent', while Matthew Whiting Rosa states that 'no resemblance exists between Murray and Carabas'.[16] Certainly, some of the descriptions of Carabas, in particular, the final confrontation between Vivian and Carabas (at the end of book four, chapter three), are highly dramatic:

'My Lord!' said Vivian.

'I will not hear you; out on your fair words! They have duped me enough already. That I, with my high character and connections! That I, the Marquis of Carabas, should have been the victim of the arts of a young scoundrel!'

Vivian's fist was once clenched, but it was only for a moment. The marquess leant back in his chair with his eyes shut. In the agony of the

moment a projecting tooth of his upper jaw had forced itself through his
under lip, and from the wound the blood was flowing freely over his dead
white countenance. Vivian left the room. (p. 160)

The language of popular melodrama, combined with the final image's
indebtedness to the waning gothic genre, conjure up a scene far exceeding
the boundaries of realism. However, Disraeli's point is surely to dramatise a scene in order to place the stoic Vivian in definite opposition to the
monstrous Carabas. The imagery serves to justify the hero's conduct without recourse to serious analysis, in the context of which Vivian and, by
extension, Disraeli himself, might not emerge so favourably. In addition,
in *Vivian Grey* Disraeli deliberately plays with modes of representation
for comic effect. The narrator is satirical throughout the novel: on poets,
'there was a Mr John Brown, a fashionable poet, and who, ashamed of his
own name, published his melodies under the more euphonious and romantic title of "Clarence Devonshire"' (p. 26); on the language of politicians,
'here his Lordship got parliamentary' (p. 30); and on intellectuals, 'surely
you have heard of his "Treatise on Man"? A treatise on a subject in which
every one is interested, written in a style which no one can understand' (p.
424). While realism and satire jostle for centre stage within the text, the
autobiographical underpinning to *Vivian Grey* remains valid.

At times the satire gives way to straightforward comedy (unless it is
the readers themselves who are being satirised). In book seven, chapter
nine, the narrator draws attention to some of the unrealistic features of
his account: 'the season, as we have often had occasion to remark in the
course of these volumes, was singularly fine' (p. 468). Earlier, in the
opening to book three, chapter seven, the narrator playfully hands over
control of his text to the reader: 'what is this chapter to be about? Come,
I am inclined to be courteous! You shall choose the subject of it. What
shall it be, sentiment or scandal? A love-scene or a lay-sermon? You will
not choose?' (p. 124). Considering the variety of stylistic techniques used
throughout the novel, it is clear that the generic contexts of *Vivian Grey*
are as wide-ranging as the social and geographical ones. It is not merely
a fashionable novel, as Vivian acidly highlights the genre's limitations:
'there was a Mr Thomas Smith, a fashionable novelist; that is to say, a
person who occasionally publishes three volumes, one half of which contain the adventures of a young gentleman in the country, and the other
volume and a half the adventures of the same young gentleman in the
metropolis' (p. 26). *Vivian Grey*'s canvas of narrative and stylistic levels
is varied and broad, reflecting its central protagonist's search for selfhood and a satisfactory outlet for his talents. However, this project is
undoubtedly grounded in *The Representative* and its fallout. In the man-

uscript of the novel, 'Chiefswood' is the name given to the character who would eventually become Lockhart. It is no coincidence that Chiefswood was the name of Lockhart's house.[17] The choice of Carabas as the name for Murray's character in the text is also significant. As Jane Ridley, among others, has pointed out, the Marquess of Carabas features in the folk tale of Puss in Boots. It is the name given to a miller's son by Puss, and the cat subsequently makes the boy's fortune through his wit and daring.[18] Therefore, the renaming of Murray in *Vivian Grey* becomes a defiant statement, expressing Disraeli's own sense of betrayal after having (from his point of view) advanced the cause of an undeserving individual. The renaming also signifies Disraeli's on-going confidence in his own acumen. *Vivian Grey* retells Disraeli's recent past and projects into his uncertain future, featuring a restless wanderer teaching and learning.

In what is an introspective novel, an important aspect of Vivian's self-conception is Byronic; in the opening chapter of book four he expresses great admiration for the recently deceased (1824) Byron: 'there was the man! And that such a man should be lost to us at the very moment that he had begun to discover why it had pleased the Omnipotent to have endowed him with such powers!' (p. 150). He shortly thereafter adds, 'Byron's mind was like his own ocean, sublime in its yeasty madness, beautiful in its glittering summer brightness, mighty in the lone magnificence of its waste of waters, gazed upon from the magic of its own nature, yet capable of representing, but as in a glass darkly, the natures of all others' (pp. 151–2). The reference to St Paul's First Letter to the Corinthians 13:12 elevates Byron to near-messianic status; he is the role model to whom Vivian aspires, especially as he too is a wanderer in the mould of Byron's Childe Harold, cruelly misunderstood by the world at large. However, Vivian experiences considerable self-doubt when he asks, 'but am I entitled, I, who can lose nothing, am I entitled to play with other men's fortunes? Am I all the time deceiving myself with some wretched sophistry?' (p. 113). Moreover, when self-doubt is not present, Vivian is concerned about the implications of his own ambition. In book three, chapter five, when Mrs Felix Lorraine tries to poison him, he thinks of her as a double of himself. Vivian thus emerges as a philosophical romantic in the Byronic mould, absorbed in his personal experiences and musing, yet he is also aware of the social implications of his philosophy, and the extent to which his self-centredness spills over into a lack of empathy for others, right up to the point at which it may mutate into ruthlessness.

An important figure in Vivian's development is Beckendorff, who enters the text in book six. He is hugely successful yet profoundly enigmatic; he establishes a character type that features frequently in Disraeli's novels, most notably in the figure of Sidonia in *Coningsby*. He guides Vivian through aphorism, 'grief is the agony of an instant; the indulgence of Grief the blunder of a life' (p. 395), and sometimes through advice which is more explicit: 'sooner or later, whatever may be your present conviction and your present feelings, you will recur to your original wishes and your original pursuits' (p. 394). This conversation occurs not long after Vivian has ruled out any return to the political realm for himself: '"Political business?" said Vivian, in an agitated voice. "You could not address a more unfortunate person. I have seen, Prince, too much of politics ever to wish to meddle with them again. . . . I thank Heaven daily that I have no chance of again having any connection with it"' (p. 355). Beckendorff's subsequent comment leaves the door open, undermining Vivian's and indeed the narrator's repudiation of political activity. Moreover, the narrator is clearly impressed by Beckendorff, as Daniel Schwarz has noted: 'Disraeli's narrative voice . . . is sympathetic with the bold, idiosyncratic monster'.[19] An older, enigmatic man becomes a guru to the young adventurer, a relationship which was to feature structurally in many of Disraeli's subsequent novels.

A political standpoint is developed within *Vivian Grey*. In the early part of the novel, when politics is at the narrative forefront, the political analysis is often vague. When Vivian's alliance with Carabas is at its warmest, he addresses a gathering of interested and influential parties:

> when the blood of the party was tolerably warmed, Vivian addressed them. The tenor of his oration may be imagined. He developed the new political principles, demonstrated the mistake under the baneful influence of which they had so long suffered, promised them place, and power, and patronage, and personal consideration, if they would only act on the principles which he recommended, in the most flowing language and the most melodious voice in which the glories of ambition were ever yet chaunted. There was a buzz of admiration when the flattering music ceased; the Marquess smiled triumphantly, as if to say, 'Didn't I tell you he was a monstrous clever fellow?' and the whole business seemed settled. (p. 91)

The precise details of 'the principles' are conspicuous by their absence. On one level the narrator is satirising the cabal from the outset, stressing their ambition as opposed to their ideas, yet it is also noteworthy that the policies of the faction headed by Carabas and fuelled by Vivian's energy are always amorphous. When Vivian makes his proposal to Cleveland he describes himself as 'uncommitted in political principles' (p. 100). Although designed to dilute Cleveland's initial hostility to a project involving his erstwhile adversary, Carabas, this comment reflects how

Vivian's own political principles have yet to be developed and enunciated. In its early stages, *Vivian Grey* is more interested in the machinery of politics than political ideologies.

When explicit political beliefs are voiced in the first volumes of the book they are often cynical. In particular, Cleveland, perceived as a politically weighty figure within Carabas's project, takes a dim view of economic fluctuations and the populace:

> there is nothing like a fall of stocks to affect what is the fashion to style the Literature of the present day, a fungus production which has flourished from the artificial state of our society, the mere creature of our imaginary wealth. Everybody being very rich, has afforded to be very literary, books being considered a luxury almost as elegant and necessary as ottomans, bonbons, and pierglasses. Consols at 100 were the origin of all book societies. The Stockbroker's ladies took off all the quarto travels and the hot-pressed poetry. They were the patronesses of your patent ink and your wire-wove paper. That is all past. Twenty per cent difference in the value of our public securities from this time last year, that little incident has done more for the restoration of the old English feeling, than all the exertions of Church and State united. There is nothing like a fall in Consols to bring the blood of our good people of England into cool order. (p. 149)

Cleveland's analysis turns the population into shallow cultural sycophants, determined passively by shifts in the economy. More worrying still is an earlier comment of Cleveland's which strikes the modern reader as an advocacy of despotism: 'make them fear you, and they will kiss your feet' (p. 146). In the early part of the novel, therefore, the little politics that does appear is reactionary, dissatisfied with the present and yet unable to construct an analytical programme for the future.

However, *Vivian Grey* does contain a more serious contribution to political thinking. This is prefigured implicitly in book two, in which Vivian demonstrates concern for the poor through his intercession in the case of John Conyers, an agricultural worker being pressurised over unpaid rent by Stapylton Toad. Vivian is able to solve the problem and in part the incident is merely a narrative opportunity to expose Vivian's heroism and Toad's villainy. However, by highlighting a concern for the rural poor and demonstrating the social conscience of the comparatively well off, Disraeli dramatises briefly a central feature of his subsequent political creed, developed fully through the Young England trilogy, in which the central characters are philanthropic and mindful of their social duty. A rural worker and an envoy of the aristocracy engage symbiotically, with Vivian's concern for the family having arisen after Conyers had attended to Vivian's unruly horse. Their harmony is, however, threatened by a money-grabbing representative of a landlord. By extrapolation, commercialism is seen as socially divisive, interrupting a state of benign reciprocity which would otherwise exist between ruler and ruled. A concern over the consequences of commercialism is further signified in book five, in which Mr Fitzloom, a former 'journeyman cottonspinner' (p. 223) is now a member of parliament. *Vivian Grey* detects change in society and is not at all comfortable with it.

While commercial prosperity was often rooted in manufacturing industry, large-scale, market speculation delivered success or failure on different terms, as rumours within the market could significantly affect valuations. Disraeli was clearly aware of this practice, hence his publications extolling the virtues of mining companies in which he had an interest. In *Vivian Grey* the vagaries of the financial markets are subjected to the narrator's satire:

> There must be something in the wind, perhaps a war. Was the independence of Greece about to be acknowledged, or the dependence of Spain about to be terminated? What first-rate Power had marched a million of soldiers into the land of a weak neighbour, on the mere pretence of exercising the military? . . . At length Fitzloom decided on a general war. England must interfere either to defeat the ambition of France, or to curb the rapacity of Russia, or to check the arrogance of Austria, or to regenerate Spain, or to redeem Greece, or to protect Portugal, or to shield the Brazils, or to uphold the Bible Societies, or to consolidate the Greek church, or to monopolise the commerce of Mexico, or to disseminate the principles of free trade, or to keep up her high character, or to keep up the price of corn. England must interfere. In spite of his conviction, however, Fitzloom did not alter the arrangements of his tour; he still intended to travel for two years. All he did was to send immediate orders to his broker in England to sell two million of consols. The sale was of course effected, the example followed, stocks fell ten percent, the exchange turned, money became scarce. . . . Rest assured that in politics, however tremendous the effects, the causes are often as trifling. (pp. 249–50)

Placing Disraeli's own speculations in the market to one side, the passage exhibits anxiety relating to the inherent precariousness of an economy in which vast sums are realigned on the basis of rumour. Given that the speculator named in this passage is Fitzloom, with whom the narrator has no sympathy, Disraeli's objections are being directed more against socially ambitious industrialists dabbling in an activity reserved for the upper classes than against speculation *per se*. Nevertheless, there is, throughout *Vivian Grey*, criticism of the increasingly dominant economic values of entrepreneurism which were changing the social fabric of Disraeli's age.

In opposition to expanding commercialism lies Vivian's final destination of Astra, a pre-industrial idyll presided over by a beneficent lord. Generous government ensures universal wealth: 'Vivian was much struck by the appearance of the little settlement as he rode through it. It did not consist of more than fifty houses, but they were all detached, and each beautifully embowered in trees' (pp. 504–5). The ruler himself has patriarchal yet gentle qualities: 'he was a tall but thin bending figure, with a florid benevolent countenance, and a quantity of long white hair. This venerable person cordially offered his hand to Vivian' (p. 505). Subjecting this incident, which occurs near the end of the novel, to a political analysis in the context of *Vivian Grey* as a whole, Disraeli's solution to the dangers of a commercialised society lies in the restoration of small, rural communities characterised by interdependence between governor and governed, a position consistent with the much more explicit political analysis presented in the Young England trilogy. *Vivian Grey* is part of the gestation of Disraeli's political vision, and the Young England trilogy is therefore the distillation of long-held thought, supplemented by a more empirical understanding of the problems of society through the first half of the nineteenth century.

The marketing of *Vivian Grey* is a tribute to the commercial sense of Disraeli himself and, particularly, to his publisher, Henry Colburn. Shortly prior to *Vivian Grey's* release, brief notes appeared in gossip columns (generally in publications owned by Colburn) announcing the imminent publication of a scandalous novel of high society. Anonymous publication, as in the case of *Tremaine* (also published by Colburn) suggested that the author was a part of the social circles he described. *Vivian Grey* was duly successful upon its release; the first two volumes, which deal with Vivian's adventures prior to his travels on continental Europe, were published on 22 April 1826, and sales were regularly reinvigorated by the publication of keys which purported to identify the real individuals behind the characters named in the text. It is likely that some if not all of these were written by Disraeli himself (one of them appeared in the seventh edition of *Star Chamber* [see below], to which Disraeli was a contributor), and thus he fuelled additional demand for his own novel. Therefore, running alongside the satire, the scandal, the disdain for commercialism and the suggestion of an alternative vision for society, Disraeli also practised the wily pragmatism of an author yearning for success. By mid-May of 1826, the discovery of the true authorship of *Vivian Grey* brought widespread criticism of Disraeli; *Blackwood's Magazine* for July 1826 referred to him as 'an obscure person for whom nobody gives a straw', while the *Monthly Magazine* suggested that the author should, 'content himself with sinking into total oblivion.'[20] By that stage, however, Disraeli was already laughing all the way to the bank, or to his creditors at least.

While *Vivian Grey* was in circulation, Disraeli continued writing, publishing (again anonymously) a satirical poem in two instalments. *The Dunciad of Today* appeared in a short-lived satirical journal, *The Star Chamber,* which ran from 19 April to 7 June 1826. *The Dunciad* commenced in issue five (10 May) and continued in issue six (17 May). Further instalments were promised but did not appear. The influence of Byron is very much to the fore in *The Dunciad of Today.* From the outset he is praised extravagantly: 'in spite of every obstacle and discouragement, his genius burst forth at once, and gave a new tone and energy, not merely to the literature of the day, but to the general taste, and feeling, and spirit of his countrymen' (p. 21ff). Within the poem itself the influence of Byron's *Don Juan* is obvious, not least in the comical rhymes that occur throughout. Disraeli rhymes 'before us' with 'semichorus', echoing Byron's method in *Don Juan* as he had, for example, rhymed 'intellectual' with 'hen-pecked you all' (canto 1, stanza 22). *The Dunciad of Today* is a savage attack on contemporary writers, from which few are immune: Chandos Leigh, Felicia Hemans, Laetitia Elizabeth Landon – all are castigated. Furthermore, the poem concludes with a call to arms to the few writers deemed worthy of any note. Disraeli denied having had a connection with *The Star Chamber,* but Michael Sadleir subsequently argued persuasively that Disraeli had in fact written *The Dunciad.*[21] The poem develops the satirical skills aired occasionally in *Vivian Grey* as it picks off, one by one, its literary targets.

In 1828 Disraeli produced another satire, published on 3 June, this time of greater length and in prose. *The Voyage of Captain Popanilla,* in common with *The Dunciad,* attacks the contemporary literary scene: 'Popanilla was waited upon by the most eminent bookseller in Hubbabub, who begged to have the honour of introducing to the public a Narrative of Captain Popanilla's Voyage. . . . Popanilla was charmed with the proposition, but blushingly informed the mercantile Maecenas that he did not know how to write. The publisher told him that this circumstance was not of the slightest importance' (pp. 42–3). There is also criticism of the fashionable novel in chapter twelve: 'BURLINGTON, A TALE OF FASHIONABLE LIFE, in three volumes post octavo, was sent forth. Two or three similar works, bearing titles equally euphonious and aristocratic, were published daily' (p. 73). However, satire in *Popanilla* has a broader remit than in Disraeli's earlier poem, with criticism also being aimed at economic and political principles common to society. More specifically, Disraeli attacks the Benthamite, utilitarian ideas which were both popular and influential: 'he did not imagine that the most barefaced hireling of corruption could for a moment maintain that there was any utility in pleasure. If there were no utility in pleasure, it was quite clear that pleasure could profit no one. If, therefore, it were unprofitable, it was injurious; because that which does not produce a profit is equivalent to a loss; therefore pleasure is a losing business; consequently pleasure is not pleasant' (p. 15). Later, Popanilla is exposed to the principle, 'that nothing is good which is not useful' (p. 46). As the text's purpose is served by satire it does not prescribe any substantial, alternative vision of society. However, there is consistency in Disraeli's writing up to this point in his career: though he plays with different genres and styles, there is a clear disdain for the commercial principles operating in English society in the early part of the century.

While the humour is overwhelmingly satirical in *Popanilla*, it is occasionally more straightforward: 'his face was so covered with hair, and the back of his head cropped so bald, that you generally addressed him in the rear by mistake' (p. 49). Moreover, in common with *Vivian Grey* the narrator sometimes plays with his audience: 'this book is so constructed that if you were even, according to custom, to commence its perusal by reading the last page, you would not gain the slightest assistance in finding out "how the story ends"' (p. 8). The narrative strategy throughout Disraeli's early works is as performative and deliberately stylistic as it is critical or instructive. The satire of politics is evident, but Disraeli's own philosophy, influenced by Byronic Romanticism, was still in an early stage of its development.

THE YOUNG DUKE

'The world seemed created solely for his enjoyment.'

The primary purpose behind Disraeli's second novel, *The Young Duke* (1831), was clear: to make money.[22] In debt as a result of his Stock Exchange misadventures and under pressure from his creditors, Disraeli saw writing as a means of providing some relief from his problems. He was already at work on *Alroy,* based on David Alroy, a twelfth-century Jewish hero, which he abandoned temporarily to concentrate on the more commercially viable *The Young Duke*, which was always likely to be a success at a time when there was a demand for fashionable novels of high society. Moreover, Disraeli had remained active as a published writer after *Vivian Grey* and *Popanilla*, contributing a number of articles to *The Court Journal* in 1829, using the pseudonym Mivartinos.[23] Between 1827 and the latter stages of 1829, Disraeli had been afflicted by an unspecified illness, thus explaining his comparatively meagre literary output during this period. His work was also put on hold for a further sixteen months by his travels in the Mediterranean and Near East (1830–1), although his experiences abroad proved to be valuable when writing the second half of *Tancred* (see chapter two). Disraeli's own assessment of his situation at the end of 1829 was blunt: 'a literary prostitute I have never yet been, tho' born in an age of general prostitution, and tho' I have more than once been subject to temptation which might have been the *ruination* of a less virtuous young woman. My muse however is still a virgin, but the mystical flower, I fear, must soon be plucked. Colburn, I suppose will be the bawd.'[24]

The Young Duke gives a thorough airing to an idea which later found full expression in the Young England trilogy. The Duke is an aristocrat but he is neglectful of his duties, indulging instead in a hedonistic lifestyle: 'having been stamped at the Mint of Fashion as a sovereign of the brightest die, he was flung forth, like the rest of his gold brethren, to corrupt the society of which he was the brightest ornament' (p. 17). The coin metaphor signifies the axiomatic corruption of the aristocracy through its preoccupation with wealth and materialism. The Duke requires correction in order to fulfil the responsibilities of his blood. The idea of a morally dormant aristocracy awaiting reinvigoration is also a key element in *Sybil* (1845), dramatised from the outset in the form of an upper class that can only be excited by the prospect of the Derby at Epsom racecourse. In *The Young Duke,* aristocrats at least bother to attend the House of Lords, but Disraeli shows them to be lethargic and devoid of inspiration: 'there was Lord Ego, who vindicated his character, when nobody knew he had one, and explained his motives, because his auditors could not understand his acts. . . . In the end, up started the Premier, who, having nothing to say, was manly, and candid, and liberal; gave credit to his adversaries, and took credit to himself, and then the motion was withdrawn' (p. 20). However, this is not the whole story:

> while all this was going on, some made a note, some made a bet, some consulted a book, some their ease, some yawned, a few slept; yet, on the whole, there was an air about the assembly which can be witnessed in no other in Europe. Even the most indifferent looked as if he would come forward if the occasion should demand him, and the most imbecile as if he could serve his country if it required him. When a man raises his eyes from his bench and sees his ancestor in the tapestry, he begins to understand the pride of blood. (pp. 20–1)

The present may be moribund but the past is glorious, and, while the future is uncertain, the Lords have heroic potential. The aristocracy is a sleeping giant, temporarily overtaken in society by commercialism and utilitarianism, yet possessed of a moral legitimacy for leadership which cannot be taken away. All it lacks is a political leader. Disraeli's first attempt to enter parliament did not occur until the year after *The Young Duke* was published, but he was clearly in the process of developing a coherent political creed, in which the historical responsibility of the aristocracy held a key role.

The Young Duke (the character's full name is George Augustus Frederick, Duke of St James) is incapable of self-reformation. His self-centredness prevents him from perceiving his own responsibilities: 'his sympathy for those he believed his inferiors was slight', yet the narrator warns us against condemning the hero: 'pity him! Pity his fatal youth!' (p. 36). By presenting his hero as an object for sympathy, Disraeli anticipates two of his central characters from later works of the 1830s, Ferdinand Armine (*Henrietta Temple*) and Plantagenet Cadurcis (*Venetia*). The aristocracy is shown to be enduring the burden of responsibility and leadership. Its extraordinary privileges receive less attention in *Henrietta Temple* and *Venetia*, but in *The Young Duke* considerable detail is given concerning the Duke's lifestyle, as determined by the aesthetic criteria for the fashionable novel. However, Disraeli plays with the genre through satirising its preoccupation with the details of opulence: 'room after room, gallery after gallery; you know the rest. Shall we describe the silk hangings and the reverend tapestry, the agate tables and the tall screens, the china and the armour, the state beds and the curious cabinets, and the family pictures mixed up so quaintly with Italian and Flemish art?' (p. 116). On society, the narrator laments: 'and this glare, and heat, and noise, this congeries of individuals without sympathy and dishes without flavour; this is society! What an effect without a cause!' (p. 165). The distance between the narrator and the characters allows Disraeli's position to coincide with May Dacre's, the character who holds the position of dominant specularity in the hierarchy of discourses in *The Young Duke*. Satire and the criticism also encourage a judgemental narrative outlook, with the Duke and his society being celebrated by numerous figures within the text but criticised from without; the shallowness of fashionable life is highlighted when the Duke is superseded by the new kid on the block, Lord Marylebone.

Given the unhealthy state of the aristocracy within the novel, the Duke's peer group are unable to assist in his reformation. For example, Lord Squib 'had inherited a fair and peer-like property, which he had contrived to embarrass in so complicated and extraordinary a manner that he had been a ruined man for years, and yet lived well on an income allowed him by his creditors to manage his estate for their benefit' (p. 74). When the Young Duke sustains his biggest losses at the hands of gamblers, one of them is Lord Dice, 'who boasted of having done his brothers out of their miserable 5,000*l.* patrimony' (p. 253). The Duke is part of a profligate class, the power of which is being eroded by its own folly and parasitism; the Duke's own gambling losses have, paradoxically, a purgatorial function as he feels 'as if he had dishonoured his ancestry' (p. 265), thus seeing beyond himself and his own desires. In addition, the King, while praised, is also not discharging his duties to their fullest extent. The King and the Duke are introduced at a dinner party: 'his Grace listened to his Majesty, and was filled with admiration. O, father of thy people! If thou wouldst but look a little oftener on thy younger sons, their morals and their manners might alike be improved' (p. 43). Disraeli's plea signifies a desire for a rejuvenated monarchy, taking on governmental as well as ceremonial roles.

The Duke's actual reformation is facilitated by the Dacre family, and in particular by May Dacre, the woman whom the Duke eventually marries. When she rejects his first proposal she tells him, 'you act from impulse, and not from principle' (p. 125), thus identifying his central problem. The acquisition of principle will involve the Duke recognising the responsibilities as well as the rights that arise from his privileged position. May acts as the catalyst for the Duke's self-realisation, infusing him with her powerful sense of duty. Considering his love for her, 'he darkly felt that happiness was too philosophical a system to be the result or the reward of impulse, however unbounded, and that principle alone could create and could support that bliss which is our being's end and aim' (p. 203). His thoughts later crystallise into a firm belief: 'happiness must spring from purer fountains than self-love. We are not born merely for ourselves. . . . Why should I live? For virtue, and for duty' (p. 245). The Duke constructs an alternative vision of his life, in which luxurious idleness is replaced by agricultural simplicity: 'I would sooner live in a cottage with May Dacre, and work for our daily bread, than be worshipped by all the beauty of this Babylon' (p. 275). In her company he gets a brief glimpse of rural life: 'many were the cottages at which they called; many the old dames after whose rheumatism, and many the young damsels after whose fortunes they enquired' (p. 290). The Duke is the first, but not the only, Disraelian hero to witness a simpler mode of life through the intercession of an empathetic female character; most notably, Egremont follows Sybil as she dispenses charity through her community (see chapter two). The excursion is educative for the Disraelian hero, presenting him with a lifestyle with which he would otherwise be unfamiliar; it also expresses Disraeli's yearning for a pastoral utopia in which the haves and the have-nots lived in a shared harmony, taking care of each other's material and spiritual welfare. The eventual union of the Young Duke with May Dacre symbolises the Duke's alignment with a more stable and sedate philosophy, in which principle and duty are paramount.

The Dacre family is Catholic. Moreover, it is conscious and proud of its religious affiliation; May Dacre speaks of how 'her father and his friends sustained their oppression and lived as proscribed in the realm which they had created' (p. 68). Following his personal reformation, the Duke speaks in favour of Catholic emancipation in Parliament, an act signifying both his new-found seriousness and the novel's implicit advocacy of the Catholic faith. Sympathetic representations of Catholicism are to be found repeatedly in Disraeli's writings, until the more hostile perspective adopted in *Lothair*. Furthermore, in 1824 Disraeli described his first encounter with the Catholic mass: 'the host raised, and I flung myself on the ground'.[25] Opposition to the Catholic Church had, until very recently, existed on an institutional level (Catholic emancipation did not occur until 1829). Disraeli could easily be perceived to be going out on a limb by voicing support for the church and its rituals. However, Disraeli was interested in the symbolic value of Catholicism rather than in the church *per se*. Dissatisfied with a commercialised present, Disraeli constructed an image of a remote past, in which a sense of spiritual commitment fostered duty and philanthropy. His early presentation of Catholicism may thus be connected with his Young England period; both place an idealised past in opposition to a corrupted present. Furthermore, the rituals of Catholicism connected with Disraeli's extravagant imagination, offering the possibility of a fabulous realm beyond ordinary experience. Catholicism lent shape to Disraeli's Byronic imagination, imbuing it with an historical pedigree.

The Young Duke undertakes a brief survey of both Houses of Parliament, with a particular focus on the debating qualities of politicians. There is qualified praise for George Canning and Robert Peel, though some of the most favourable comments are reserved for Sir Francis Burdett: 'he was full of music, grace, and dignity, even amid all the vulgar tumult; and, unlike all mob orators, raised the taste of the populace to him, instead of lowering his own to theirs' (p. 308). The suggestion of a warm relationship between upper-class ruler and lower-class ruled is another feature of the Young England trilogy, and lends itself to the 'two nations' dualism by which Disraeli's explicitly political novels of the 1840s are best remembered. However, the relationship constructed by Disraeli in *The Young Duke* implies that the lower orders are the recipients of upper-class consideration; there is no suggestion of an equal exchange between the social classes. A similar strategy is adopted in *Coningsby*, in which the friendship of the young, upper-class hero bene-fits the son of an industrialist. Disraeli's parliamentary overview in *The Young Duke* also considers Robert Peel, fifteen years before the men became rivals in the House of Commons. Peel is described as being 'the model of a minister', though his parliamentary rhetoric is thought to be 'fluent without the least style' (p. 310), signifying Disraeli's unenthusiastic attitude towards the man who would be his Party leader. At the end of the chapter (book five, chapter six) the narrator makes some concluding points regarding debates in both Houses of Parliament: 'one thing is clear, that a man may speak very well in the House of Commons, and fail very completely in the House of Lords. There are two distinct styles requisite: I intend, in the course of my career, if I have time, to give a specimen of both' (p. 310). He did, though he had to wait until 1876 before making his début in the Lords as the Earl of Beaconsfield.

A seemingly incidental conversation in the latter stages of the novel enables Disraeli to attack his principal ideological enemy of the 1820s and 1830s, utilitarianism. The Duke travels on a coach with 'a hard-featured, grey-headed gentleman, with a somewhat supercilious look, and a mingled air of acuteness and conceit'. His pomposity and inflexibility are implied through his appearance, and are soon reinforced by his language: 'don't talk to me of beauty; a mere word'. His politics are also soon apparent: 'men begin to ask themselves what the use of an aristocracy is'. Disraeli uses the character to attack an ideology, dramatising a creed he felt to be inimical to human nature and threatening to the long-standing political and social conventions of the nation. The Duke becomes the topic of the conversation, without the utilitarian knowing the identity of his fellow traveller: '"don't talk to me of poor souls. There is a poor soul," said the utilitarian, pointing to an old man breaking stones on the highway. "That is what I call a poor soul, not a young prodigal, whose life has been one long career of infamous debauchery. . . . It's the system, the infernal system. If that man had to work for his bread, like everybody else, do you think he would dine off bank notes? No! to be sure, he wouldn't!"' (pp. 312–15). The utilitarian presents a vigorous and cred-ible, anti-aristocratic argument. The Duke lives partly off rents paid on his land, and thus he is supported by the labour of the working people beneath him. However, Disraeli does not present the utilitarian as a poten-tial liberator because, for Disraeli, utilitarianism degraded people by reducing them to a theoretical, even arithmetical, phenomenon. When the utilitarian espouses the merits of the 'Screw and Lever Review' (based according to Robert Blake on the *Westminster Review*[26]), and the Duke encounters one of its writers, Duncan Macmorrogh, the (imaginary) article exposes the fallacies (as Disraeli saw them) at the heart of utilitarianism.

> Rivers he rather patronised; but flowers he quite pulled to pieces, and proved them to be the most useless of existences. Duncan Macmorrogh informed us that we were quite wrong in supposing ourselves to be the miracle of Creation. On the contrary, he avowed that already there were various pieces of machinery of far more importance than man; and he had no doubt, in time, that a superior race would arise, got by a steam-engine on a spinning jenny. (p. 321)

The chapter as a whole makes only a slight narrative contribution. Its primary purpose is political, attacking an influential, anti-aristocratic philosophy. The chapter's placement in the novel is significant; it occurs after the Duke has reformed and thus any pertinence in the utilitarian's argument is lost. Had it been placed in the first two-thirds of *The Young Duke* it would have generated quite different meanings. We have to side with the Duke as a character first, prior to accepting the class and the ideology that he represents.

The Young Duke is a story about personal reform, but it is also an admonition to an aristocracy that was not living up to its responsibilities. Redemption in the novel is achieved through the intercession of a Catholic family, signifiers of steadfastness and duty in an otherwise frivolous society. The novel also takes an indolent parliament to task, and berates a philosophy perceived by Disraeli to be most threatening to the territorial aristocracy. The hero's triumph as a character (he gains both sobriety and May Dacre) signifies the potential for the aristocracy to be revivified, but the catalyst for renewal comes from outside the aristocracy itself.

In 1832 Disraeli collaborated with Baron de Haber on an anti-Whig publication, *England and France: or a Cure for Ministerial Gallomania*.[27] In the conclusion, Disraeli declares, 'I have, in these pages, endeavoured to elucidate that obscure subject, which all men talk about and very few understand – French politics' (p. 254), yet his primary focus is a critical assessment of British foreign policy under Earl Grey's government, to which end there are also chapters on other countries, including Poland and Belgium. *England and France* is also useful because it contains one of Disraeli's briefest synopses of his political creed: 'my politics are described by one word, and that word is ENGLAND' (p. 13). From Romantic beginnings he had begun to acquire historical awareness, which was leading him towards a political philosophy rooted in patriotism. Disraeli also found time in 1832 to contribute to the *New Monthly Magazine*, publishing 'Ixion in Heaven' in December 1832 and February 1833, subsequently followed by 'The Infernal Marriage', published between July and October 1834. Both texts are satirical. Ixion meets Mercury, who reiterates Disraeli's distinction between deeds and words: 'study and action will not combine' (p. 116). Ixion's self-belief and determination call to mind Disraeli's own fortitude as he embarked upon literary and political life, as Ixion proclaims, 'he who laughs at Destiny will gain Fortune', and later adds, 'I have done much: what I may produce we have yet to see' (pp. 122 & 129). However, his most telling assertion is 'adventures are to the adventurous' (p. 129), a belief reiterated more than a decade later by Sidonia in *Coningsby*. The adventurous Disraeli also undertook his first critical inspection of his hero, Byron, in 'Ixion in Heaven', in which the character of Apollo, clearly modelled on Byron, 'was a somewhat melancholy lack-a-daisical looking personage, with his shirt collar thrown open, and his long curls theatrically arranged'. Apollo's ennui, 'immortality is a bore', anticipates the jaded aristocrats in the opening to *Sybil*.

'Ixion in Heaven' is counterbalanced by 'The Infernal Marriage', which is set in hell. From a standard Disraeli perspective, the narrator criticises Pluto as a politician, who opts for expediency rather than principle in his dealings with Orpheus and Eurydice, while Saturn criticises a lack of reverence in society: 'I look upon the Spirit of the age as a spirit hostile to Kings and Gods' (p. 191). However, one of the most significant characters in 'The Infernal Marriage' is Tiresias who, as a mythological seer, embodies many of the qualities of Disraeli's fictional gurus, while also anticipating the stock character's fully developed and secular manifestation in Sidonia. Tiresias's wide mistrust, 'I never trust any one, either God or man' (p. 179), finds an echo in Sidonia's wilful solitude. Both 'Ixion in Heaven' and 'The Infernal Marriage' are satirical, yet the characterisation of Apollo in 'Ixion . . .' also demonstrates the fact that Disraeli was changing, abandoning wholehearted Romanticism in favour of more substantial and constructive engagement with society.[28]

The year 1832 was important for Disraeli, for it marked his first attempt to get into Parliament, as a member for High Wycombe, standing as the Radical candidate. A by-election in June saw him appealing to an electorate of just thirty-two (he lost by twenty votes to twelve). For the December election the constituency had swollen to 298 votes, but Disraeli came last in a field of three candidates. In this second campaign he spoke warmly of the political principles of Lord Bolingbroke,[29] who was to become a larger influence when Disraeli came to write *A Vindication of the English Constitution* (see below). In October 1832 he published his address to the electorate, in which he expressed mistrust of both the Whigs and Tories. He sought to improve 'the condition of the lower orders', and phrased his essential position in the following terms: 'rid yourselves of all that political jargon and factious slang of Whig and Tory – two names with one meaning, used only to delude you – and unite in forming a great national party which alone can save the country from impending destruction'.[30] The ambition which had emerged in the letters sent to John Murray from Scotland in 1825 gains a more palpable form here: Disraeli's intention was nothing less than the complete transformation of the political landscape. Disraeli had high expectations of his developing creed of Romantic patriotism; the electorate had other ideas.[31]

CONTARINI FLEMING

'I swore by the Nature that I adored, that, in spite of all opposition, I
would be an author; ay! the greatest of authors; and that far climes and
distant ages should respond to the message of my sympathetic page.'

The second novel in Disraeli's trilogy of selfhood is *Contarini Fleming*, first published in May 1832. The eponymous hero is unquestionably based on Disraeli himself. As Paul Smith has pointed out, the hero's 'name deliberately embodies that mingling of northern and southern strains which it was now his need explicitly to recognise and explore'.[32] Furthermore, whereas *Vivian Grey* is written in the third person, *Contarini Fleming* a first-person narrative. On one level this is merely a literary device, and therefore a confessional text is not necessarily implied by Disraeli's authorial perspective. However, enough of Disraeli's personal adventures and misadventures are replayed in *Contarini Fleming* to justify an autobiographical reading, and letters written home during his trip to Italy in 1826 are reproduced word for word.[33]

A Byronic influence is still present in *Contarini Fleming*, especially in the characterisation of the hero. At the beginning of the novel he hears the wind whisper to him: 'child of Nature, learn to unlearn!' (p. 2). While this is a typical romantic aspiration it is also implicitly narcissistic, with Contarini being singled out by nature. Elsewhere in the text this criticism becomes explicit as, in the course of two dreams, Contarini first sees his portrait alongside Julius Caesar's, and then dreams that 'a long line of Venetian nobles, two by two, passed before me, and as they passed they saluted me' (p. 208). The confidence of Disraeli's central character had clearly grown since the time of *Vivian Grey*. Whereas Vivian questioned his right to interfere with the lives of others, Contarini assumes his own genius.

Contarini Fleming also has its own enigmatic guide, after *Vivian Grey*'s Beckendorff and before *Coningsby*'s Sidonia. In book one, chapter thirteen, Contarini meets an unnamed stranger, 'seated on a mass of ancient brickwork', with 'an air of acuteness in his countenance which was striking' (p. 48). After speaking enigmatically with Contarini for a while, he gives him 'some talismanic rules' which conclude the chapter in block capitals:

> BE PATIENT: CHERISH HOPE. READ MORE: PONDER LESS. NATURE IS MORE POWERFUL THAN EDUCATION: TIME WILL DEVELOP EVERY THING. TRUST NOT OVERMUCH IN THE BLESSED MAGDALEN: LEARN TO PROTECT YOURSELF. (p. 57)

Disraeli's gurus specialise in broad generalisations. They signify, at this stage in his development, Disraeli's inability to construct concrete, political possibilities out of his current situation, beyond an appeal for a rejuvenated monarchy. Although he was attempting to get into Parliament, his political allegiance shifted from the Radicals to the Conservatives and, according to Paul Smith, 'he might have condescended to the Whigs had they done so to him', though it is my own contention that Disraeli would never have joined the Whigs (see below).[34] In Disraeli's characters' statements of wisdom there is dissatisfaction with the present, and a consideration of some of the factors that have brought this about, but the analysis does not extend into the future, which remains amorphous. In the Young England trilogy a remedy is proposed that, paradoxically, involves reaching back into the past. We learn little about Disraeli's spiritual guide in *Contarini Fleming*, yet it is significant that when we first encounter him he is, literally, in touch with the ancient: his wisdom and authenticity are linked to the context in which he is first seen.

Contarini Fleming also demonstrates dramatically Disraeli's interest in Catholicism. He undergoes an epiphany and a conversion:

> six large burnished lamps were suspended above, and threw a magical light upon a magical picture. It was a Magdalen kneeling and weeping in a garden. Her long golden hair was drawn off her ivory forehead, and reached to the ground. Her large blue eyes, full of ecstatic melancholy, pierced to heaven, while the heavy tears studded like pearls her wan but delicate cheek.
>
> I gazed upon this pictured form with a strange fascination. I came forward, and placed myself near the altar. At that moment the organ burst forth, as if heaven were opening; clouds of incense rose and wreathed around the rich and vaulted roof; the priest advanced, and revealed a God, which I fell down and worshipped. From that moment I became a Catholic. (pp. 46–7)

The introduction of the heroine of *Sybil* has some of the same mystical qualities, signifying that she is as much a religious icon as a convincing character. Disraeli's early fascination with Catholicism is a correlative of his equally fastidious interest in enigmatic characters possessed of wisdom. Both hint at metaphysical truth while declining to give it concrete form. Although, in *Contarini Fleming*, the stranger advises against putting too much faith in the Magdalen, he offers a not dissimilar spiritual experience. Whether it is ritual itself or ritualistic phrases, the form of expression (a message transcribed or a ceremony enacted) holds meaning as it adopts a position of high seriousness. Furthermore, the rich and emotive world of Catholicism in *Contarini Fleming* is countered by the sterner, protestant world of the hero's father.[35] Disraeli's wider dualistic tension between spiritual–imaginative possibilities and practical considerations assumes dramatic form. In his diary, Disraeli wrote, 'the Utilitarians in politics are like the Unitarians in religion: both omit imagination in their systems, and imagination governs mankind'.[36] Disraeli's visionary streak generated extravagant imaginative possibilities, yet ultimately he needed the temperate influence of pragmatism to bring his ideas to fruition.

Just as *Vivian Grey* offered a rural idyll, *Contarini Fleming* follows suit as Contarini, in book one, encounters the Winter family. He meets them after having been robbed; the father of the family is first described as 'an ancient woodman . . ., a comely and venerable man'. His impact on Contarini is instantaneous: 'I began to long to be a woodman, to pass a quiet, and contemplative, and virtuous life, amid the deep silence and beautiful scenery of forests' (p. 78). Contarini remains there for three days, before returning to the city. The episode is a pastoral interlude, placed between betrayal and robbery on the one hand, and immersion in urban and political life on the other.

Two of the most prominent features of *Contarini Fleming* are the demands of literature and politics. Disraeli believed, wrongly, as it transpired, that *Contarini Fleming* would cement his literary reputation; in fact, only 614 copies of the first edition were sold, creating a mere £56 profit. Within the novel the hero, like Disraeli, has his first attempt at novel writing rejected by a publisher and, like Disraeli, Contarini writes a scandalous bestseller which lampoons a number of prominent figures both within and beyond the writer's immediate circle. Just as *Vivian Grey* allowed Disraeli to recount the story of *The Representative*, so *Contarini Fleming* allows Disraeli to present his version of events regarding *Vivian Grey*. Contarini calls his book 'Manstein', publishes it anonymously, and records what happened once his authorship was discovered, in terms which replay the fallout that ensued when Disraeli was exposed as the author of *Vivian Grey*.

All the people who had read 'Manstein,' and been very much amused with it, began to think they were quite wrong, and that it was a very improper and wicked book, because this was daily reiterated in their ears by half-a-dozen bores, who had gained an immortality which they did not deserve. Such conduct, it was universally agreed, must not be encouraged. Where would it end? Everybody was alarmed. Men passed me in the street without notice; I received anonymous letters, and even many of my intimates grew cold. As I abhor explanations I said nothing; and, although I was disgusted with the folly of much that I had heard, I contradicted nothing, however ridiculously false, and felt confident that, in time, the world would discover that they had been gulled into fighting the battle of a few individuals whom they despised. I found even a savage delight in being an object, for a moment, of public astonishment, and fear, and indignation. (p. 180)

Through Contarini, Disraeli turns on his critics, accusing them of mounting a conspiracy against him. Contarini becomes the victim: stoic and morally superior in his silence, he also claims to have found a perverse enjoyment in being in the limelight. Contarini later claims to have successfully fought a duel, echoing a similar narrative incident in *Vivian Grey*, following the collapse of the Carabas faction. Therefore, Disraeli's characters do occasionally resort to violent, aggressive tactics against their tormentors when the need arises. In real life, Disraeli did become embroiled, in 1835, in a challenge to a duel with Daniel O'Connell, the Irish Nationalist leader, but it was never fought. However, Disraeli does periodically imbue his (autobiographical) literary characters with qualities of orthodox masculine heroism. His characters are shown to be thrusting, dynamic individuals, unafraid to take fearsome risks, recapturing the noble fighting spirit of their ancestors in combat.

In *Contarini Fleming*, the hero is confident regarding his literary vocation: 'I buried my face in my hands; I summoned my thoughts to their last struggle; I penetrated into my very soul; and I felt the conviction, that literary creation was necessary to my existence, and that for it I was formed' (p. 182). Shortly thereafter, Contarini has another one of his epiphanies: 'and I arose, and lifted up my arm to heaven, and waved it like a banner, and I swore by the Nature that I adored, that, in spite of all opposition, I would be an author; ay! The greatest of authors; and that far climes and distant ages should respond to the magic of my sympathetic page' (p. 183). However, for Contarini's creator, the critical and commercial failure of *Contarini Fleming* did nothing to develop his reputation. In fact, it was not long after the disappointing release of *Contarini Fleming* that Disraeli first sought election to Parliament. It is possible that Disraeli, increasingly the pragmatist as well as the visionary, immersed himself in politics when he realised that his ambitions could not be fully realised within literature. Moreover, given that the failure of *Contarini Fleming* coincided with a period of intense political interest and uncertainty arising out of the Reform Bill, Parliament was no doubt an attractive proposition for an ambitious and a dynamic young man. Paul Smith has pointed out that literature was at the heart of Disraeli's career in the 1820s and early '30s: 'from *Vivian Grey* until the publication of *Contarini Fleming* in 1832 – perhaps until the fiasco of the *Revolutionary Epick* in 1834 – literature was the principal medium of his pursuit not only of fame but of himself'.[37] In *Contarini Fleming* and other texts, Disraeli was gestating a political philosophy long before he entered politics. The political arena was a logical destination for an author concerned with developing a philosophy of government.

Contarini's father is the Secretary of State for Foreign Affairs. Contarini goes to see him and is struck by the conduct of his staff: 'at the end two young men were fencing. Another, seated at a round table, covered with papers, was copying music, and occasionally trying a note on his guitar. A fourth was throwing himself into attitudes before a pier-glass; and the fifth, who was the only one whose employment was in any degree of a political nature, was seated at his desk, reading the newspaper' (pp. 90–1). There is a similarity between this description and the opening to *Sybil*; it is also reminiscent of the first House of Lords scene in *The Young Duke* (discussed above). Although the characters are administrators rather than aristocrats there is a prevailing image of disinterested lethargy. The political process is lifeless, awaiting a charismatic figure to rejuvenate it. By early 1833 Disraeli had a fairly good idea of who that individual might be; in a letter to his family he stated, 'I was never more confident of anything than that I could carry everything before me in that House. The time will come.'[38] Disraeli's literary ambitions, thwarted by *Contarini Fleming*'s lack of success, were increasingly being redirected towards politics in the 1830s.

Politics becomes an increasingly central theme to *Contarini Fleming*. In book two, Contarini's father is made Prime Minister and Contarini himself becomes an under secretary of state. At the end of chapter nine of book two, Contarini burns his first book after it is rejected by a publisher, a metaphorical abandonment of literature; the subsequent relocation of the action to the political realm signifies the discovery of a new vocation. The opening to chapter ten sees Contarini immersing himself fully in political and governmental work on behalf of his father, a narrative development which prefigures Disraeli's own subsequent shift in attention from literature to politics. Furthermore, Contarini is clearly intoxicated by his new environment: 'it was enchanting to be acquainted with the secrets of European cabinets, and to control or influence their fortunes' (p. 153). His father later informs him, 'my son, you will be Prime Minister of . . . ; perhaps something greater' (p. 173). However, these narrative incidents are interwoven with Contarini's account of 'Manstein': there was still a tension, for Disraeli, between the competing attractions of literature and politics. Moreover, the word 'enchanting' suggests a child-like euphoria and wonderment at the process of government, arising out of an association with high circles.

In the final two books of the novel Contarini is able to make some more considered remarks concerning the political process, such as 'the most successful legislators are those who have consulted the genius of the people' (p. 331). Given that the novel was published at a time when electoral reform was a subject of paramount importance, Disraeli was reacting with considerable confidence to the new composition of the electorate, even though he felt that the 1832 Reform consolidated a Whig oligarchy. For Disraeli, 'the genius of the people' was not to be found in its elected representatives in the House of Commons. In addition, the position adopted at this point in *Contarini Fleming* is consistent with aspects of the Young England trilogy, as the instinctive goodness of the populace is relied upon, when they are guided by a suitably enlightened ruler.

The conclusion that Contarini Fleming comes to concerning politics is voiced in the last chapter: 'when I examine the state of European society with the unimpassioned spirit which the philosopher can alone command, I perceive that it is in a state of transition, a state of transition from feodal [sic] to federal principles. This I conceive to be the sole and secret cause of all the convulsions that have occurred and are to occur' (pp. 363–4). Anxiety about the loss of feudal principles (which, in Disraeli's eyes, centred on the symbiosis between ruler and ruled) remained at the heart of Disraeli's political thinking. His analysis is naïve for two reasons. First, it portrays a rose-tinted view of feudal societies. Second, in identifying a single root cause for the recent social turmoil across Europe, it unwittingly neglects the plethora of economic and social forces which were, combined, bringing about great changes in England at the time. However, Disraeli's observation also signifies a level of consistency in the development of his political vision, which had been aired in *Vivian Grey* and which was to achieve a more sustained representation in Disraeli's literary output of the 1840s.

ALROY

*'Out on Society! 'twas not made for me. I'll form my own, and be the
deity I sometimes feel.'*

The year 1833 saw the publication of *The Wondrous Tale of Alroy*, as
well as a shorter work, *The Rise of Iskander*, both of which were published in March.[39] *Alroy* saw Disraeli change from the fashionable novel
to historical fiction, a move which brought him an advance of £300
from the publishers Saunders and Otley, thereby enabling him to address
his most pressing debts. His hero is based superficially on a twelfth-century Jewish hero, David Alroy, described by Daniel Schwarz as 'a
self-appointed messiah in Kurdistan during a period of severe tribulation
and unusual suffering for the Jews'.[40] However, Disraeli's Alroy is not
the historical figure brought to life, but the typical Disraelian hero projected onto an historical canvas. Disraeli's Alroy is brought down by
misdirected ambition and a seductive female, and eventually he is exe-
cuted.

Alroy is without parents but, like Vivian Grey and Contarini Fleming
before him, has a yearning to rise to great heights, proclaiming, 'toil
without glory is a menial's lot' (p. 6). His sister, Miriam, invests all her
hope in her brother in a manner which calls to mind the devotional attitude of Disraeli's own sister, Sarah. The catalytic moment for the narrative
occurs when Alroy kills Alschiroch, a Moslem lord who had attempted to
seduce Miriam. Alroy escapes on a horse, whose appearance signifies by
association his rider's potential: 'his haughty crest, his eye of fire, the glory
of his snorting nostril, betokened well his conscious pride, and pure
nobility of race' (p. 20). Thereafter, having fallen asleep in the desert,
Alroy wakes up to find himself face to face with a lion. Their encounter
comprises the whole of chapter three of book two.

> He awoke; his gaze met the flaming eyes of the enormous beast fixed upon
> him with a blended feeling of desire and surprise. He awoke, and from a
> swoon; but the dreamless trance had refreshed the exhausted energies of the
> wanderer; in an instant he collected his senses, remembered all that had
> passed, and comprehended his present situation. He returned the lion a
> glance as imperious, and fierce, and scrutinising, as his own. For a moment,
> their flashing orbs vied in regal rivalry; but at length the spirit of the mere
> animal yielded to the genius of the man. The lion, cowed, slunk away,
> stalked with haughty timidity through the rocks, and then sprang into the
> forest. (p. 25)

Subsequently, a bird appears, 'and thrice with circling grace it flies around the head of the Hebrew Prince. Then by his side it gently drops a bunch of fresh and fragrant dates' (p. 26). The animal kingdom recognises the ferocious and regal qualities of Alroy. Beneath a corrupt society (in which the Jewish people are enslaved), a proper and beneficent order exists within nature; Disraeli's Romantic beliefs thus persist in *Alroy*, developing into an insurrectionary political and military programme.

An important figure in Alroy's rise to prominence is Jabaster, who performs the role of surrogate father, providing wisdom and guidance to Alroy, inspired by a devout Jewish faith. In this sense Jabaster is the most explicit prefiguration of Sidonia, as his Jewish faith is central to his characterisation. However, Jabaster is counterbalanced by the character of Honain, his brother, who is far more worldly and calculated. As long as Alroy is advised by Jabaster he is safe and successful, but when he is drawn away from the visionary and beguiled into a materialistic outlook by Honain, he suffers. Disraeli thus dramatises the conflict between principle and expediency, a familiar struggle for his central characters.

Alroy's ambitions are validated by a vision he experiences, in which he gains the blessing of Solomon, who passes him a sceptre, which he retains even after the vision has finished. Alroy is thus privileged to the point of being deified, a level of esteem and supremacy far in excess of that apportioned to any of Disraeli's other heroes, even the Young Duke. *Alroy* clearly represents Disraeli's 'ideal ambition', as the mutilated diary attests, as his hero's potential is unlimited. Alroy moves from one military victory to another, pausing only to share his triumph with Miriam, and to ennoble Jabaster by making him High Priest of Israel. The encounter with Miriam, prior to a departure for another battle, is placed in a pastoral setting and presented in intimate terms: 'one arm was wound round her delicate waist, and with the other he clasped her soft and graceful hand. The heavy tears burst from her downcast eyes, and stole along her pale and pensive cheek. They walked in silence, the brother and the sister, before the purity of whose surpassing love even ambition vanished. He opened the lattice gate. They entered into the valley small and green; before them was the marble fountain with its columns and cupola, and in the distance the charger of Alroy and his single attendant' (p. 129). The incident allows a momentary departure from the narrative and suggests that there is value in life beyond the pursuit of material reward. While much of the novel is interested in ambition, conquest and glory, when Alroy loses touch with his spiritual and emotional roots, he also loses his empire. *Alroy* is thus interested in the proper conditions for success as well as its pursuit. A similar pastoral episode within a general landscape of conflict is also presented in *Sybil* (see chapter two), signifying the possibility of happiness within a natural environment once conflict is dissolved.

Alroy's greatest military conquest is Baghdad. Prior to its capture he confidently announces, 'there is no career except conquest', and, 'say what they like, man is born for action' (pp. 131–2), the latter calling to mind Disraeli's pronouncement, 'I wish to *act* what I *write*.'[41] Following Baghdad's capture, Alroy is petitioned by Honain, in Jabaster's presence. Alroy allows the inhabitants of Baghdad to retain their own faith, with lukewarm support from Jabaster. This is Alroy's first departure from strict adherence to the tenets of his faith, and it paves the way for his eventual undoing. The novel thus encourages the reader to view faith as the basis for progress; it is a central element of his 1847 novel, *Tancred*, which subsequently endorses this position, while, much later, in *Lothair*, the purity of faith is compromised by the politics of confrontation and manipulation.

Alroy's triumphant arrival in Baghdad is phrased in the biblical idiom employed frequently in the novel, thereby enabling Disraeli to magnify the messianic qualities of his hero: 'march, onward march, ye valiant tribes, the hour has come, the hour has come! All the promises of ages, all the signs of sacred sages, meet in this ravishing hour. Where is now the oppressor's chariot, where your tyrant's purple robe? The horse and the rider are both overthrown, the horse and the rider are both overthrown!' (p. 144). The repeated labelling of Alroy as 'the chosen one' emphasises his religious qualities, yet it is at this point that the hero has his first confrontation with Jabaster. In reply to Alroy's comment, 'we must beware of dreamers', Jabaster replies, 'Dreams are the oracles of God.' Alroy's retort includes his insistence on the point, 'I must have practical men about me, practical men' (p. 147). The hero's separation from the visionary, together with his new stern pragmatism, aligns him with the utilitarians of Disraeli's own day; the novel becomes an allegory for Victorian England's philosophy as espoused by Bentham and J. S. Mill, rejecting the use of biblical language and authority.

Alroy's imminent marriage to Schirene places greater distance between himself and Jabaster. Alroy becomes less a spiritually-inspired visionary, more a politician.

> 'What is this?' continued Alroy, as Jabaster offered him a scroll. 'Ah! Your report. "Order of the Tribes," "Service of the Levites," "Princes of the People," "Elders of Israel!" The day may come when this may be effected. At present, Jabaster, we must be moderate, and content ourselves with arrangements which may ensure that order shall be maintained, property respected, and justice administered.' (pp. 158–9)

In the tension between visionary potentiality and concrete potentiality, ambition versus practicality, which characterises Disraeli's writings during this period, *Alroy* clearly prioritises the visionary above the pragmatic, yet it is important to remember that Disraeli identified the novel as his '*ideal* ambition' (emphasis added). *Alroy* demonstrates what can be achieved by the unfettered visionary, who is only laid low by the worldliness and corruption of others. His attraction to practical government alienates him from the narrator's support, at a time when Disraeli's own politics had yet to settle into a commitment to the values and strategy of a specific political party.

Jabaster's similarity to Sidonia is especially true with regard to his views on women and on racial purity. Sidonia remains determinedly single and insists, 'all is race' (*Tancred*). Jabaster, in a reference to Schirene, states, 'this Delilah may shear thy mystic locks' (p. 163) and is insistent on the need for Jewish separatism: 'we must exist alone. To preserve that loneliness is the great end and essence of our law. What have we to do with Bagdad [sic], or its people, where every instant we must witness some violation of our statutes? Can we pray with them? Can we eat with them? Alike in the highest duties, and the lowest occupations of our existence, we cannot mingle. From the altar of our God to our domestic boards, we are alike separated from them. Sire, you may be King of Bagdad, but you cannot, at the same time, be a Jew' (p. 164). Long before *Lord George Bentinck* presented Disraeli's detailed views on race and Jewishness (repeating, incidentally, the 'all is race' dictum), he presented these views in a condensed and abbreviated form in *Alroy*. Jabaster, now speaking in the third person to Alroy, highlights the consequences of Alroy's separation from his roots: 'the genius of the people, which he shared, raised him; and that genius has been formed by the law of Moses. Based on that law, he might indeed have handed down an empire to his long posterity; and now, though the tree of his fortunes seems springing up by the water-side, fed by a thousand springs, and its branches covered with dew, there is a gangrene in the sap, and to-morrow he may shrink like a shrivelled gourd. Alas! alas! for Israel' (p. 165). When the outburst is reported to Honain, he announces, 'my pious brother wishes to lead you back to the Theocracy' (p. 166), yet it is the spiritual vacuity of Honain that is, in part, responsible for Alroy's downfall. Disraeli's views on contemporary society and politics depicted a brusque, utilitarian pragmatism draining politics, and life in general, of its spirituality and imagination.

Part of Alroy's problem is that he attributes his success entirely to his own talents, forgetting the firm spiritual foundation on which his early triumphs were based. However, his empire lacks stability, precisely because he has neglected its spiritual foundation. Alroy's prophetess,

Esther, turns upon him and attempts to kill him, but not before she has highlighted a structural inequality in society: 'man made society, and made us slaves' (p. 195). Disraeli was a quiet advocate for women's rights at many points in his career, arguing for suffrage for women in 1866 (see chapter three). Alroy puts down the rebellion, but not before exposing his own weakness: 'I was not born to die in a civic broil. I bear a charmed life' (p. 198). His increasing separation from any sense of his own fallibilities creates the conditions in which he can be manipulated by those around him. Schirene urges him to kill Jabaster, who is held responsible for the rebellion. When Alroy recommends banishment instead, Schirene replies, 'to herd with rebels. Is this thy policy?' (p. 204). Like Macbeth and Lady Macbeth, Alroy and Schirene lose contact with reality; her taunts and his sense of his own omnipotence combine to shift the tone and indeed, temporarily, the genre of *Alroy*. Comparisons with *Macbeth* are further validated when Alroy self-torturously examines his own conduct, culminating in a vision or hallucination of the dead Jabaster, supposedly 'self-strangled' (p. 206) but, as it turns out, murdered by Honain and Schirene. Immediately prior to Jabaster's appearance, Alroy complains, 'all about me seems changed, and dull, and grown mechanical' (p. 214). Having lost touch with his spiritual dimension, personified through Jabaster, Alroy has also lost his inspiration. He is reduced to the role of an automaton, acting out a role with no sense of purpose. The loss of the sceptre of Solomon symbolises Alroy's alienation from his roots, an act of signification confirmed when Alroy has a further dream or vision in which he witnesses a grand procession, and 'the form of Solomon extended its arm, and took the sceptre, and instantly the mighty assembly vanished!' (p. 218).

Alroy is now powerless when he discovers the truth concerning Jabaster's murder. Schirene, though corrupted irredeemably, is still a figure of massive influence for Alroy: 'his judgement fluctuated in an eddy of passion and reason. Passion conquered. He dismissed from his intelligence all cognizance of good and evil; he determined, under all circumstances to cling ever to her; he tore from his mind all memory of the late disclosure' (p. 222). Alroy remains capable of energetic, even inspired, conduct, yet he has been corrupted at source by Schirene. Without spiritual foundations he betrays Jabaster in death as he betrayed him in life. Disraeli shows how Alroy's reason, his practicality, swamps the visionary within him, yet reason itself is subject to sexual passion. The prophetess Esther is similarly a slave to her own desires, as her attempt upon Alroy's life is born primarily of sexual jealousy. Disraeli demonstrates in *Alroy* not only the importance of spiritual foundation but also, paradoxically, its vulnerability; the maintenance of inspiration requires ongoing renewal and commitment. Without Jabaster this was no longer possible for Alroy. Disraeli's ideal ambition, though utopian, was not naïve; *Alroy* voices his recognition that ambition needs to be nurtured out of a belief system. The same emphasis on faith as a necessary precursor for successful action is also at the heart of *Tancred*.

Deposed by a second rebellion, Alroy flees to the desert with a residue of followers. In a brief, Romantic episode the transformation is restorative as, removed from the corruption of the city and once more in touch with nature, Alroy is able to connect with those around him, 'and merry faces were not wanting when at night they assembled in the amphitheatre for their common meal' (p. 230). However, he is betrayed from within his camp, captured, and returned to Baghdad: 'his clothes were soiled and tattered. The children pelted him with mud. An old woman, with a fanatic curse, placed a crown of paper on his brow. With difficulty his brutal guards prevented their victim from being torn to pieces. And in such fashion, towards noon of the fourteenth day, David Alroy again entered Bagdad' (p. 235). Disraeli shows graphically the extent of Alroy's fall; he had one reliable guide, whom he rejected, and thereafter he was vulnerable. Disraeli takes the opportunity of having Alroy in captivity to offer an exposition on the feeling of loss, conjuring up a sense of depression which may relate to his own lengthy yet unspecified illness of 1827–9: 'an awful thing it is, the failure of the energies of a master-mind. He who places implicit confidence in his genius will find himself some day utterly defeated and deserted. 'Tis bitter! . . . Like a dried up fountain, the perennial flow and bright fertility have ceased, and ceased for ever. Then comes the madness of retrospection' (pp. 238–9). Many of Disraeli's early ambitions with regard to both politics and literature were thwarted, and while his persistence and indomitability were both obvious qualities, he was not indifferent to defeat. *Alroy* articulates loss, coming from one who knew the experience repeatedly in his youth.

In the period before his execution Alroy regains his integrity by refusing to renounce his faith in exchange for his life. The defining encounter in this final section of the novel is not with his betrayers, Honain and Schirene, but with his sister, Miriam. She reassures him about the value of his life and deeds: 'you have shown what we can do and shall do. Your memory alone is inspiration. A great career, although baulked of its end, is still a landmark of human energy. Failure, when sublime, is not without its purpose. Great deeds are great legacies, and work with wondrous usury. By what Man has done, we learn what Man can do; and gauge the power and prospect of our race.' Miriam is a stoic and reliable character in the novel; her views reflect Disraeli's own outlook. Miriam believes that how one fights the battle is more important than whether one wins the war: consistent with the perspective adopted throughout *Alroy*, she values the visionary above the practical. Her assertion that 'our race' will benefit from Alroy's example reminds us that a sense of group identity is also important in *Alroy*: voiced by Honain, echoed by Miriam, it is developed into a full statement of belief by Disraeli later in his career as a novelist. Miriam then goes on to imply Disraeli's own role in the production of *Alroy*: 'perchance some poet, in some distant age, within whose veins our sacred blood may flow, his fancy fired with the national theme, may strike his harp to Alroy's wild career, and consecrate a name too long forgotten?' (p. 235). A link is thus forged between the twelfth-century hero and the nineteenth-century novelist. Furthermore, the connection is clearly constructed along racial lines; the sense of his own Jewishness was an important aspect of Disraeli's self-conception, even at this early stage in his career. The fact that Miriam dies after having made her proclamation imbues her words with even greater significance. Disraeli the chronicler is destined to become the next great Jewish leader.

Disraeli's Alroy is a more spectacular figure than the twelfth-century leader on whom he is based. It is also possible to read *Alroy* as an allegory of competing philosophies in the 1830s, or to see it as dramatising the conflict between ambition and practicality. In this sense the characters represent different sides of the argument and, given that *Alroy* elevates the imagination above pragmatism, fall into the category of either visionary or utilitarian, although this analysis fails to anticipate the complexity of the narrative. Honain is Jabaster's brother, and is also his alter-ego. While Jabaster inspires Alroy to strive for others, Honain encourages him to serve a narrower base of interests; Daniel Schwarz says of Honain, 'his own welfare is at the centre of his value system'.[42] Despite this, the two important characters are still brothers, and Honain, in an early part of the novel, acts with Solomon-like wisdom when he adjudicates on the ownership of a ring in Alroy's favour (book five, chapter two). Furthermore, a conversation between Honain and Schirene demonstrates some depth in the characters.

> 'I suppose common people are never tired,' said the Princess.
> 'Except with labour,' said the Physician; 'care keeps them alive.'
> 'What is care?' asked the Princess, with a smile.
> 'It is a god,' replied the Physician, 'invisible, but omnipotent. It steals the bloom from the cheek and lightness from the pulse; it takes away the appetite, and turns the hair grey.' (p. 70)

The sympathy for the poor illustrated in their conversation foreshadows some of the ideas developed in the Young England trilogy, especially *Sybil*. It reinforces the idea that *Alroy* is as much concerned with Disraeli's own period as it is with the twelfth century. Disraeli takes the genre of historical fiction (including enough environmental detail, drawn from his own travels in the East, to render his setting credible) and then imbues it with contemporary anxieties in order to air and develop the views at the centre of his gradually evolving philosophy.

The Rise of Iskander is a short text (approximately 3,500 words), yet its two main characters, Iskander and Nicaeus, embody separately Alroy's conflicting nature: Iskander is noble and self-sacrificing, Nicaeus is passionate but lacking in wisdom. The tension between the conflicting demands of imagination and reason occurs frequently in Disraeli's heroes; indeed, Disraeli himself, in a diary entry dated 1 September 1833, referred to his own 'awful ambition and fiery passions'.[43] The young man who transformed a journalistic proposal into a political one when he visited Lockhart in Scotland in 1825 was fuelled by ambition and vision rather than pragmatism.

Iskander is a Christian and a fierce warrior, brought up under the care of the Turkish sultan. Although he is distinct from Alroy in terms of his faith, he is, like the hero of Disraeli's earlier novel, on a mission to renew a nation – in his case, Epirus. The capital, Croia, fulfils a Disraelian ideal through its proximity to abundant nature: 'the city was surrounded by a beautiful region of cornfields and fruit-trees. The road was arched with the overhanging boughs. The birds chirped on every spray.' Iskander's effect on his homeland is midway between that of Aubrey Bohun in *A Year at Hartlebury*, and Alroy: 'the name of Iskander acted as a spell. They stopt not to inquire. A magic sympathy at once persuaded them that this great man had, by the grace of Heaven, recurred to the creed and country of his fathers' (p. 235). Iskander is thus a messianic figure with a political agenda.

Iskander and Nicaeus become love rivals for a princess, Iduna. Her kidnap leads to a daring escape directed by Iskander, who defends a bridge against pursuers while Nicaeus and Iduna complete their escape. It is at this point that betrayal threatens *The Rise of Iskander*, as Nicaeus, himself a prince, imprisons Iduna with a view to seducing her. The narrator's comment, 'the Prince of Athens, with many admirable qualities, was one of those men who are influenced only by their passions, and who, in the affairs of life, are invariably guided by their imagination instead of their reason' (p. 267), signifies Disraeli's gradual movement away from wholehearted endorsement of the Romantics' celebration of the unfettered imagination. *The Rise of Iskander* differs from *Alroy* in the sense that it advocates balance; the hero's nationalistic agenda is tempered by an active and rational intelligence. The defeat of Nicaeus's plan, followed by his purgatorial death in battle on Iskander's behalf, results in a happy conclusion, in which integrity thwarts the rogue elements. Unlike Alroy, Iskander does not lose his focus, nor is he lulled into complacency by his own victories. Disraeli's biographer, Monypenny, claimed that *The Rise of Iskander* 'has nothing that is peculiar to Disraeli nor any special significance in the story of his inner development'.[44] This is not so; *The Rise of Iskander* highlights the gains to be drawn from marrying a visionary imagination with a practical strategy for application. Moreover, Disraeli applauds his fictional hero's vigilance, alongside his strategically underpinned ambition, at a time when Disraeli himself was attempting to construct practical outlets in Parliament for his imaginative impulses.

On the political front Disraeli sought to stand for the constituency of Marylebone in April 1833, but the expected vacancy did not occur. He also published a pamphlet in connection with the anticipated parliamentary contest, *What is He? By the author of Vivian Grey,* which urged the formation of a national party, created out of an alliance between the Tories and the Radicals: 'if the Tories indeed despair of restoring the aristocratic principle, and are sincere in their avowal that the State cannot be governed with the present machinery, it is their duty to coalesce with the Radicals, and permit both political nicknames to merge in the common, the intelligible, and the dignified title of a National Party' (pp. 19–20).[45] Disraeli was not alone in advocating the formation of a national parliamentary party; the same remedy for the country's ills was proposed by Edward Bulwer-Lytton in *England and the English,* also published in 1833. *What is He?* attributes the destruction of the aristocratic principle to the Reform Bill, and the overall tone, while spirited, is generally measured, and the approach analytical. Disraeli is resigned to the new political settlement and states that it is, 'absolutely necessary to advance to the new or the democratic principle' (p. 18). However, as *What is He?* concludes it becomes positively symphonic, rising to a conclusion which implies social redemption by messianic means: 'great spirits may yet arise, to guide the groaning helm through the world of troubled waters; spirits whose proud destiny it may still be, at the same time to maintain the glory of the Empire, and to secure the happiness of the People!' (p. 22). More prosaically, there is clear intellectual continuity between *What is He?* and the Young England trilogy: the upper classes and the populace are urged to unite under a leadership which is assumed to be benign and socially responsible. He also repeats, albeit in slightly different terms, the claim of *Contarini Fleming,* that there had occurred a shift in power from the 'aristocratic' to the 'democratic', which correlates with the feudal and the federal in the earlier novel; indeed, Disraeli writes in *What is He,* 'that Europe for the last three centuries has been more or less in a state of transition from Feudal to Federal principles of government' (p. 22). A landowning class has given way to a collection of interests which Disraeli is more capable of identifying by name, the Whigs, than by overt ideology.

In July 1833, another work of Disraeli's, 'Walstein; or, A Cure for Melancholy' appeared in *The Court Magazine*. Walstein's tendency to elevate the visionary above the practical is tempered by the advice of a physician, Schulembourg, who sees the need to balance the two. When Walstein proclaims, 'I have become convinced that man is not a rational animal. He is only truly great when he acts from passion', Schulembourg counters with a metaphor which signifies the shifting current of Disraeli's thoughts: 'passion is the ship, and reason is the rudder' (p. 349). Schulembourg further states that 'action' is the sole cure for Walstein's melancholy (p. 350), and the physician's subsequent overview urges the application of inner thoughts and feelings to the wider environment: 'when a man has a peculiar structure, when he is born with a predisposition, or is, in vulgar language, a man of genius, his content entirely depends upon the predisposition being developed and indulged' (p. 356). 'Walstein' expresses Disraeli's ongoing inner debate between the visionary and the expedient. The hero, unable to meld the two, is steered away from melancholy by Schulembourg's advice, along with the sympathetic attention of the physician's wife. 'Walstein' also mentions a writer named Sidonia: while the character is of little consequence, the name was set to be important within Disraeli's literary *oeuvre*.[46]

A YEAR AT HARTLEBURY

'"Agitate," replied his principal, "agitate, agitate. That magic word is the main essence of all political success."'

One of Disraeli's more curious novels of the 1830s was *A Year at Hartlebury*, first published by Saunders and Otley in March 1834.[47] It was co-authored by his sister, Sarah, and published under the pseudonyms of Cherry and Fair Star. It has been established that Sarah wrote the bulk of the novel, with Benjamin's most sustained contribution being the first nine chapters of volume two, which involve an election for the constituency of Fanchester. Through this episode, Disraeli offers a version of his first campaign for Parliament, though in the novel he is successful. Therefore, the novel occurs at a cusp period in Disraeli's career, when his commitment to literature was waning and his immersion in politics increasing. He had campaigned for a seat in High Wycombe twice in 1832, before switching his attention to Bucks county, and then Marylebone in April 1833. He had little time left over for literature, though he had also been working on a poem, *The Revolutionary Epick*, which is one of the reasons why he handed the completion of *A Year at Hartlebury* over to his sister. It seems most likely, according to John Matthews, that he stopped contributing material for the novel before the end of 1833.[48] Speculation has arisen concerning the choice of pseudonyms, and it has led to further conjecture, namely that Disraeli was the author of a theatrical work, *Cherry and Fair Star or, The Children of Cyprus*, which was staged successfully at the Theatre Royal, Covent Garden in the spring of 1822. It would explain how Disraeli came to have money to speculate on the stock market in the 1820s, but the matter is as yet unresolved.[49]

There is a significant autobiographical element in *A Year at Hartlebury*. Bradenham, the Disraeli's home, becomes Hartlebury Manor, Benjamin becomes Aubrey Bohun and Sarah is the heroine, Helen Molesworth. Like Vivian Grey or Contarini Fleming, Aubrey Bohun is a vivacious, dynamic character: 'to sigh over the unchangeable past was not in the nature of Aubrey Bohun. The exciting present was the world in which he lived, and remorse or regret were phantoms that never disturbed his reveries' (p. 57). At times, the characterisation of Bohun anticipates the hero of *Sybil*, Egremont: 'they found Mr Bohun, in every respect, the reverse of what they expected. If Mr Chace was astonished at detecting in him a complete man of business, they were not less so at finding a man of sense. Graceful and easy in his address, mild and unaffected in his manners, he seemed as eager to please as he appeared agreeably impressed by them' (p. 59). However, when the campaign itself is in full flow, Bohun exudes all the ostentatious, unbounded confidence of Vivian Grey, or Disraeli himself in his *Representative* phase:

> the music became louder and louder, the advanced flags approached, and passed them. The cheering seemed to rend the skies. Bounding with matchless grace on an Arab steed and at the head of nearly a thousand of his tenantry and neighbours covered with boughs of laurel, Aubrey Bohun appeared. (p. 131)

The imagery here is imperial, even messianic. Bohun is a saviour, determined to liberate Fanchester from narrow-minded Whig commercialism. In a diary entry, Disraeli himself decorates his future career in similarly grandiose terms: 'my career will probably be more energetic than ever, and the world will wonder at my ambition'.[50] This is remarkably similar to Bohun's thoughts during the election: 'if I live I *must* be a great man' (p. 141).[51] Matthews has pointed out other parallels between Bohun's career and Disraeli's. Both seek parliamentary seats in boroughs rather than in the county. This is primarily because Bohun perceives it as being less of a risk to upset urbanites as opposed to his friends in the country, while Disraeli's fiction always applauded the homogeneity of rural communities. Both position themselves between the two main political parties, but with greater hostility to the Whigs than to the Tories (Disraeli did not stand as an official Conservative candidate until 1835). Therefore, Bohun parallels the aspiring parliamentarian who chased a seat so energetically in the 1830s.

There is a consistency of outlook between the two authors of *A Year at Hartlebury*. This is not surprising: the two were close as individuals and were frequent correspondents – agreement regarding wider issues is to be expected. The novel commences in the idyll of Hartlebury, 'a rural green, encircled by cottages, and embosomed in wood-crowned hills' (p. 3). It is the home of Arthur Latimer, a clergyman and one of the few characters to emerge from the novel with credit. His values are established swiftly: 'in proportion as people were rich and educated so he thought they ought to be virtuous and religious' (p. 5); on a less spiritual and more social level he later states, 'it is the sympathy of the landlord which above all elevates the moral feelings of his poorer neighbours' (p. 9). Such views were essential to Benjamin Disraeli's philosophy, a state of benign reciprocity prevailing within communities, generated through philanthropy. Hartlebury is also home to Kate Medley, an orphan, whose life illustrates the principles set forth by Latimer: 'she was brought up the child of parish bounty; but instead of belonging to no one, she was a subject of common interest to all' (p. 46). Helen Molesworth is similarly loving and loved: 'these almshouses were Helen's favourite resort. Here she took many lessons, not only in the mysteries of knitting but in the knowledge of cheerfulness and the art of content' (p. 10). Under these conditions Hartlebury is a Little England utopia, characterised by local collectivism, propelled by benevolent rule.

However, Hartlebury is not immune to the social changes sweeping through the country, the consequences of the Industrial Revolution. In chapter two, Mr Gainsborough, a rich tradesman, has built a new mansion, signifying the emergence of a new and powerful, commercial class. The same literary device is used when Aubrey Bohun returns to reinvigorate Bohun Castle: 'as he passed over the draw-bridge, a porter threw open the massive gates, which no longer creaked upon their hinges' (p. 63). The return of the castle's rightful owner is restorative, both architecturally and, as the novel develops, politically. The landscape to which Bohun returns is in a state of flux. Mr Gainsborough's mansion has been built while long-established modes of living are under threat. Sarah Disraeli (assuming that she is sole author of the first volume) castigates dominant political principles for having brought this state of affairs about. In one episode we are introduced to Mr Ford, 'a fine specimen of a once numerous and noble race, now alas! nearly extinct – the blunt, the honest, the true old English yeoman' (p. 98). He lives on 'one of the few small farms which still managed to struggle on, in spite of political economy' (p. 97). Sarah Disraeli's defence of her fictional character and, more pertinently, her criticism of political economy, echoes the stance adopted six years earlier by her brother in *Popanilla*. Her analysis is also expressed through other characters in *A Year at Hartlebury*. In chapter nineteen, Helen Molesworth's father speaks with Aubrey Bohun: "'there was no cholera when I was a boy," observed Mr Molesworth, "and then we were indeed an aristocratic nation. That is past. We are now a people of political economists. Ricks are burnt and machines shattered, and the people are starving, but then we have the advantage of being destroyed by the most scientific legislation"' (p. 77). By association, political economy becomes a virulent disease; it is associated with social discontent and violence. This quote further suggests that the lower classes are unhappy with their lot and potentially disruptive, an anxiety voiced earlier in the novel when a question is asked of Mr Gainsborough: "'I don't think an English mob would kill children, do you Mr Gainsborough?" "It is impossible to say what an infuriated populace would do," solemnly replied the politician. "It appears to me," said Arthur Latimer, "that the transition from incendiarism to the most horrible murder is not very difficult"' (p. 31). Mr Gainsborough's reply is ambiguous, retaining the suggestion of violence. However, Arthur Latimer enjoys the narrator's trust, and he recognises the destructive potential of the lower classes. Connecting Sarah Disraeli's position with her brother's, the conversation in *A Year at Hartlebury* prefigures aspects of the concluding section of *Sybil*, as a lower-class mob of Chartist persuasion goes on the rampage. The apparent contradiction here is that the contented servility of the lower orders is transformed into angry violence. The difference is one of guidance: when the populace are spearheaded by a political militant they become monstrous. When they have no aspirations to advance as an organised class and instead submit voluntarily to benevolent, paternalistic rule, they are the happy beneficiaries of charity and sympathy.

Parliamentary life is mentioned in volume one, prior to volume two's focus on the electoral process. Whereas Benjamin Disraeli's *The Young Duke* showed the House of Lords to be a dormant place, the collaborative *A Year at Hartlebury* deals briefly with the Commons: 'trying to get in is some amusement. But every man I know in the House tells me he is bored to death. There's Crawford – Crawford never could sleep 'till he got into parliament; and Harry Stair, he always says it cured his dyspepsia. There is no place in the world where you sleep so soundly as in the House of Commons' (p. 77). There is humour in this passage but also a deep cynicism. Parliament slumbers, according to the Disraelis: while the more natural leaders of the House of Lords await a catalyst, the Commons is truly moribund.

In the election chapters of volume two, the villains are clearly identified as the Whigs. They attack long-standing institutions, 'sapping the foundations of that church which was the only barrier against their barbarising creeds and customs' (p. 103). Their perceived subversive qualities have scarcely any limits as far as Benjamin Disraeli is concerned: 'if ever a revolution come round in this once happy country, we may trace all our misery to the influence of the low Whigs. These are the real causes of Manchester massacres, though they are always abusing the magistracy; these are the men who, though they think they are only snuffing the candle in their own miserable hard-hearted parlours, are in fact lighting the torch of every incendiary in the kingdom' (p. 103). The Whigs are personified in the figure of Mr Jenkins, 'a sharp, square-built, acute looking man, with a peculiarly unamiable expression of countenance, and somewhat bald' (p. 131); in the heat of the election 'he gnashed his teeth' (p. 143). Disraeli's portrayal of the Whigs can be linked to his own career: though he associated with Radicals (and stood for election as one) prior to his movement into the Conservative camp in the mid-1830s, he rarely ever held anything other than contempt for the Whigs. Disraeli's stance here also counters the accusation that he was merely an opportunist who allied himself with whatever faction was in the ascendant; in the period surrounding the Reform Bill, the Whigs were unquestionably the dominant party in the country.[52] For Disraeli, however, the Whigs represented the ascendancy of commercialism and, simultaneously, the degradation of the institutions upon which, Disraeli believed, the prosperity and stability of the nation was based. The Whigs of *A Year at Hartlebury* are stern and parasitical; Disraeli was never going to find his political home among them.

Bohun's victory in the Fanchester election is Disraeli's imaginary compensation for actual defeat. Bohun goes on to make a sparkling maiden speech in Parliament. However, this angel transpires to have feet of clay, as he has sexually betrayed Helen Molesworth, the woman he is set to marry. He is found shot dead and his assassin remains undetected. Sarah Disraeli wrote the conclusion to the novel and it is not easy to speculate on what her intentions may have been. It could conceivably have been an outlet for suppressed, aggressive feelings towards her brother, but it could just as easily have been a deliberately dramatic and unresolved conclusion in order to create the conditions in which a sequel would be required; this was certainly the view taken by one of the critics who reviewed the novel upon its publication.[53]

While Sarah Disraeli was working on *A Year at Hartlebury*, her brother was completing his epic poem (while also finding time to contribute 'The Infernal Marriage' to the *New Monthly Magazine*), *Revolutionary Epick*. The first volume was published in March 1834. The title page announced that the poem was 'the Work of Disraeli the Younger, Author of "The Psychological Romance"' (*Contarini Fleming*).[54] It was all a far cry from the anonymous publication of *Vivian Grey*, suggesting that Disraeli was very confident with regard to his new work. Two more volumes of *Revolutionary Epick* appeared in June. In a characteristically grand gesture Disraeli asked permission to dedicate it to the Duke of Wellington, but this was declined. The concept underpinning the *Revolutionary Epick* could hardly have been more grand.

> Now for the Epic! It appears to me that all great works that have formed an epoch in the history of the human intellect have been an embodification of the spirit of their age. An heroic age produced in the Iliad an *heroic* poem. The foundation of the Empire of the Caesars produced in the Aeneid a *political* poem. The revival of letters produced in the Divine Comedy a *national* poem. The Reformation & its consequences produced in the Paradise Lost a *religious poem.*
>
> Since the revolt of America a new principle has been at work in the world to which I trace all that occurs. This is the *Revolutionary* principle, and this is what I wish to embody in *The Revolutionary Epic.*[55]

Disraeli's starting point in the *Epick* was to have the advocates of feudalism and federalism plead their causes before the almighty: feudalism is represented as the character of Margos, federalism becomes Lyridon and the almighty is Demogorgon. The poem makes a clear case for government by the nobility.

> Deep in the strata of the human heart,
> The seeds of aristocracy are sown.
> A vigorous plant, and soon a nation's pride,
> That ardent atmosphere, its lusty buds
> Calls forth to taste the promise of their Spring;
> And when the glowing summer of their fortunes
> Leads on its dazzling pageant, mark ye well
> To lustrous bloom those lusty buds expand,
> And fill the air with splendour and perfume! (p. 45)

Disraeli's metaphors associate the aristocracy with natural growth, suggesting that they emerge organically out of society, and have the capacity to spread their goodness throughout the community. In the following stanza, entitled 'Portrait of a true Noble', Disraeli clarifies his understanding of the ideal aristocrat. The nobleman, 'from his elevated station views, / As from some noble mount, or lofty tower, / The wide spread region of society' (p. 45). He becomes a deified figure and a representative of a class which guarantees a nation's welfare: 'This pledge that in the tempests of the world / The stream of culture shall not backward ebb, / This is the noble that mankind demands, / And this the man a nation loves to trust' (p. 46). The beneficent government promised by the nobleman represents Disraeli's ideal, a wise patriarch superintending his community in a climate of mutual trust and public adoration. Conversely, federalism offers savage destruction; whilst considering equality, in the context of the French Revolution, Disraeli refers to it as 'The maddening charm', having a degrading effect, 'And man becomes more savage than the beasts' (p. 62). Reform appears as 'bold Subversion' (p. 81). The contention of Magros is that 'GRADATION is the spell of Nature's sway' (p. 65); inequality is presented as a law of nature, with the aristocracy having the innate right and responsibility to govern.

In common with *Contarini Fleming*, Disraeli had high hopes for *The Revolutionary Epick*. A recitation of some of the work took place in January 1834, and one of those present reported Disraeli's view of his poem: 'he proceeded . . . to ask why, as the heroic age had produced its Homer, the Augustan era its Virgil, the Renaissance its Dante, the Reformation its Milton, should not the Revolutionary epoch, in which we live, produce its representative Poet?'[56] With this level of ambition it is hard to see how any response could live up the poet's expectations, and thus it proved: the *Epick* received nothing more than an indifferent response from the critics. However, it is noteworthy that Disraeli discontinued the work after volume three, despite the high ambition with which it had commenced; in a letter of December 1833 he stated that the work 'could not be completed under 30,000 lines'.[57] The visionary in Disraeli was now effectively countered by the pragmatist. While his early literary works celebrate visionary characters, they also demonstrate a developing preoccupation with the need to balance inspiration alongside practical considerations. Furthermore, this tension is not only evident within Disraeli's early novels, it is also apparent in his early literary career.

In July 1834 Disraeli was introduced to Lord Melbourne, then Home Secretary, subsequently Prime Minister. In response to an enquiry from Melbourne concerning his future plans, Disraeli stated, 'I want to be Prime Minister.'[58] At the end of 1834 he launched another (unsuccessful) attempt to enter Parliament, standing for Wycombe as a Radical. The Tories contributed £500 towards his election expenses, but this was less an expression of wholehearted support than the discreet and politically sensible backing of the anti-Whig candidate. A speech he delivered to the electorate on December 16 was subsequently published as a pamphlet: *The Crisis Examined by Disraeli, the Younger*, in which he condones the Peel government's acceptance of the Whig Reform Act, justifying it in the context of a larger formula, laced with a generous measure of self-justification: 'the truth is, gentlemen, a statesman is the creature of his age, the child of circumstances, the creation of his times. . . . I laugh, therefore, at the objections against a man that at a former period of his career he advocated a policy different to his present one: all I seek to ascertain is whether his present policy be just, necessary, expedient.'[59] Here the visionary of the novels is tempered by the practical considerations of the prospective parliamentarian, mindful of the accusations of political insincerity which could be made against him. Disraeli the aspiring politician was even more bothered by other people's perceptions than Disraeli the novelist. His literary works granted him a degree of imaginative freedom; his political ambitions were less accommodating, forcing him to respond to the demands of the time. In any event, his more tactical presentation to the electorate did him no good, and he again finished last in a field of three.

Disraeli's major publication of 1835 was *A Vindication of the English Constitution in a Letter to a Noble and Learned Lord by Disraeli, the Younger*.[60] By this stage his conversion to the Conservative cause was complete, an act signified by his application to join the Carlton Club, the main and most influential point of assembly for the party which had emerged out of the post-Reform Act parliament. Furthermore, in the same year he stood as a Conservative candidate for the first time, losing a by-election at Taunton. *A Vindication* is primarily a defence of the House of Lords, but it contains within it Disraeli's ideas about history and politics, ideas which were to resurface later in both *Coningsby* and *Sybil*. He condemns the Whigs as the 'anti-national party' on the grounds that they were in alliance with Daniel O'Connell's Irish Nationalists in the House of Commons. Thus, by a blunt process of elimination, 'the Tory party in this country is the national party; it is the really democratic party of England' (p. 216), a point which Disraeli was to emphasise and develop as his career progressed. The publication of *A Vindication* was also timely; Catholic Emancipation in 1829 and the Reform Act of 1832 had challenged already existing power structures. Monarchic influence was reasserted in 1834 with William IV's dismissal of Lord Melbourne as Prime Minister, declining only in the 1840s when Queen Victoria adopted a non-partisan role. Therefore, Disraeli was writing at a time when long-standing modes of government in England were under threat. Disraeli's desire to conserve British institutions identified him unambiguously as a Tory.

Disraeli personifies political virtue in the form of Lord Bolingbroke, though his description owes more to Disraeli's personal vision of a charismatic political saviour than to the Bolingbroke of history. He writes that Bolingbroke 'incurred the common-place imputation of insincerity and inconsistency', a charge frequently levelled against Disraeli, while also pointing out that, 'from the moment that Lord Bolingbroke, in becoming a Tory, embraced the national cause, he devoted himself absolutely to his party' (pp. 218–19). Disraeli uses his subject to advocate his own cause, implying a parallel between himself and Bolingbroke in a manner which suggests that the Tories would benefit from Disraeli's involvement.

Elsewhere in *A Vindication*, Disraeli declares a nostalgic position: 'this moderate, prudent, sagacious, and eminently practical application of principles to conduct has ever been, in the old time, the illustrious characteristic of our English politicians' (p. 121). He attacks indirectly the attraction to theory which, he felt, was one of the chief faults of the utilitarians. His opposition to theory is voiced more explicitly when he writes that, 'political institutions, to be effective, must be founded on the habits and opinions of the people whom they pretend to govern' (p. 129). Good government, for Disraeli, was practically an organic phenomenon, growing out of a community in which the aristocracy was paramount but not despotic; he writes of 'the sympathy which has ever subsisted between the English and their aristocracy' (p. 154). Therefore, change should be gradual: 'are we never to learn that a Constitution, a real Constitution, is the creation of ages, not of a day, and that when we destroy such a Constitution we in fact destroy a nation?' (p. 133). On the matter of electoral reform he argues, 'a free government on a great scale of national representation is the very gradual work of time, and especially of preparatory institutions' (p. 145). His objections to the Reform Act of 1832 centred not on the fact that the electorate had been expanded, but on the manner in which the task had been undertaken, the effect of which (for Disraeli) was the strengthening in government of a Whig oligarchy: 'although their representatives may be chosen by three hundred thousand men instead of one hundred thousand, they are still only the representatives of a limited and favoured class of the kingdom' (p. 169). He reinforces this point in his concluding paragraph: 'the Reform Act has placed the power of the country in the hands of a small body of persons hostile to the nation' (p. 225). Subsequent commentary has provided vindication of Disraeli's view by pointing out the limits in the extension of the franchise, while also identifying how the new electoral arrangements affected the working classes. According to Philip Davis: 'the Reform Act only extended the franchise, cautiously, to the new economically successful and respectable middle classes, forestalling any further unrest from this newly powerful section of the populace. But as the harbinger of democracy, it helped create a volatile new class-consciousness and, in particular, served only to increase the working classes' consciousness of exclusion.'[61] The potential saviour of the nation in *A Vindication* was to be the Conservative Party, ideally strengthened by the presence of a new Bolingbroke. *A Vindication* takes the anti-utilitarian, pro-aristocratic spirit of Disraeli's early literary works and gives them a clear political form for the first time. His ideas would be developed still further in his novels of the 1840s, in which he used the genre of the novel to dramatise the ongoing political tensions of his time.

Disraeli also wrote two short stories in 1835, 'The Carrier Pigeon' and 'The Consul's Daughter', for a fashionable annual with a predominantly female readership, *Heath's Book of Beauty*. 'The Carrier Pigeon' features a hero named Lothair in a romantic yet illicit relationship, sustained by messages carried by pigeon. The death of the creature suggests that Disraeli knew the limitations of the long-distance romance genre: 'alas! Alas! The blood gushes from thy breast, and from thine azure beak! Thy transcendent eye grows dim – all is over! The carrier-pigeon falls to the earth!' (p. 307). 'The Consul's Daughter' features a hero named Lord Bohun who temporarily goes by the name of Ferrers, names which look back to *A Year at Hartlebury* and forward to *Endymion*. The heroine of the tale is named Henrietta, which may seem indecorous in view both of Disraeli's private life at the time, and the subject matter of his next novel.

HENRIETTA TEMPLE

'. . . and here, perhaps, I should remind the reader, that of all the great distinctions in life none perhaps is more important than that which divides mankind into the two great sections of Nobs and Snobs.'

Henrietta Temple, A Love Story, completed by the autumn of 1836 but first published in 1837, records in fiction Disraeli's real-life affair with a married woman, Henrietta Sykes.[62] Henrietta used the pet name 'Ammin' for Disraeli; it is no coincidence that the hero in *Henrietta Temple* is Ferdinand Armine. However, it would be incorrect to read *Henrietta Temple* as purely autobiographical. Robert Blake notes that, 'Armine bears no resemblance whatever to Disraeli. Henrietta, who is only eighteen, bears little to the real Henrietta, except for her physical description, and her letters to Ferdinand.'[63] *Henrietta Temple*, therefore, takes autobiographical detail and then places it within an ongoing internal debate in Disraeli's writings between principle and expediency.

Within the novel, the Armine family are Catholic, symbolising solidity and continuity. The hero's grandfather, also called Ferdinand Armine, was impetuous and reprobate by nature, while Ferdinand junior's father, Sir Ratcliffe Armine, is conservative and conventional. The conflicting influences of these two figures are both at work inside Ferdinand, enabling Disraeli to depict the tension between desire and practicality operating within the central character. Ferdinand's mother is 'Constance, the eldest daughter of Lord Grandison' (p. 8). She is a 'pious and dutiful' woman (p. 12), thereby imbuing the hero with nobility and seriousness. The Armine family is completed by the character of Adrian Glastonbury, a Catholic scholar. Consequently, Ferdinand Armine is endowed with the qualities required for the Disraelian hero to embark upon a successful career. At the age of ten he possesses, 'the wild and careless grace of childhood [and] the thoughtfulness and self-discipline of maturer age' (p. 22), expressing his radically contrasting influences. His potential volatility is signified by the fact that he is attracted to, and resembles, the figure of his grandfather: 'he would sometimes stand abstracted for many minutes before the portrait of Sir Ferdinand in the gallery, painted by Reynolds, before his grandfather left England, and which the child already singularly resembled' (p. 23). In Ferdinand's internal tensions, impetuosity will periodically triumph over decorum.

The driving force behind *Henrietta Temple* is financial problems. Ferdinand's task is to restore the family's fortunes, to which end he first becomes an ensign in the Royal Fusileers. On the night before his departure, in a revealing conversation with his mother, Ferdinand exposes the anxiety generated by the burden which has been placed upon him, 'all now depends on me, you know. I must restore our house' (p. 48). By the standards of the Young Duke or Alroy, his task is not Herculean, but it is set to determine and constrain his actions; Disraeli presents a branch of the aristocracy which, far from being ostentatious and profligate, is having to act defensively in order to retain its position. His mother presents him with his grandfather's sword, which acquires a symbolic value, a bond between the recipient and the original holder. Lady Constance imbues the incident with additional significance by stating, 'I am very superstitious about that sword, and while you have it I am sure you will succeed' (p. 50). However, in taking the sword Ferdinand assumes a closer relationship with the character of his reckless grandfather.

As Ferdinand leaves, early the following morning, he surveys his surroundings in a manner which reflects the concluding, pastoral idyll of *Vivian Grey,* while simultaneously anticipating the advocacy of rural life and values found later in *Coningsby* and *Sybil*:

From the green knoll on which he stood he beheld the clustering village of Armine, a little agricultural settlement formed of the peasants alone who lived on the estate. The smoke began to rise in blue curls from the cottage chimneys, and the church clock struck the hour of five. It seemed to Ferdinand that those labourers were far happier than he, since the setting sun would find them still at Armine; happy, happy Armine! (pp. 50–1)

The responsibility of the aristocracy as social leaders is here presented as a burden rather than a blessing. Ferdinand is attending to his responsibilities, despite the personal discomfort this brings about. The peasant community is idyllically depicted as being content in its containment, removed from the anxiety of leadership.

The military context allows the influence of Ferdinand's grandfather to become more prominent: 'he was the best rider among them, and the deadliest shot, and he soon became an oracle at the billiard-table, and a hero in the racket-court' (p. 58). It is not surprising that he also starts to accumulate debts, with comments offered on the nature of debt and its consequences: 'if youth but knew the fatal misery that they are entailing on themselves the moment they accept a pecuniary credit to which they are not entitled, how they would start in their career! how pale they would turn! how they would tremble, and clasp their hands in agony at the precipice on which they are disporting! Debt is the prolific mother of folly and of crime; it taints the course of life in all its dreams' (pp. 60–1). The exaggerated, exclamatory tone here encourages us to think that the writer is being ironic, yet Disraeli was no stranger to financial worries. Debt threatened to derail his career on many occasions prior to his marriage to a relatively well-off widow in 1839, whereafter he still endured another further decade of substantial financial anxiety. *Henrietta Temple* presents debt as a crushing determinant, and while Disraeli displayed considerable skill in evading his creditors, simultaneously testing (and, to an extent, exploiting) the patience of his friends and benefactors (most notably, at this point in his career, Benjamin Austen) he knew personally the extreme difficulties that owing money could cause. His comments on debt in *Henrietta Temple* are more impassioned than ironic.

Ferdinand's insurance rests in his belief that his mother's father, Lord Grandison, will leave everything to him in his will. However, it all goes to Ferdinand's cousin, Katherine. Immediately, Ferdinand resolves to marry his cousin: 'the future, not the past, must be my motto. To retreat is impossible; I may yet advance and conquer. Katherine Grandison: only think of my little cousin Kate for a wife!' (p. 63). The military metaphor is partly a reflection of the context in which Ferdinand has been placed, yet the complete absence of emotional or romantic feeling is also noteworthy. Ferdinand is not presented as a callous character in the novel, but his attitude towards Katherine is entirely calculated; the maintenance or the restoration of the aristocracy is the primary goal, and anything that serves the ends of the aristocracy is justified. Although Ferdinand has a particular duty which transcends personal feelings, he also has a personal motive for pursuing Katherine, as, with her new-found wealth, she is in a position to discharge his debts.

Irrespective of motive, he is successful in his pursuit, and Katherine falls in love with him. Ferdinand is now able to think of himself in heroic terms. His actions are motivated by an illegitimate selfishness and therefore undermine his relationship with Katherine. Moreover, he feels the burden of his situation: 'there are moments I almost wish that I had no father and no mother; ay! not a single friend or relative in the world, and that Armine were sunk into the very centre of the earth. If I stood alone in the world methinks I might find the place that suits me; now everything seems ordained for me, as it were, beforehand' (p. 71). Having completed his task with a satisfactory outcome, he is surprised to find himself so restless and dissatisfied: 'there is, there must be, something better in this world than power and wealth and rank' (p. 74). Like the Young Duke, he searches for something beyond material reward and, like the earlier hero, he finds it in love, because it is at this point that he sees Henrietta Temple for the first time. She represents the opportunities, regarding his future, which he has forsaken in the successful romantic pursuit of his cousin. Henrietta attracts him intensely, but he has renounced one aspect of his selfhood in the satiation of another: he may have staved off his financial crisis and restored his family's position, but he has necessarily set aside some of his personal desires in so doing.

Ferdinand has fallen in love at first sight, and duty is overwhelmed by desire. Accommodating *Henrietta Temple* within the dualistic tension which characterises Disraeli's writings during this period, the heroine represents what ambition would have, while Katherine stands for what is demanded in practice by society. Henrietta's effect upon Ferdinand is transformative. The narrator, dwelling on the state of being in love, highlights its overwhelming impact upon the lover: 'revolutions of empire, changes of creed, mutations of opinion, are to him but the clouds and the meteors of a stormy sky' (p. 77). The outer world, the canvas on which the Disraelian hero strives to make an impression, is temporarily forgotten when juxtaposed against the interior world of feelings. Furthermore, for Ferdinand, society transforms from a long-standing order to be maintained into a set of oppressive restrictions. Ferdinand does not lose a sense of purpose once he has met Henrietta. Instead, his task, his aspiration, takes on a new form, one which is likely to test him far more than his effortless pursuit of Katherine. The dilemma for the aristocracy in

Henrietta Temple is that duty determines conduct; its privileges are understated, its responsibilities emphasised.

The portrayal of Henrietta anticipates that of the heroine of *Sybil*; both signify their beneficent and charitable nature through their work among their own communities. Henrietta is welcomed by her humble, rural neighbours: 'the thin grey smoke that rose in different directions was a beacon to the charitable visits of Miss Temple. It was evident that she was a visitor both habitual and beloved. Each cottage-door was familiar to her entrance' (p. 113). Ferdinand is attracted to the mode of living to which he is introduced by Henrietta and, anticipating the concerns of the Young England trilogy, yearns for rural simplicity in opposition to the increasingly materialistic values of the urbanites and city-dwellers: 'why should his love for her make his heart a rebel to his hearth? Money! horrible money! It seemed to him that the contiguous cottage and the labour of his hands, with her, were preferable to palaces and crowds of retainers without her inspiring presence' (p. 114). His conversion to pastoral values stands in contrast to his previously mercenary lifestyle: 'it was not the profligacy of his ancestor, it was not the pride of his family then, that stood between him and his love; it was his own culpable and heartless career!' (p. 115).

The crisis created by his love for Henrietta alongside his betrothal to Katherine provides an opportunity for character growth, but Ferdinand fights against this by invoking the spirit of his dead grandfather as a means of justifying a self-gratifying course of action. His impetuous grandfather provides a template for his own errant conduct; Disraeli shows implicitly the consequences of the aristocracy failing to live up to its responsibilities. Ferdinand now has to amputate himself from his own class and his own history, the narrator asserting that 'the past, the future, should be nothing; he would revel in the auspicious present' (p. 131). The practical outcome of this commitment is that he has to renounce his mother and father: 'as for those parents, so affectionate and virtuous, and to whom he had hitherto been so dutiful and devoted, he turned from their idea with a sensation of weariness, almost of dislike' (p. 164). By affronting the values of his class, Ferdinand also cuts himself off from the support of his benefactors.

Presented with the conundrum of having to adopt an antipathetic stance towards his hero Disraeli digresses temporarily from the complexities of the narrative. He discusses the effect of women upon men: 'few great men have flourished, who, were they candid, would not acknowledge the vast advantages they have experienced in the earlier years of their career from the spirit and sympathy of woman. . . . A female friend, amiable, clever, and devoted, is a possession more valuable than parks and palaces; and, without such a muse, few men can succeed in life, none be content' (p. 170). Disraeli's comments anticipate his marriage to Mary Anne Lewis, who remained a source of support and solidity for Disraeli throughout his career. Furthermore, his observations can be read as his gesture beyond the text to his relationship with Henrietta Sykes, and perhaps also his relationship with Sara Austen, on whose patronage (and that of her husband) he had often relied. Disraeli also comments on the nature of love: 'for love can illuminate the dark roof of poverty, and can lighten the fetter of the slave' (p. 194). This view is later modified in the Young England trilogy, where we see, in the description of the weaver's cottage in *Sybil*, personal relations compromised because of the gruelling effects of poverty (this passage in discussed in greater detail in chapter two). Given that *Henrietta Temple* was given the sub-title *A Love Story*, Disraeli stresses love as the main theme, yet his reappraisal of the determining effects of economic conditions in the Young England trilogy implies development in his thinking. In Disraeli's writings of the 1840s love loses its transcendence; poverty, its causes and effects, are foregrounded.

At a later point in *Henrietta Temple*, during a conversation between Katherine Grandison and Henrietta Temple, Disraeli uses the authorial voice, through the characters, to express his views of contemporary literature:

'I wonder why all this class of writers aim now at the sarcastic. I do not find life the constant sneer they make it.'

'It is because they do not understand life,' said Henrietta, 'but have some little experience of society. Therefore their works give a perverted impression of human conduct; for they accept as a principal, that which is only an insignificant accessory; and they make existence a succession of frivolities, when even the career of the most frivolous has its profounder moments.'

'How vivid is the writer's description of a ball or a dinner,' said Miss Grandison; 'everything lives and moves. And yet, when the hero makes love, nothing can be more unnatural. His feelings are neither deep, nor ardent, nor tender. All is stilted, and yet ludicrous.'

'I do not despise the talent which describes so vividly a dinner and a ball,' said Miss Temple. 'As far as it goes it is very amusing, but it should be combined with higher materials. In a fine novel, manners should be observed, and morals should be sustained; we require thought and passion, as well as costume and the lively representation of conventional arrangements; and the thought and passion will be the better for these accessories, for they will be relieved in the novel as they are relieved in life, and the whole will be more true.' (pp. 357–8)

The above conversation is a thinly disguised criticism of the fashionable novel and a plea for greater psychological depth in literature. Disraeli's first novels, *Vivian Grey* and *The Young Duke*, were both fashionable novels, though *Vivian Grey* may also be read as a *Bildungsroman*, and Disraeli subtitled *The Young Duke*, 'a moral tale, though gay'. As the 1830s progressed, however, Disraeli experimented with other literary forms, from love story to drama to epic verse. When, therefore, Henrietta Temple argues for the inclusion of substantial emotions in novels, she is articulating her creator's own desire for a modified literary form which includes psychological depth in the interests of greater realism.

Within the shifting narrative of *Henrietta Temple*, Glastonbury represents solidity and continuity, achieved through his devotion to his faith: 'there was ever open to the pious Glastonbury one perennial source of trust and consolation. This was a fountain that was ever fresh and sweet, and he took refuge from the world's harsh courses and exhausting cares in its salutary flow, and its refreshing shade, when, kneeling before his crucifix, he commended the unhappy Ferdinand and his family to the superintending care of a merciful Omnipotence' (pp. 237–8). The character of Glastonbury suggests the existence of a realm which transcends human machinations. The challenge for the characters in *Henrietta Temple* is to achieve alignment with the higher power, which will be apparent in the gratification of its representative, Glastonbury, whose Catholicism implies a narrative endorsement of that particular faith.

The engagement between Ferdinand and Katherine is severed through Katherine's rationality, which neutralises the emotional impact of the split. However, while one source of conflict in the novel is lessened, others remain, most notably the tension between the interior and the outside world. The narrator expresses the insistent nature of desire: 'the heart, the heart, the jealous and despotic heart! It rejects all substitutes, it spurns all compromise, and it will have its purpose or it will break' (p. 264). Furthermore, personal dilemmas are placed explicitly in opposition to political crises: 'what are those political revolutions, whose strange and mighty vicissitudes we are ever dilating on, compared with the moral mutations that are passing daily under our own eye; uprooting the hearts of families, shattering to pieces domestic circles, scattering to the winds the plans and prospects of a generation, and blasting as with a mildew the ripening harvest of long cherished affection!' (p. 267). *Henrietta Temple* argues that personal ambitions and individual needs are more important than social theories and the 'mutations' of the wider milieu, yet Disraeli also believed that the aristocracy had the responsibility of leadership, at the sacrifice of personal desires. In order for Ferdinand Armine to fall within Disraeli's broader conception of ideal government, his personal desires have to be tempered by a sense of social obligation. The resulting internal tension creates character development and narrative movement, while keeping us in mind of the dualistic tension around which many of Disraeli's early literary works are constructed: the aspirational is repeatedly challenged by the practical.

One of the principal reasons for Ferdinand's loss of Henrietta is the fact that she has another suitor, one who is favoured by her family: Lord Montfort. He clearly also enjoys the narrator's approval: 'the young marquis was an excellent specimen of a class inferior in talents, intelligence, and accomplishments, in public spirit and in private virtues, to none in the world, the English nobility' (p. 265). Disraeli's eulogy of the English aristocracy is developed when he contrasts Lord Montfort with Ferdinand, identifying the latter's impulsiveness as the chief difference between them.

> And yet Lord Montfort was a man of deep emotions, and of a very fastidious taste. He was a man as of romantic a temperament as Ferdinand Armine; but with Lord Montfort, life was the romance of reason; with Ferdinand, the romance of imagination. The first was keenly alive to all the imperfections of our nature, but he also gave that nature credit for all its excellences. He observed finely, he calculated nicely, and his result was generally happiness. Ferdinand, on the contrary, neither observed nor calculated. His imagination created fantasies and his impetuous passions struggled to realise them. (p. 290)

Ferdinand's Byronic tendencies would have made him the unambiguous hero of an earlier Disraeli novel such as *Vivian Grey*. However, the progress of Disraeli's novels in the 1830s demonstrates that his romantic, Byronic idealism was being altered by a more pragmatic input, directing the actions of the aspiring parliamentarian. Furthermore, within *Henrietta Temple*, Ferdinand does not always enjoy unqualified narrative support, yet, paradoxically, it is his impetuosity which guides him towards Henrietta and his ultimate happiness. While the triumph of lovers over adversity is a generic convention of the love story, it also suggests that Disraeli still had uses for, or admiration of, impulsive behaviour.

Impulsiveness is often read as a sign of immaturity, a view consolidated by Ferdinand's response to Henrietta's betrothal to Lord Montfort: 'he was alone, with a broken heart and worse than desperate fortunes, and all for her sake, his soul became bitter: he reproached her with want of feeling; . . . he cursed her caprice; he denounced her infernal treachery; in the distorted phantom of his agonised imagination she became to him even an object of hatred' (p. 300). His aggressive feelings are subsequently developed still further: 'he was enraged, he was disgusted, he despised himself for having been her slave; he began even to hate her. Terrible moment when we first dare to view with feelings of repugnance the being that our soul has long idolised! It is the most awful of revelations. We start back in horror, as if in the act of profanation' (pp. 340–1). Ferdinand's character does little to commend itself to the reader at this point, yet Disraeli is using his hero to explore the obsessional aspect of being in love. When played through in the form of an impulsive character such as Ferdinand, obsession in the face of romantic disappointment transforms into feelings of hatred for the love-object. Ferdinand's raw, almost naïve, emotionalism is also emblematic of a youthful idealism. The loss of this idealism – manufactured through the loss of Henrietta – results in a tempering of ambition, a regression into mediocrity as acceptable situation. World-weariness of this kind is the standpoint adopted by the narrator, not long after Ferdinand has plunged into his despair: 'as men advance in life, all passions resolve themselves into money. Love, ambition, even poetry, end in this' (p. 368). Finance is represented as a process of degradation. The narrator's comment reflects Disraeli's own pressing debts, which could easily have resulted in him forming the view that financial concerns were all-pervasive. More generally, within the scheme of Disraeli's novels up to this point, the loss of idealism emerges as an unavoidable necessity in order for the subject to achieve an accommodation within mainstream society, yet this process is also impregnated with a sense of loss and melancholy.

The love between Ferdinand and Henrietta creates widespread division. Henrietta reveals the truth to her father, who tells her, 'take this Armine once more to your heart, and you receive my curse, the deepest, the sternest, the deadliest that ever descended on a daughter's head' (p. 397). Ferdinand fares no better, as his father states, 'Madman! You know not what you have done!' (p. 401). In both cases, the families react badly because the relationship between Ferdinand and Henrietta threatens to disrupt the smooth flow of wealth and influence from one generation of the aristocracy to the next. The loss of Katherine Grandison is also the loss of her money, without which the Armine family may lose its estate. The seriousness of Ferdinand's situation is impressed upon him: 'my life, your mother's, the existence of our family, hang upon your conduct' (p. 402). Ferdinand becomes, in effect, a representative for a class which, from Disraeli's perspective, had far-reaching responsibilities placing onerous burdens upon its members' shoulders. Hindered from making life-choices according to its personal preferences, the aristocracy is shown by Disraeli to be a self-sacrificial group within society, organising its conduct for the benefit of the nation as a whole. Aside from the primary romantic narrative in *Henrietta Temple*, Disraeli is commending a more considerate and empathetic approach towards those who he felt were born to lead.

Ferdinand's debts result in his imprisonment, yet it is at this point, when his fortunes are at their lowest ebb, that he is liberated. First, the romantic complications are resolved briskly, even abruptly, when it transpires that Lord Montfort is to marry Katherine Grandison. Secondly, he is relieved of his debts by a friend's good fortune in a gaming-house, while further money is donated for his benefit by the combined efforts of Katherine and Grandison. While Ferdinand may appear to be undeserving of such extraordinary good fortune, Lord Montfort cites the grounds on which he is to be vindicated: 'whatever career you pursue, so long as you visibly possess Armine, you rank always among the aristocracy of the land, and a family that maintains such a position, however decayed, will ultimately recover' (p. 429). Ferdinand's noble birth is the guarantee of his success; Disraeli presents aristocracy as a responsibility which functions symbiotically with society as a whole, as the world will pardon Ferdinand in return for his willingness to fulfil the commitments consequent upon his noble birth.

Ferdinand describes his own career as being akin to 'dancing on a volcano' (p. 437). Disraeli would use the same phrase again in his final completed novel, *Endymion* (chapter sixty-four). However, Ferdinand tempers his extremes and, at the close of the novel, he is rewarded with a seat in Parliament and, in a narrative detail signifying full reconciliation with his family and his responsibilities, a son named Glastonbury. *Henrietta Temple* fulfils the generic conventions of a love story (with an autobiographical infusion arising out of Disraeli's relationship with Henrietta Sykes), though Disraeli also manages to put distance between himself and the discourse of romantic love through jocular and ironic chapter titles, such as, 'In which some light is thrown on the title of this work' (I.4) and 'Containing a conversation not quite so amusing as the last' (IV.6). In addition, *Henrietta Temple* explores the aristocracy: their responsibilities, their anxieties and the hard decisions they have to make. Through the character of Lord Montfort, Disraeli presents his ideal aristocrat, a template to which Ferdinand must aspire.

VENETIA

'Literature to Herbert was now only a source of amusement and engaging occupation. All thought of fame had long fled his soul.'

The evidence of the 1830s suggests that Disraeli's ideas about writing were changing markedly, a point made by B. R. Jerman: '*Henrietta*

Temple and *Venetia* are transitional works. They follow his introspective novels and precede his political fiction.' This view is echoed in part by Paul Smith: 'the vein of autobiography, however, was almost extinct, and in *Venetia* disappeared, as Disraeli made his genuflection to the figures of Byron and Shelley'.[64] Viewed more prosaically, *Venetia* was written when Disraeli was heavily in debt, and thus the presence of two central characters modelled on Byron and Shelley was always likely to attract interest, boost sales and thereby assuage some of Disraeli's creditors. Despite this, however, *Venetia* remains an important text within Disraeli's *oeuvre* as it traces the development of the romantic idealist into the social pragmatist.[65]

The novel commences with a romantic idyll, as the young Venetia is brought up by her mother, far removed from the corruption of society. Venetia thinks of herself as living 'in an enchanted wilderness' (p. 12). However, civilisation intrudes upon their enclave through narrative observation: 'the peasants on the estate, or labourers as they are now styled, a term whose introduction into our rural world is much to be lamented, lived in the respective farmhouses on the lands which they cultivated' (p. 13). By pointing out a change in nomenclature, Disraeli presents the background of industrialisation. Venetia's life is also set to be uprooted by the introduction into the text of Lord Plantagenet Cadurcis, clearly based upon Byron. He is boisterous and rebellious: 'his favourites among the peasantry were ever those who excelled in athletic sports; and, though he never expressed the opinion, he did not look upon the poacher with the evil eye of his class' (pp. 59–60). His radical approach to life and politics is further signified when he runs away from home and joins a gypsy encampment. The incident demonstrates narrative sympathy for the outsider, a position which was familiar to Disraeli in his considerations of Catholicism and, later, Judaism. The beneficent gypsies give a welcome to Cadurcis, 'rough as was the fare, it was good and plentiful'. The encampment's harmony with nature also expresses the gypsy idyll: 'the fire was replenished, its red shadow mingled with the silver beams of the moon; around were the glittering tents and the silent woods' (p. 73). Cadurcis's whereabouts remains a mystery to those in mainstream society, where his disappearance takes on more sinister, conspiratorial contours; Squire Mountmeadow, for instance, is certain that 'Rome is at the bottom of it' (p. 78). In its early stages, therefore, *Venetia* is distinctly romantic, with an unimaginative and prejudiced society contrasted against the beneficence and excitement of nature.

The death of Cadurcis's mother and the young boy's departure for Eton shifts the focus of the novel onto the identity of Venetia's father, whose portrait is kept in a locked room, a gothic touch intended to intensify the enigma surrounding his identity. He is revealed to be Marmion Herbert, a poet and a figure of notoriety. Herbert is based on Percy Shelley, who had similarly abandoned his first wife, Harriet Westbrook. The gothic tone of this section of *Venetia* is stressed when Cadurcis, on a visit from Eton, argues with Venetia.

> 'I am glad you have not read his works,' said Lord Cadurcis, with increased bitterness. 'As for his conduct, you mother is a living evidence of his honour, his generosity, and his virtue.'
>
> 'My mother!' said Venetia, in a softened voice; 'and yet he loved my mother!'
>
> 'She was his victim, as a thousand others may have been.'
>
> 'She is his wife!' replied Venetia, with some anxiety.
>
> 'Yes, a deserted wife; is that preferable to being a cherished mistress? More honourable, but scarcely less humiliating.' (p. 206)

The intensity of their conflict increases, with Cadurcis calling Herbert 'a traitor to his king and an apostate from his God!', leading Venetia to respond, 'words cannot express the disgust and the contempt with which you inspire me'. The chapter concludes with Cadurcis's proclamation: 'Woman! Henceforth you shall be my sport! I have now no feeling but for myself. When she spoke I might have been a boy; I am a boy no longer. What I shall do I know not; but this I know, the world shall ring with my name; I will be a man, and a great man!' (p. 210). The romanticism of the early chapters of *Venetia* has shifted into its darker gothic undercurrent, symbolising the lost idealism and rational development of the characters. The next book of *Venetia* is set in fashionable society, where Cadurcis's poems are the subject of gossip and fascination; a movement through chronological literary genres is evident in *Venetia*.

A digression from the narrative allows the developed presentation of the character of Marmion Herbert. Like Shelley he left Oxford and, again like Shelley, he is a radical: 'in politics a violent republican, and an advocate, certainly a disinterested one, of a complete equality of property and conditions, utterly objecting to the very foundation of our moral system, and especially a strenuous antagonist of marriage, which he taught himself to esteem not only as an unnatural tie, but as eminently unjust towards that softer sex, who had been so long the victims of man' (p. 224). The character information about Herbert is important, not least because Cadurcis, in a *volte face*, has become one of his fiercest devotees. Incidental details about Cadurcis further align him with Byron, with Cadurcis keeping a bear at university, as Byron is thought to have done. Disraeli clearly intends the reader to admire Cadurcis, concluding chapter three of book four with the comment, 'he had risen, and still flamed, like a comet as wild as it was beautiful, and strange as it was brilliant' (p. 240). However, Lady Annabel Herbert, Venetia's mother, draws a distinction between Herbert and Cadurcis, to the discredit of the latter: 'great as might have been the original errors of Herbert, awful as in her estimation were the crimes to which they had led him, they might in the first instance be traced rather to a perverted view of society than of himself. But self was the idol of Cadurcis' (p. 280). While her judgement is informed by her ongoing feelings for Herbert, she is articulating a valid critique of romantic verse, which can be visionary but which can also (through its focus on the individual's experience) veer into narcissism. The narrator's unqualified admiration for Cadurcis is tempered by Lady Herbert's opinions; *Venetia* questions romantic characters as much as it celebrates them. Bishop Masham underlines this idea by saying, of Cadurcis, 'he is not prompted by any visionary ideas of ameliorating his species' (p. 281). It was to be left to Coningsby, Egremont and Tancred, the heroes of Disraeli's novels of the 1840s, to turn their attentions to the improvement of the condition of the people.

Cadurcis's notoriety leads him into trouble. Social hypocrisy and the character of the urban lower classes now come to the fore. Society is presented as a capricious and callous organism, as shown at the beginning of chapter eighteen, book four.

> It has been well observed, that no spectacle is so ridiculous as the British public in one of its periodical fits of morality. In general, elopements, divorces, and family quarrels pass with little notice. We read the scandal, talk about it for a day, and forget it. But, once in six or seven years, our virtue becomes outrageous. We cannot suffer the laws of religion and decency to be violated. We must make a stand against vice. We must teach libertines that the English people appreciate the importance of domestic ties. Accordingly, some unfortunate man, in no respect more depraved than hundreds whose offences have been treated with lenity, is singled out as an expiatory sacrifice. (pp. 335–6)

Disraeli attacks hypocrisy and the culture of victimisation. He is implicitly defending figures of infamy – Shelley and Byron (through Herbert and Cadurcis) on the one hand and himself, less spectacularly, on the other.

Disraeli's presentation of the urban lower classes in *Venetia* anticipates the assault upon the heroine in *Sybil*, when she searches for her father in a disreputable area of London (see chapter two). Cadurcis attempts to leave Parliament on horseback and, in a general climate of hostility, 'a bolder ruffian, excited by the uproar, rushed forward and seized Cadurcis' bridle. Cadurcis struck the man over the eyes with his whip, and at the same time touched his horse with his spur, and the assailant was dashed to the ground. This seemed a signal for a general assault, which commenced with hideous yells. His friends at the house, who had watched everything with the keenest interest, immediately directed all the constables who were at hand to rush to his succour.' Cadurcis is besieged by a lower-class mob and is only saved by the police. Like Ferdinand Armine, Cadurcis effectively bites the hand that feeds him; his poetry shocks mainstream society, yet that same society will intervene to defend him, not least because of his nobility. Cadurcis's assailants, in contrast to his friends, are presented in savage terms, their 'hideous yells' placing them at the same level as beasts. Conversely, police violence is presented as a matter for delectation: 'the charge of the constables was well timed; they laid about them with their staves; you might have heard an echo of many a broken crown' (p. 341). However, the attack upon Cadurcis continues until troops arrive and the mob disperses; a second, more powerful, layer of the state defending the nobleman. In the aftermath of the incident, he begins to realise where his allegiances and interests lie: 'he had experienced, indeed, some kindness that he could not forget, but only from his own kin' (p. 343). Like *Henrietta Temple*, *Venetia* presents an aristocrat whose rebellious behaviour softens alongside a growing appreciation of the merits of his own class. However, while *Henrietta Temple* rarely moves beyond the world of aristocrats, *Venetia* takes a look at the masses but sees only an animalistic mob. The same representation appears in *Sybil*, yet, in the Young England novel, it is qualified substantially by the examination of the economic forces that prompt degradation.

Plantagenet has an eminently respectable alter ego in the form of his brother, George Cadurcis, whose credentials are stressed by his reputation in Parliament, 'of all the members of the House of Commons he was perhaps the only one that everybody praised' (p. 354). His introduction provides the narrative with ballast as events speed up, with Venetia and Lady Annabel in turn meeting Herbert. Lady Annabel's first reaction is hostile, leading the narrator to speculate on human misery: 'want of love, or want of money, lies at the bottom of all our griefs' (p. 396). In common with *Henrietta Temple*, the narrator exudes a sense of cynicism and world-weariness, though in *Venetia* human sadness is depicted as being a multi-faceted, multi-layered condition, not merely a result of financial impoverishment. While *Henrietta Temple* is a love story, *Venetia*, paradoxically, is more interested in the complexity of human emotions, as Lady Annabel and Herbert have to reconstruct their love out of pain and betrayal.

As the novel nears its end the four main characters are brought together. Full reconciliation is fuelled by the rebels, especially Herbert, returning to the establishment. The narrator signifies Herbert's new found maturity by stating that, 'literature to Herbert was now only a source of amusement and engaging occupation. All thought of fame had long fled his soul' (p. 419). His political position is now less radical and is in accord with some of Disraeli's fundamental views concerning the importance of continuity. Herbert claims that, 'what America is deficient in is creative intellect. It has no nationality. Its intelligence has been imported, like its manufactured goods. Its inhabitants are a people, but are they a nation? I wish that the empire of the Incas and the kingdom of Montezuma had not been sacrificed. I wish that the republic of the Puritans had blended with the tribes of the wilderness' (pp. 422–3). Like Disraeli, Herbert is hostile to the importation of ideas that are not indigenous to the territory in which they are played out. Disraeli's opposition to utilitarianism was based on its theoretical rigidity and the fact that it was imposed on political and social life in the form of a metadiscourse.

In a conversation between Herbert and Cadurcis, the latter's conversion to a more orthodox perspective is signified by his assessment of the attack and his escape: 'a brutish mob in a fit of morality about to immolate a gentleman, and then scampering off from a sentry. I call that human nature!' (p. 434). He has lost his idealism, but this is a necessary part of personal development for the Disraelian heroes of the second half of the 1830s. Cadurcis undertakes the same journey as Ferdinand Armine, albeit in a different context. Herbert, with greater age and experience than Cadurcis, adopts a broader perspective: 'political revolutions, changes of empire, wrecks of dynasties and the opinions that support them, these are the marvels of the vulgar, but these are only transient modifications of life' (p. 435). His radicalism has dissolved into sanguine acceptance and, in his final speech to Cadurcis, he offers advice, 'I am not altogether void of the creative faculty, but mine is a fragmentary mind; I produce no whole. Unless you do this, you cannot last; at least, you cannot materially affect your species' (p. 458). It is hard here not to hear an echo of the mutilated diary, in which Disraeli stated he had 'a revolutionary mind'.[66] Herbert voices his creator's frustration at a time when Disraeli's political ambitions had found no outlet. The death at sea of Herbert and Cadurcis is suggestive of Shelley's demise, yet the loss of the two main characters from *Venetia* also paves the way for the marriage between George Cadurcis, now Lord Cadurcis, and Venetia. His unblemished past and character ensures the smooth and commendable movement of wealth and influence through the generations. The dramatised versions of Byron and Shelley in *Venetia* could not be fully assimilated into a society on which both real-life characters had turned their backs, yet both Cadurcis and Herbert renounce their radicalism in favour of co-operation with a system which will grant them privilege in return for a measure of compromise and a willingness to engage with the responsibilities to which both were elected by birth. An effective companion piece to *Henrietta Temple*, *Venetia* depicts a definite movement towards conformity, a journey which Disraeli himself was undertaking as he sought to renounce his own past as a dandy and gain respectability and influence in Parliament. *Venetia* is thus the final shedding of Disraeli's own Byronic persona.

Disraeli's last literary work of the 1830s is probably the strangest. *The Tragedy of Count Alarcos* is a five-act play written in verse.[67] It reads like a Jacobean tragedy, with the Infanta Solisa losing her lover, Alarcos, because of her mother's attempts to seduce him. Alarcos's wife, Florimonde, is the victim of an attempted seduction by Sidonia. Solisa attempts to kill Florimonde, yet it is Alarcos who actually ends up killing her, just prior to learning that Solisa has been killed by a bolt of lightning. It is difficult to accommodate *Alarcos* within Disraeli's work; he was an experimental writer in the sense that he played with different genres and, given that, between 1834 and 1837, he had published a love story, a fictional account of Byron and Shelley and an epic poem, it is not altogether surprising that he also tried his hand at drama. Furthermore, according to Monypenny and Buckle, Disraeli's venture into drama was clearly well-timed: 'there had been in recent years a marked revival of interest in serious drama. Talfourd's *Ion* had been produced in 1836, and had been followed at no long interval by Bulwer's *Lady of Lyons*. Disraeli was determined not to be behindhand, and set to work on *Alarcos*.'[68] The play is action-packed, and most of the dialogue serves merely to propel the narrative. However, in act one, scene four, Solisa protests to her father: 'A sacrificial virgin, must I bind / My life to the altar, to redeem a state, / Or heal some doomed people?' (p. 20). Again the plight of the nobility is stressed, with Solisa being encouraged to marry in order to cement political alliances. Like many Disraelian aristocrats, she is characterised by her responsibilities more than by her privileges. *Alarcos* was not produced on stage around the time it was written, but Monypenny and Buckle noted that it did receive an airing in the 1860s, riding on the fame of its author: 'when Disraeli was Prime Minister in 1868, an adaptation was produced at Astley's Theatre Royal. It ran for five weeks, "with the loudest demonstrations of applause from delighted audiences," as the courtly manager wrote to the author at the close, but, unfortunately, as he had to add, with heavy losses to himself as the penalty of his enterprise'.[69]

In 1837, and at the fifth attempt, Disraeli was finally elected to the House of Commons as the member for Maidstone. Although it is true that Disraeli's early novels are more interested in character portrayal and debt-paying than politics, it would be wrong to neglect the extent to which they contributed to the next phase of his career, both on the literary and the political level. Disraeli wished, of course to *act* what he *wrote*, not vice versa. In other words, he wasn't putting to paper already-gathered political thoughts. Subsequent commentators, among them John K. Walton, have also remarked on the value of Disraeli's early works in the context of his later career: 'a recurrent motif of his literary output in the 1830s, *before* the more overtly political novels of the famous "Young England" trilogy, is the need for a politics based on tradition and national unity, rather than a competitive individualism which divided and threatened the social order'.[70] From his earliest works there is a disdain for what he perceived as petty-minded commercialism and, conversely, approbation for aristocratic structures of power. *Vivian Grey* finally offers a contented rural idyll governed by a titled patriarch, which stands in stark contrast to some of the corrupted communities visited by Vivian in the course of his adventures. Satires of the late 1820s continued to berate the shortcomings of contemporary political and literary life, while *The Young Duke* highlighted the need, as Disraeli saw it, for aristocratic renewal.

Contarini Fleming, the second part of Disraeli's 'secret history of my feelings', locates both his hero and his context in a transitional phase. Contarini contends with the conflicting demands of literature and politics, while Europe is, in Contarini's view, shifting from feudal to federal principles. Furthermore, the failure of the novel did not affect significantly Disraeli's outlook; in his diary he continued to regard *Contarini Fleming* as 'the perfection of English Prose'.[71] *A Year at Hartlebury* is of interest primarily because it offers some insights regarding Disraeli's perspective on the electoral process yet, paradoxically, it contains less of a political vision than some of Disraeli's other works in the 1820s and '30s. We learn of Bohun's opposition to Whiggism but comparatively little of his own specific political programme. Conversely, when Disraeli releases his creative energies, unhindered by any direct or immediate political motive, a bold critique and vision emerge. The social effects of economic policy are perceived as damaging because commercialism distorts the social fabric, altering long-standing relationships in the process. The vision emerging out of this critique is nostalgic, and it is additionally problematic in the sense that it hearkens back to an idyll that probably only ever existed in English myths and fairy-tales. However, the vision *is* forward-looking to the extent that a once powerful yet presently dormant aristocracy lacks nothing more than effective leadership from an inspired visionary, purged of his own excesses, rather like the poetic heroes of *Venetia*. Enter the newly elected member for Maidstone.

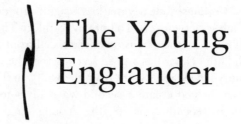

Chapter Two | The Young Englander

'There are great bodies of the working classes of this country nearer the condition of brutes, than they have been at any time since the conquest.'
Sybil

In Disraeli's general preface to the 1870 collected edition of his novels, he summarised the purpose of the Young England trilogy: 'CONINGSBY, SYBIL and TANCRED form a real Trilogy; that is to say, they treat of the same subject, and endeavour to complete that treatment. The origin and character of our political parties, their influence on the condition of the people of this country, some picture of the moral and physical condition of that people, and some intimation of the means by which it might be elevated and improved, were themes which had long engaged my meditation.'[1] Disraeli's assessment of the trilogy is a retrospective rather than a compositional judgement; he had originally intended to handle all these issues in *Coningsby*, but found that he required greater space in which to elaborate his themes. In this chapter I will explore the trilogy, as well as examining Disraeli's 1851 political biography, *Lord George Bentinck*. As will be revealed an explicit political philosophy is presented and argued for within Disraeli's literary output of the period. Consistency in Disraeli's ideas themselves – based on political and religious atavism – and in the ways he chose to structure and present his material, will also be revealed.

CONINGSBY

'A political institution is a machine: the motive power is the national character.'

Coningsby, first published in May 1844,[2] has been described by Robert Blake as 'the first and most brilliant of English political novels, a genre which he [Disraeli] may be said to have invented'.[3] Whatever the truth of this claim (it has been argued, for example, that John Galt's *The Member* (1832), which focused on parliamentarianism, was the first political novel),[4] *Coningsby* clearly marked a significant departure from Disraeli's early high society novels. To borrow Kathleen Tillotson's phrase, Disraeli was involved in 'the extension of the social frontiers observed in fiction',[5] though Philip Davis has argued recently that there are elements of literary continuity in Disraeli's work from the 1820s to the 1840s: 'it was Disraeli who then helped create a second-wave silver-fork in the 1840s, transformed by social concern: the Young England novels written in aristocratic support of the old feudal society'.[6] Thus, Disraeli's trilogy draws from his first generation of novels, yet, in so doing, *Coningsby*, *Sybil* and *Tancred* move progressively further away from the observation of the surface details of society, and into an investigation of that society: its political, economic and spiritual foundations.

Disraeli had conscious political designs for *Coningsby*, as evidenced by his preface to the fifth edition, published in 1849: 'it was not the intention of the writer to adopt the form of fiction as the instrument to scatter his suggestions, but, after reflection, he resolved to avail himself of a method which, in the temper of the times, offered the best chance of influencing opinion'.[7] The intention of *Coningsby* was propagandist, with Disraeli seeking to promote his own views outside Parliament, through the medium of fiction. He was clearly successful in this sense, as the first thousand copies of *Coningsby* were sold in a fortnight.[8] The public attention which it claimed was sufficient for two parodies to be published: *Anti-Coningsby; or, The New Generation Grown Old*, purportedly the work of 'An Embryo, M.P.', and William Makepeace Thackeray's *Codlingsby*, published in *Punch*. The former features the Queen sending for Coningsby to form a government upon the resignation of Sir Robert Peel. The new Prime Minister enjoys the support and patronage of Ben Sidonia, portrayed complete with Hasidic curls. *Codlingsby* is blatantly anti-Semitic and draws attention to deficiencies in the characterisation of Sidonia (see below). Even Charles Dickens satirised *Coningsby* in his serial, *The Chimes*.[9] Insensitive and often cruel, their very publication signifies the extent to which *Coningsby* had made an impact, and thus the parodies serve to emphasise, rather than detract from, the importance of the work.

The first book of *Coningsby* is set in 1832, the year of the Reform Act. The measure is condemned by the narrator, who views the qualifications set down for the vote as, 'arbitrary, irrational and impolitic' (p. 39). It is further claimed that this initial error concerning the dispensation of the vote was responsible for Chartism (a movement generated by *The People's Charter*, calling for universal suffrage for men, secret ballot voting, and other controversial reforms) and that, 'the country was going to be given over to a rapacious oligarchy' (p. 24). The provisions of reform legislation amount to a virtual coup d'état in *Coningsby*: political power has been seized by a small clique rather than dispersed through the classes. The idea that legislation was responsible for Chartism, however, is unreasonably reductive. As a political movement with substantial mobilised support, Chartism was more heavily motivated by the economic pressures preceding reform legislation which had generated grievances and anxieties; for example, population growth and the movement of people in response to the opportunities and needs of an industrialising economy.

Ingrained problems in the aristocracy are personified through the character of Lord Monmouth, based on the Third Marquess of Hertford, whose debauched lifestyle, culminating in his death in the company of courtesans in March 1842, was a matter of widespread public knowledge. He also provided the model for Lord Steyne in William Makepeace Thackeray's *Vanity Fair*. In *Coningsby*, Lord Monmouth is Coningsby's grandfather and despite his disreputable habits he is not without some good qualities: 'in height above the middle size, but somewhat portly and corpulent. His countenance was strongly marked; sagacity on the brow, sensuality in the mouth and jaw. His head was bald, but there were remains of the rich brown locks on which he once prided himself' (p. 19). The remnants of nobility are undermined by the consequences of a lifestyle driven by appetites, a contrast expressed most lucidly through Monmouth's face: his sagacious brow suggests a thoughtful mind, while the lower half of the face signifies a habit of satiating physical desires.

When we first encounter Coningsby his appearance is similarly telling: 'his short upper lip indicated a good breed' (p. 2). His early education took place at a 'homely, rural school, where he had been well grounded by a hard-working curate, and affectionately tended by the curate's unsophisticated wife' (p. 11). Having experienced Disraeli's ideal, pastoral simplicity away from the corruption of the social world, he goes on to be esteemed by his peer group at Eton. Therefore, Coningsby's character has been determined by rural benevolence and the adoration of the elite. He is clearly a leader and, significantly, he is free from any taint of middle-class influence; the 'rapacious oligarchy' will not claim him for itself, and they, in turn, will form no part of his constituency. However, he does meet Oswald Millbank at Eton, the son of a successful industrialist: 'he was a good-looking boy, somewhat shy, and yet with a sincere expression in his countenance' (p. 42). His appearance signifies that he will be no threat to Coningsby in the leadership stakes. His most significant narrative contribution in the first book is that he serves to provide Coningsby with an opportunity to display his heroism. Coningsby saves Millbank from drowning, the rejuvenated aristocracy coming to the aid of honest industry. Millbank complements rather than compromises Coningsby's character and purpose because, despite his linkage to industry, he is in need of guidance and support. Coningsby is crucial to his survival.

Book two moves forward to the latter stages of 1834, drawing attention to the moribund and degraded condition of politics, before offering restorative potential through Coningsby and his cohorts. This section of the novel is thus an advocacy of the Young England movement, a group of idealistic Conservatives, emerging out of the Oxford Movement, who congregated around Disraeli in the early and mid-1840s.[10] A number of characters in *Coningsby* are modelled on leading figures in the Young England movement: Coningsby is based on Lord George Smythe, who also appears as Waldershare in Disraeli's final novel, *Endymion* (1880). While Disraeli was the dominant Parliamentary figure in the movement, Smythe also had a significant input and may well have influenced the theory of English history presented by Disraeli in both *Coningsby* and *Sybil*.[11] The character of Lord Henry Sydney is based on another leading figure from Young England, Lord John Manners; Buckhurst is based upon Alexander Baillie-Cochrane; and Oswald Millbank is purportedly John Walters of *The Times*.[12] Smythe, Manners and Baillie-Cochrane had joined Disraeli in the House of Commons by the end of 1841, and Young England could therefore legitimately claim to have limited political influence. In 1846 Smythe accepted a post as Under Secretary for Foreign Affairs, a move which, in effect, rounded off Young England, though it had suffered from diminishing parliamentary coherence since 1844, a fact which is thought to have adversely affected initial sales of *Sybil*.[13] Prior to Smythe's move into government, the production of a short-lived weekly newspaper, *Young England or, the Social Condition of the Empire,* from January through to April 1845, signified that the movement had made some impact, though Disraeli was not involved in the publication, nor did he approve of it.[14] Furthermore, the Young England name had been spread far and wide thanks to sympathetic coverage in *The Times*. Young England can be considered in the context of other nationalistic organisations in Europe at the time, such as Guiseppe Massini's Young Italy, Young Germany and Young Ireland. Indeed, Disraeli used the phrase 'Young England' in a letter to his wife concerning one of his parliamentary speeches, in 1842: 'all young England, the new members etc., were deeply impressed'.[15] However, the argument that Young England was part of an international fraternity with a common goal is difficult to sustain, mainly because Disraeli and his associates did not style themselves with the name as such – they had the name applied to them, first by the Radical M.P. Joseph Hume in 1843. Disraeli's primacy within Young England may be gauged by the fact that, in 1843, the then Home Secretary, Sir James Graham, wrote to Croker, stating that Disraeli, 'is the ablest man among them'.[16]

The Young England movement was described by Robert Blake as 'the reaction of a defeated class to a sense of its own defeat'.[17] Nostalgia was a governing principle of the movement, which constructed as much as resurrected a benign, hierarchical system of the Middle Ages, in which the various strata of society attended to each other's needs in a spirit of reciprocity. Karl Marx was unsympathetic to Young England, attacking its 'total incapacity to comprehend the march of history'.[18] Young England did not produce a direct manifesto or a specific programme for reform, though aspects of both may be gleaned from some of the published works of its most prominent members, with Lord John Manners's *A Plea for National Holy-Days* (1843) being the most notable example. In it, Manners laments the loss of 'the old parish church' and 'the merry green, where youth shall disport itself, and old age, well pleased, look on', in language which calls to mind William Blake's 'The Echoing Green', though without the earlier work's irony.[19] Manners further argues that, in the Medieval period, 'it was the Church that then was the defence of the poor and the weak against the rich and the strong'.[20] Such a stymied and stunted perspective on history reinforces claims that Young England neglected analytical rigour in the pursuit of nostalgia; yet the movement cannot be accused of insincerity, at least as far as most of its central figures are concerned. Furthermore, Young England was not solely about aristocratic nostalgia. Richard Faber cites an illustrative example of the potential application of the movement's principles: 'on 15 August 1843 Manners asked the Attorney-General about the fining of some young men for playing cricket on a Berkshire common after divine service. If the fining was legal, "was it legal for the rich to have their horses and carriages and other enjoyments at the same time?"' Faber also claims that 'Cochrane and Manners were prepared to envisage governmental interference in factories'.[21] Here we see that distinct sense of class sympathy and social justice that impregnates *Sybil,* where working-class recreation in 'The Temple of the Muses' is fondly described. Examining Disraeli's position in relation to Young England, there is no direct and simple equation between his own politics and that of the movement with which he was associated: while there were very significant levels of correspondence between the two (Disraeli, addressing his parliamentary constituents in 1843, had extolled the values of the Church and the landed interest[22]), Disraeli found in the otherwise homogeneous grouping of idealistic, university educated young men a convenient platform from which to present his own political vision to a wider audience. Early in 1842, when the group was still in its infancy,

Disraeli wrote to his wife: 'I already find myself without effort the leader of a party, chiefly of the youth and new members'; Disraeli was willing to associate with Young England, but for reasons of ambition more than principle.[23]

In *Coningsby*, Disraeli is wittily disparaging about the government of England in the aftermath of the Napoleonic Wars: 'these men, indeed, were the mere children of routine. They prided themselves on being practical men. In the language of this defunct school of statesmen, a practical man is a man who practises the blunders of his predecessors' (p. 72). The narrator also considers the social consequences of rapid economic development: 'an illimitable currency; an internal trade supported by swarming millions, whom manufactures and inclosure-bills summoned into existence; above all, the supreme control obtained by man over mechanic power, these are some of the causes of that rapid advance of material civilisation in England, to which the annals of the world can afford no parallel. But there was no proportionate advance in our moral civilisation. In the hurry-skurry of money making, men-making, and machine-making, we had altogether outgrown, not the spirit, but the organisation, of our institutions' (p. 73). The narrator is acutely aware of the effects of industrialisation, but all he sees are the moral fissures, the erosion of venerable practices and institutions, and political betrayal undertaken by intellectually and imaginatively redundant statesmen.

While the Whigs are the primary villains in *Coningsby*, the Tories fare little better. The narrator does state that the government of the Duke of Wellington and Sir Robert Peel was 'distinguished by a spirit of enlightened progress and comprehensive amelioration' (p. 77), yet within two years Disraeli was ruthlessly engineering Peel's downfall. The most heartfelt assessment of Peel in *Coningsby* is therefore the denunciation of the Tamworth Manifesto, the document which expressed the central features of Conservatism in the post-reform era. The details and significance of the Tamworth Manifesto and Peel's contribution to the development of the Conservative Party has been thoroughly discussed elsewhere.[24] It is, however, relevant to note that *Coningsby* explicitly states: 'the Tamworth Manifesto of 1834 was an attempt to construct a party without principles'. The passage goes on to ask the key question of conservatives, 'what will you conserve?', before providing an answer which implicitly accuses Peel of the betrayal of long-standing institutions: 'the prerogatives of the Crown, provided they are not exercised; the independence of the House of Lords, provided it is not asserted; the Ecclesiastical estate, provided it is regulated by a commission of laymen'. He concludes that the Party, 'offers no redress for the Present, and makes no preparation for the Future' (pp. 104–5).

The real-life political and parliamentary assault on Peel, occurring \
the publication of *Coningsby* and *Sybil,* was certainly opportunistic, a
capitalised on discontent among the landed interest over reform of the
Corn Laws. Disraeli himself, after he had become Conservative leader in
the House of Commons, dropped his opposition to the repeal of the Corn
Laws, which suggests that principle was not the primary motivating factor
in his attack on his then parliamentary leader. However, it would be incorrect to assert that Disraeli held no principled opposition to Peel's
programme. His criticism of the Tamworth Manifesto is not a departure
from earlier views put forward in the pre-parliamentary phase of his
career; rather it develops and solidifies those views into an explicitly party
political critique. The Young England movement, together with the
landed interest of the Conservative Party in the House of Commons
provided Disraeli with an opportunity to achieve prominence, but his
opposition to the general direction being taken by his Party was deeply
rooted in views he had held since the 1820s pertaining to the importance
of long-standing institutions in Britain, especially the monarchy. Disraeli
stood out against structural, political change: the new electoral franchise
of the 1830s, and the lessening of parliamentary support for the agricultural interest in the 1840s were, for Disraeli, symptoms of a wider, and
undesired, constitutional overhaul.

Against the bleak background of Whig dominance and Conservative
passivity, there is the potential for a better future through the values of
Coningsby and his devotees. Early on in book two we are informed that
'great minds must trust to great truths and great talents for their rise, and
nothing else' (p. 69). This proves prophetic when Coningsby assumes
prominence over his talented circle of friends, a process referred to by the
narrator as 'the destiny of genius' (p. 109). Coningsby's friends 'talked of
him, they quoted him, they imitated him' (p. 110). We also meet Henry
Sydney's father, who 'had that public spirit which became his station . . .
He was munificent, tender and bounteous to the poor, and loved a flowing hospitality' (p. 86); it is thus made clear that some individual
aristocrats in *Coningsby* continue to uphold ungrudgingly the generous
practices of which Disraeli approves. More importantly, book two charts
the developing friendship between Coningsby and Oswald Millbank, representing fellow-feeling that is capable of transcending the class divide:
'there had risen up between Coningsby and Millbank mutual sentiments
of deep, and even ardent, regard. Acquaintance had developed the superior qualities of Millbank' (p. 109). Millbank is made the beneficiary of
this intercourse: it is assumed that Coningsby will have more to offer,
given his superior class status. However, Millbank does have a significant
hand in the development of Coningsby's social awareness, though his role

in this respect is not strictly consciously instructive: 'Coningsby liked very much to talk politics with Millbank. He heard things from Millbank which were new to him.' Millbank also extends Coningsby's political knowledge: 'but in conversing with Millbank, he heard for the first time of influential classes in the country, who were not noble, and were yet determined to acquire power' (pp. 110–11). Through Millbank, Coningsby is made aware of the full extent of industrialisation and its consequences. He equips Coningsby with a breadth of perspective which later contributes to his dismissal of Lord Monmouth's patronage. However, while Coningsby benefits from Millbank's acquired knowledge, Millbank benefits from Coningsby's innate qualities, signifying Disraeli's faith in the superiority of the upper class.

Book three of *Coningsby* introduces the character of Sidonia. He becomes the hero's guru: fabulously wealthy and influential, enigmatic and aphoristic in his speech. Not for the first time, a Disraelian hero is propelled towards enlightenment by a character who shares some common features with a religious revelation. Robert Blake, however, argues that Sidonia is 'that strange fantasy fulfilment of a cross between Baron de Rothschild and Disraeli himself'.[25] Blake also describes Sidonia as 'Disraeli's revenge for Fagin', the stereotyped Jew of *Oliver Twist*; Disraeli's Sidonia is a champion of positive Judaic strengths.[26] Sidonia is an idealised Disraeli, distilled from real life into a character imbued with intellectual certainty and racial purity. Immediately prior to his meeting with Sidonia, Coningsby is luxuriating in his pastoral surroundings. The scene is set by 'huge and vigorous oaks, intersected with those smooth and sunny glades, that seem as if they must be cut for dames and knights to saunter on' (p.116). The Young Englander is busy at work here, with the deliberate appropriation of a medieval setting. Coningsby 'threw himself under the shade of a spreading tree, and stretched his limbs on the turf for enjoyment rather than repose'. Coningsby, it is revealed, 'was blessed with that tenderness of soul which is sometimes linked with an ardent imagination' (p. 117). The reverie is, however, broken by a storm, which forces Coningsby to take shelter in an inn before heralding Sidonia's arrival: 'a flash of lightning illumined the whole country, and a horseman at full speed, followed by his groom, galloped up to the door' (p. 120). Metaphorically, Sidonia's appearance is a call to action for Coningsby: musing is at an end, a sense of direction is at hand.

Disraeli's description of Sidonia's appearance does not offer much in the way of specific detail, focusing more on his general qualities: 'he was above the middle height, and of a distinguished air and figure; pale, with an impressive brow, and dark eyes of great intelligence' (p. 120). Almost immediately, he impresses his homespun wisdoms upon Coningsby:

'every moment is travel, if understood. .... Adventures are to the adventurous' (p. 121). The latter comment appears in 'Ixion in Heaven' (see chapter one), and in one of Disraeli's personal notebooks for 1842.[27] Having established an electric, captivating aura, through a combination of the narrator's admiration and Coningsby's receptivity, Sidonia presents the essence of his philosophy to Coningsby in the context of a conversation about the meal served to them at the inn.

> "Tis but simple fare,' said Coningsby, as the maiden uncovered the still hissing bacon and the eggs, that looked like tufts of primroses.
>   'Nay, a national dish,' said the stranger, glancing quickly at the table, 'whose fame is a proverb. And what more should we expect under a simple roof! How much better than an omelette or a greasy olla, that they would give us in a posada! 'Tis a wonderful country, this England! What a napkin! How spotless! And so sweet; I declare 'tis a perfume. There is not a princess throughout the South of Europe served in the cleanliness that meets us in this cottage.' (p. 122)

Sidonia, like Disraeli, sees goodness at the heart of England. Pride and effort underpin even the most mundane of tasks, and it follows therefrom that any national malaise springs from a failure of political leadership, not a dearth of human potential. It is unlikely, however, that Disraeli's readers would have found Sidonia's eulogising of bacon and eggs as representative of English nationhood and heritage. William Makepeace Thackeray lampoons the incident, as his Sidonia in *Codlingsby*, Rafael Mendoza, declines 'a luncheon of many courses', opting instead for the rather acerbic meal of 'a couple of dates and a glass of water'.[28]

As the conversation develops between Coningsby and Sidonia, the latter clarifies his thoughts on leadership: '"The age does not believe in great men, because it does not possess any," replied the stranger. "The Spirit of the Age is the very thing that a great man changes."' Sidonia's anonymity at this point underlines his enigmatic nature. He is as much an oracle as a character. Coningsby questions Sidonia's comments and receives a firm answer: '"But are these times for great legislators and great conquerors?" urged Coningsby. "When were they wanted more?" asked the stranger. "From the throne to the hovel all call for a guide"' (p. 124). In the first part of the Young England trilogy, therefore, one of the central dilemmas of *Sybil* is anticipated through Sidonia's and Coningsby's conversation: how can a suffering nation be unified and given a sense of purpose? In *Sybil* the solution is achieved through the restoration of the heroine to her rightful status of nobility, a healing process which covers the wounds of so-called progress. Her marriage to Egremont emphasises the point that a new phase of responsible aristocratic rule has arrived. In

Coningsby the wounds are healed by a symbolic alliance of aristocracy and industry through the marriage of the hero and heroine, providing a basis for challenging the oligarchy which, Disraeli believed, was responsible for discord within the nation.

Sidonia leaves Coningsby with more words of wisdom and advice, echoing to a degree the written message left by a departed stranger for Contarini Fleming: 'nurture your mind with great thoughts. To believe in the heroic makes heroes' (p. 127). Thereafter, Coningsby travels to Beaumanoir where an extended debate is presented between the rival political philosophies of the period. Lord Everingham represents Whiggism, while the families of Lord Henry Sydney and Mr Lyle challenge him in the name of tradition, generosity and ceremony. The numerically uneven nature of the contest reflects Disraeli's own position in the debate. Lord Everingham 'looked upon the New Poor Law as another Magna Carta' (p. 140). The provisions of the Poor Law (1834) had centralised relief for the poor, the new system having replaced local administration. Disraeli, with his support for the principles of small communities and his hostility to centralisation in general, was opposed to the new provisions. In a later debate, the importance of ceremony is considered. Lord Everingham refers to it 'a thing as much gone by as tilts and tournaments'.

> 'I am sorry that they have gone by,' said Lady Theresa.
> 'Everything has gone by that is beautiful,' said Lord Henry.
> 'Life is much easier,' said Lord Everingham.
> 'Life easy!' said Lord Henry. 'Life appears to me to be a fierce struggle.'

Everingham subsequently underlines his position by stating, 'civilisation has no time for ceremony' (p. 150). He is outnumbered in the conversation and thus the argument against him has greater substance and depth, especially as his words are characterised by a belligerent tone. It is noteworthy that an argument whose focus lies across the whole mainstream political spectrum is conducted exclusively amongst aristocrats. Disraeli could not have placed a representative of another class amongst them, as serious political discussion in a social context was unlikely to have taken place across the class divide in the real world. It is also possible that Disraeli was simply being consistent with his broader view, that the aristocracy were the natural leaders of the people, and therefore no participant beyond their circle was required in order to host a comprehensive debate.

Conversely, *Sybil* demonstrates development in Disraeli's examination of politics, in the sense that the working classes do not remain voiceless. Disraeli took advantage of material presented to parliamentary committees in *Sybil* and used it to imbue some of his working-class characters with a sense of authenticity.

In the same visit, Coningsby is introduced to Mr Lyle, from a Roman Catholic family. The novel has already informed us where the narrator stands in relation to Catholicism; in book two, Catholic Emancipation (1829) is referred to as 'the rescue of our Roman Catholic fellow-subjects from the Puritanic yoke' (p. 78). Disraeli was attracted to Catholicism because it had seemingly withstood outside influences and thus functioned as a present, live expression of an uncorrupted past. The same principle is at work in *Coningsby*; Lord Henry Sydney tells Coningsby that the Lyles are 'about the oldest [Roman Catholic family] we have in the country, and the wealthiest' (p. 146). It is therefore little surprise when the Lyle family transpires to be conspicuous by its generosity and sense of social obliga-tion. Twice a week, charity is dispensed among Mr Lyle's neighbours, generating loyalty and gratitude across generations of families: 'the old man, who loved the pilgrimage too much to avail himself of the privilege of a substitute accorded to his grey hairs, came in person with his grand-child and his staff'. Furthermore, Lyle's generosity has a clear purpose: 'I wish the people constantly and visibly to comprehend that Property is their protector and their friend' (p. 153). Disraeli constructs the Lyle family and their practices in order to illustrate a broader point about socially responsible living. Benign pastoral reciprocity is seized as a template for national government. Given the narrative approval heaped upon Mr Lyle, his assessment of the Conservatives has the blessing of his creator: 'this party treats institutions as we do our pheasants, they preserve only to destroy them' (p. 155). Disraeli objects to a lack of rever-ence for tradition and ceremony. Moreover, these ancient, inherited practices are held to have a practical application, as they provide a basis for national renewal. In this respect, *Coningsby* follows the Young England line enthusiastically.

In the fourth book, Coningsby meets an industrialist, Mr Millbank, the father of Oswald. However, far from being a parsimonious utilitarian, Millbank is a benevolent patriarch presiding over his employees. The novel is determined to present the reader with both representatives of a corrupted and narrow-minded present, and embodiments of a potentially better future. Mr Millbank's daughter, Edith is Coningsby's eventual bride. Millbank's factory is the economic base for an entire community, the architecture of which is designed for aesthetic pleasure, while being mindful of the social value of strong institutions: 'about a quarter of a mile further on, appeared a village of not inconsiderable size, and remark-able from the neatness and even picturesque character of its architecture, and the gay gardens that surrounded it. On a sunny knoll in the background rose a church, in the best style of Christian architecture, and near it was a clerical residence and a school-house of similar design' (p. 169). The factory itself, in Coningsby's eyes, is making a bolder and more explicitly political statement: 'the building had been fitted up by a capitalist as anxious to raise a monument of the skill and power of his order, as to obtain a return for the great investment' (p. 172).

When Millbank appears, he is described as having 'a visage of energy and decision' (p. 171). In conversation he represents the responsible, philanthropic industrialist, concerned about the errant conduct of the aristocracy. One of his clerks talks about 'how he [Millbank] had built churches, and schools, and institutes; houses and cottages on a new system of ventilation; how he had allotted gardens; established singing classes' (p. 172). Millbank is a localised version of Disraeli's ideal ruler, motivated by the desire to provide for those within his care, rather than pursuing a selfish, personal agenda. He is less important as an industrialist than as an embodiment of Disraeli's preferred form of government. Even his name, containing both industrial and rural elements, signifies his connection to the traditions Disraeli holds so dear. In similar fashion, the aural connection between Lyle and 'loyal' should not be overlooked, as it signifies steadfastness and continuity. Millbank voices an opinion which could just as easily come from Disraeli: 'I do not understand how an aristocracy can exist, unless it be distinguished by some quality which no other class of the community possesses' (p. 178). However, he develops this point in order to form a criticism of the role and composition of the aristocracy across three centuries: 'we owe the English peerage to three sources: the spoliation of the Church; the open and flagrant sale of its honours by the elder Stuarts; and the boroughmongering of our own times. Those are the three main sources of the existing peerage of England, and in my opinion disgraceful ones' (p. 179). Given Disraeli's faith in aristocratic renewal and the prospects this would offer the country, it appears Millbank deviates from the author's own beliefs at this juncture. However, Disraeli condemned the dissolution of the monasteries and, in his own time, viewed the limited extension of the electoral franchise as an essentially corrupt act designed to perpetuate a Whig oligarchy. Millbank draws an implicit connection between these acts of ruling-class betrayal, a position with which Disraeli would sympathise and identify. Ultimately, however, Disraeli viewed aristocratic misbehaviour as an abrogation brought about by errant individuals, rather than a symptom of a fundamental, structural flaw within the aristocracy itself. The true aristocracy, in Disraeli's view, had been deflected from its path by malign influence, yet it remained as an untapped source of national renewal.

Millbank's home offers two further attractions for Coningsby. The first is the food: 'the dinner was plain, but perfect of its kind' (p. 175). In common with the meal served to Coningsby and Sidonia at the inn, food is an important signifier, representing English attributes – honesty, decency and integrity. In the case of the Millbanks, it underlines the modest generosity expressed through the architecture of the community. The second attraction is Edith Millbank. She is young, 'apparently she could scarcely have counted sixteen summers'. Furthermore, 'she was delicate and fragile, but as she raised her still blushing visage to her father's guest, Coningsby felt that he had never beheld a countenance of such striking and such peculiar beauty'. Moving from a general tone of admiration to more specific qualities, Disraeli writes that, 'it was a radiant face, one of those that seem to have been touched in their cradle by a sunbeam, and to have retained all their brilliancy and suffused and mantling lustre' (p. 174). Following this striking introduction, Edith continues to enchant Coningsby and, despite the complexities of a plot in which the long-standing animosity between Millbank and Lord Monmouth (rooted in romantic rivalry) impedes the progress of true love, there is a certain inevitability to the marriage between Coningsby and Edith.

Book four also sees the reintroduction of Lord Monmouth and Sidonia. Monmouth's incorrigibility is central to his character, yet the arrival of Coningsby has a partially restorative effect: 'it would be an exaggeration to say that Lord Monmouth's heart was touched; but his good-nature effervesced, and his fine taste was deeply gratified'. However, calculation overpowers sentiment as Monmouth regards his grandson as, 'a brilliant tool' (p. 195). A more significant development emerges through the presentation of Sidonia's background, as it is to Sidonia that Coningsby looks for inspiration, rather than to his hedonistic grandfather: 'Sidonia was descended from a very ancient and noble family of Arragon, that, in the course of ages, had given to the state many distinguished citizens. In the priesthood its members had been peculiarly eminent' (p. 220). Such a description imbues the family with mystery, spirituality and good breeding. This general family background is overshadowed by Sidonia's specific religious affiliation, which dominates this section of the text. In what had been a climate of intolerance, the Sidonia family 'secretly adhered to the ancient faith and ceremonies of their fathers; a belief in the unity of the God of Sinai, and the rights and observances of the laws of Moses' (p. 221). For Disraeli personally, Judaism was starting to supersede Catholicism, emerging as a central feature of his personality. The Judaistic tradition formed a substantial part of Disraeli's own ancestry. Although his father had converted to Christianity in 1817, and ensured that his children followed suit, Benjamin Disraeli's growing preoccupation with Judaism found expression repeatedly in his writings, first as a dramatic effusion in *Alroy* and then, subsequently, in a more thoughtful and considered form in Disraeli's literary works from the 1840s onwards. In *Coningsby*, the narrator claims that 'the Hebrew is an unmixed race' (p. 232). Disraeli's fascination with Judaism now becomes politically unhealthy. It is but a small step from here to launch a claim for racial superiority, which subsequently happens. It is sufficient at this point to note that Disraeli admires the Jewish community because it is defined by its religious and, to a lesser extent, its ethnic affiliation, rather than by explicit hostility to any other, similarly defined groups within society. Nevertheless, the preoccupation with racial purity becomes the most disturbing aspect of Disraeli's philosophy as his literary works unfold.

Sidonia presents his ideas on the Jewish religion in the course of a conversation with Coningsby in chapter fifteen of book four. He begins by informing Coningsby that 'the Jews . . . are a race essentially monarchical', going on to give them a more explicitly political colouring: 'yet the Jews, Coningsby, are essentially Tories. Toryism, indeed, is but copied from the mighty prototype which has fashioned Europe' (p. 263). Leaving aside the reductive nature of Sidonia's analysis, we can, adopting Disraeli's view for the moment, better understand his attraction and eventual commitment to the Conservative Party, despite his earlier affiliation with the Radicals. Conservatism, through its perceived connection with ancient institutions, ceremonies and practices, becomes the political correlative for Judaism. Immediately thereafter, Sidonia's praise for the Jewish faith leads him into a discussion about race: 'the fact is, you cannot destroy a pure race. . . . The mixed persecuting races disappear; the pure persecuted race remains' (p. 263). Having established his general position, Sidonia presents a roll call of European Ministers of Finance, claiming, quite falsely, that all were Jewish.[29] Disraeli's Judaism claims were also ridiculed by Thackeray who, at the end of *Codlingsby*, has Rafael Mendoza claiming that the Pope is Jewish.

Aside from his analysis of race, Sidonia undertakes a survey of the present state of politics in England. Unsurprisingly, he is dissatisfied with what he sees. His assessment of the prospects for national renewal rests on strength of character rather than economic and social forces. Concerning the extension of the electoral franchise, he states, 'it is not the Reform Bill that has shaken the aristocracy of this country, but the means by which that Bill was carried' (p. 236), echoing the views of Disraeli, who argued that parliamentary reform merely consolidated the power of one of the existing groups in Parliament, rather than genuinely enfranchising a wider portion of the country. Sidonia backs up his view with a historical analysis of the decline of Parliament.

For one hundred and fifty years Power has been deposited in the Parliament, and for the last sixty or seventy years it has been becoming more and more unpopular. In 1830 it was endeavoured by a reconstruction to regain the popular affection; but, in truth, as the Parliament then only made itself more powerful, it has only become more odious. As we see that the Barons, the Church, the King, have in turn devoured each other, and that the Parliament, the last devourer, remains, it is impossible to resist the impression that this body is also doomed to be destroyed; and he is a sagacious statesman who may detect in what form and in what quarter the great consumer will arise. (p. 250)

On the surface, this is a teleological argument of the kind espoused by the early, Hegelian-influenced Karl Marx. Dialectical tension has brought about the diffusion of power down from the monarch to the Parliament with an agitated working class potentially standing next in line to take control under the banner of Chartism. However, Sidonia goes on to refute explicitly any form of economic determinism: 'there is no error so vulgar as to believe that revolutions are occasioned by economical causes'. By way of an example he cites the English Civil war which, given that it was (in Sidonia's judgement) brought about by a religious movement, demonstrates that 'the imagination of England rose against the government'. This leads Sidonia to conclude that 'a political institution is a machine; the motive power is the national character' (pp. 251–2). This is an argument of a metaphysical nature, incorporating political consciousness in society: change is brought about not by the material conditions of a society but by the imaginative power of individuals. However, the power still resides within the population to change the condition of their lives, and from this perspective Sidonia recognises the transformative potential of people.

Sidonia is predictably hostile to utilitarianism and the political predominance of reason: 'it was not Reason that besieged Troy; it was not Reason that sent forth the Saracen from the Desert to conquer the world. . . . Man is only truly great when he acts from the passions.' He applies his argument to an analysis of England since the end of the Napoleonic Wars: 'since the peace, there has been an attempt to advocate a reconstruction of society on a purely rational basis. The principle of Utility has been powerfully developed' (p. 253). Sidonia acts as a wise, self-assured mouthpiece for Disraeli's own views, channelling the energies of Coningsby and enabling him to acquire the potential to become a transformative force in the realm. Sidonia rounds off the chapter with a metonymic condemnation of the nation's political history: 'England is governed by Downing Street; once it was governed by Alfred and Elizabeth' (p. 254). Having earlier said that 'Man must ever be the slave of routine: but in the old days it was routine of great thoughts, and now it is a routine of little ones' (p. 241), it is clear that Sidonia perceives a gradual process of political degradation, whereby grand monarchical power has percolated down to uncharismatic, narrow, party political influence.

The fundamental fact of Sidonia's identity is his economic power: 'he was lord and master of the money-market of the world, and of course virtually lord and master of everything else' (p. 225). We are thus presented with an unresolved paradox: Sidonia prioritises imaginative power over economic power, yet the narrator asserts that it is Sidonia's financial muscle which determines his importance and influence. Furthermore, Sidonia is practically bleached clean of his human traits by Disraeli: 'he was a man without affections' (p. 229). This maintains the enigma that surrounds him, casting him in the role of oracle rather than three-dimensional character. Indeed, he is connected with 'those subterranean agencies of which the world in general knows so little, but which exercise so great an influence on public events' (p. 231). Sidonia later tells Coningsby 'that the world is governed by very different personages from what is imagined by those who are not behind the scenes' (p. 265). Disraeli always maintained throughout his life his belief and anxiety that there were international power structures beyond those controlled by governments or monarchs, a view which flies in the face of his successful career as a politician who moved in the highest circles. However, conspiratorial theories remained a constant feature of his thought.

In book five, Coningsby ferments the political ideas and phenomena to which he has been exposed. He considers three of the most important individuals to whom he has been introduced: Eustace Lyle (the son of Mr Lyle and, supposedly, based on the real-life Young England supporter, Ambrose Lisle Philipps[30]), Mr Millbank and Sidonia. Coningsby finds a common denominator between them: 'he curiously meditated over the fact, that three English subjects, one of them a principal landed proprietor, another one of the most eminent manufacturers, and the third the greatest capitalist in the kingdom, all of them men of great intelligence, and doubtless of a high probity and conscience, were in their hearts disaffected with the political constitution of the country' (p. 271). Coningsby thus arrives at a firm conclusion regarding the problems at the heart of the nation, all of which relate to obstacles or deficiencies that lie in the way of genuine progress: 'a Crown robbed of its prerogatives; a church controlled by a commission; and an Aristocracy that does not lead'. Moreover, Coningsby perceives the social consequences of institutional failure: 'the Crown has become a cipher; the Church a sect; the Nobility drones; and the People drudges' (p. 277). From this state of discontent, Coningsby begins to establish a confederacy and a programme to instigate national renewal. At one point Coningsby makes a passionate plea to Lord Vere:

> Do what I am doing, what Henry Sydney and Buckhurst are doing, hold yourself aloof from political parties which, from the necessity of things, have ceased to have distinctive principles, and are therefore practically only factions; and wait and see, whether with patience, energy, honour, and Christian faith, and a desire to look to the national welfare and not to sectional and limited interests; whether, I say, we may not discover some great principles to guide us, to which we may adhere, and which then, if true, will ultimately guide and control others. (p. 279)

While the oratorical style of Coningsby's speech is conspicuous, the novel thus far has shown how his position has gestated out of a political malaise, from which he has been elevated through the intercession of significant others, each of whom has voiced the concerns of a specific interest group (although Sidonia's words have a transcendent quality, rather than limiting themselves solely to the articulation of the concerns of international financiers). In book five, Sidonia argues that the movement towards substantial parliamentary democracy is, paradoxically, not progressive, but regressive: 'the tendency of advanced civilisation is in truth to pure Monarchy'. However, in the same conversation with Coningsby, he aligns himself with modernity by identifying the power of the press: 'the Printing-press is an element unknown to classic or feudal times. It absorbs in a great degree the duties of the Sovereign, the Priest, the Parliament; it controls, it educates, it discusses' (p. 319). Disraeli's construction of Sidonia's philosophy involves the application of ancient beliefs to a modern context; hence he can shift from being a disciple of 'pure monarchy' to an acute observer of the terms and conditions of political influence within a parliamentary system without any great tonal shift. The character of Sidonia is raw and under-developed in some instances, but this rawness also lends Sidonia his oracular quality.

Book five presents two further, significant narrative developments. The first is the prospect of a parliamentary election in Darlford. The fact that the Conservative candidate is Rigby, the sycophantic assistant to Lord Monmouth (not to mention Disraeli's revenge on Croker for alleged betrayal during *The Representative* débâcle) underlines the extent of the corruption in contemporary politics. Disraeli's placing of Millbank senior as Rigby's electoral rival implies support for the anti-Conservative candidate. Disraeli thus declares opposition to his own party (although, as this is done through a fictitious third-party character, Disraeli is able to escape official censure). The second development is the introduction of Princess Lucretia Colonna. The difficulties that she will cause are prefigured at an early stage. Her voice 'was the voice of the serpent; indeed, there was an undulating movement in Lucretia, when she approached you, which irresistibly reminded you of that mysterious animal' (p. 306). Disraeli's female characters are frequently presented as extremes: either wholly virtuous (thinking of Edith Millbank in *Coningsby* or the eponymous heroine of *Sybil*) or they are wholly reprehensible, hell-bent on intrigue or destruction, even (as in the case of Mrs Felix Lorraine in *Vivian Grey*) attempting to poison the hero. It is not known the extent to which Disraeli's representations of women characters may have reflected his own views; however, it is relevant to note how they fit into Disraeli's general symbolic political landscape, in which principled and noble characters, with strong connections to the territory they inhabit, vie with interlopers who plot for their own, selfish purposes.

Sidonia is impervious to the attractions of women. In book six he thinks of relationships as another form of politics or militaristic conflict: 'he detested the diplomacy of passion: protocols, protracted negotiations, conferences, correspondence, treaties projected, ratified, violated. He had no genius for the tactics of intrigue; your reconnoiterings, and marchings, and counter-marchings, sappings and minings, assaults, sometimes surrenders and sometimes repulses.' Sidonia's callous assessment of emotional engagement is compounded by his fundamental, albeit sinister, reason for steering clear of relationships: he 'would never diminish by marriage the purity of his race' (pp. 334–5). Although from any modern narrative perspective Sidonia would stand condemned for his emotional nullification predicated upon a perception of racial superiority, he continues to enjoy narrative approval despite holding objectionable ideas. This is because his disposition towards women is necessary within the context of the novel as a whole: immersion in a love affair would dilute the enigma that surrounds him. His mysterious qualities are an integral part of his authoritative status and the loss of the former would involve the loss of the latter.

The connection of his abstinence from relationships with a wider creed on race renders Sidonia's character problematic, even objectionable. Racial prejudice informs Sidonia's outlook on other subjects, yet it does not necessarily follow therefrom that Disraeli himself was racist (at least in the modern sense of the term), despite the clear narrative approval bestowed upon Sidonia throughout the text. For Disraeli, race signified the presence of an uncorrupted past within a traumatic present. It also suggested restorative potential, as a re-connection with the past in all its forms could, Disraeli believed, spare the nation from the tyranny of oligarchical rule. Book six also features the seemingly incidental Carlists (supporters of the pretender to the Spanish throne, Don Carlos), guests of

Lord Monmouth. Their narrative contribution is slight, yet they are important in the sense that they stand as a living example of the ideal aristocracy: 'they are the phantoms of a past, but real Aristocracy; an Aristocracy that was founded on an intelligible principle; which claimed great privileges for great purposes' (pp. 328–9). It is appropriate that they are guests of Monmouth, as their sense of duty is the antithesis of his hedonism. Shadowy, insubstantial figures within *Coningsby*, they are also shadows of history, the presence of a real aristocracy in the house of its corrupted form.

Book seven sees the further development of Coningsby's political philosophy. In particular he launches a stern critique of the Conservative Party. Disraeli uses Coningsby to voice his own dissatisfaction with the direction being taken by the Conservative Party under the leadership of Sir Robert Peel.

> Thus they are devoted to the prerogatives of the Crown, although in truth the Crown has been stripped of every one of its prerogatives; they effect a great veneration for the constitution in Church and State, though every one knows that the constitution in Church and State no longer exists; they are ready to stand or fall with the 'independence of the upper house of Parliament,' though, in practice, they are perfectly aware that, with their sanction, 'the Upper House' has abdicated its initiatory functions, and now serves only as a court of review of the legislation of the House of Commons. (p. 371)

Coningsby sees the Conservatives as being complicit in the realignment of power. Furthermore, their position is worse than that of the Whigs, as Coningsby accuses them of rallying to various institutions, the character of each of which has been weakened with tacit Conservative approval. The word 'betrayal' is not mentioned here, but it is implicit through the whole passage. Disraeli's parliamentary attacks on Peel in 1846 are prefigured in his novel.

Coningsby's outburst occurs within the context of a lengthy conversation with Oswald Millbank. The episode is a set piece for the presentation of Coningsby's political philosophy. Millbank is the sincere and reasonable advocate of democracy: 'it is the only power by which we can sweep away those sectional privileges and interests that impede the intelligence and industry of the community'. Coningsby's retort is that class can be transcended: 'the only way to terminate what, in the language of the present day, is called Class Legislation, is not to entrust power to classes. . . . The only power that has no class sympathy is the Sovereign' (pp. 372–3). Coningsby's position (and, by extension, Disraeli's) is at its weakest here. Society is structured around class, and the economic factors that generate class relationships. Furthermore, to argue that the monarch has no position with regard to class, certainly in Disraeli's class-dominant era, is simply untrue. The monarchs represented – and, to an extent, still do today – a whole distinct, superior class themselves, hence their ability to 'elevate' ordinary citizens to a higher class level through Knighthoods and so forth. Coningsby's position is more disregard of reality than a cogent argument for the transcendence of class within government. However, he does try to produce evidence to reinforce his position: 'Parliament is not sitting at this moment, and yet the nation is represented in its highest as well as in its most minute interests.' He also picks up on Sidonia's point concerning the importance of the press: 'Opinion is now supreme, and Opinion speaks in print. The representation of the Press is far more complete than the representation of Parliament' (p. 374). This comment is ambiguous; it could be extolling the press, or it could be cautioning against its dangers. However, given the influence of Sidonia's thinking over Coningsby's, and the consequent overlap between the two, it is worth reconsidering Sidonia's teleological analysis of government in book four. Sidonia believed that the fall of parliamentary rule was a historical inevitability, yet was unsure what would follow such an event. Taking on board Coningsby's view, and identifying Disraeli as the common denominator beneath both characters, Disraeli was expressing an anxiety that the press would turn legislator, swaying opinion and determining policy in a parliament which would merely be a place of enactment for measures produced by powerful opinions within a mass market. His own involvement with *The Representative* had signified a belief that a newspaper could be used to effect political change. For the present, however, Coningsby sees a tyranny of the lower house, which he phrases in Napoleonic rhetoric, fully mindful (it would seem) of the anxiety that this might engender amongst his readership: 'the House of Commons is absolute. It is the State. "L'Etat c'est moi"' (p. 377).

Coningsby and Oswald Millbank are able to resolve their argument to their mutual satisfaction by moving away from the political terrain to the spiritual. Millbank sees a possibility of salvation in the younger clergy: 'the parochial system, though shaken by the fatal poor-law, is still the most ancient, the most comprehensive, and the most popular institution of the country; the younger priests are, in general, men whose souls are awake to the high mission which they have to fulfil, and which their predecessors so neglected; there is, I think, a rising feeling in the community, that parliamentary intercourse in matters ecclesiastical has not tended either to the spiritual or the material elevation of the humbler orders'. Coningsby develops this point and sees the youth of the nation embarking upon a spiritual quest to save the nation. The conclusion of his point, and Millbank's response to it, gives the passage an epiphanous quality.

> 'It is a holy thing to see a state saved by its youth,' said Coningsby; and then he added, in a tone of humility, if not of depression, 'But what a task! What a variety of qualities, what a combination of circumstances is requisite! What bright abilities and what noble patience! What confidence from the people, what favour from the Most High!'
>
> 'But he will favour us,' said Millbank. 'And I say to you as Nathan said unto David, "Thou art the man!"' (pp. 379–80)

Although it is difficult to read this passage in isolation without irony, within the context of the conversation between Coningsby and Millbank it is clear that none is intended. Millbank, the son of the industrialist, anoints Coningsby as the leader of the spiritually charged national youth movement, intent upon rescuing the nation. Less hyperbolically, the full conversation between Coningsby and Millbank relates to the structure of the Young England trilogy, as there is consideration of party politics, the allegedly woeful state of the nation, and the pursuit of renewal and restoration through spiritual reawakening.

Following his conversation with Oswald Millbank, Coningsby is reintroduced to Edith. They go for a walk, Coningsby sits at her feet, 'and assuredly a maiden and a youth more beautiful and engaging had seldom met before in a scene more fresh and fair' (p. 394). From the image itself, through to the idiom in which it is described, Disraeli presents an ideal of Young England: an uncorrupted, pre-industrial land of innocent and unblemished love. Yet this scene also demonstrates the utopian and self-deluding aspects of Young England. In this natural landscape, history is reversed and ignored. Book seven concludes with a storm, witnessed by Coningsby and Oswald Millbank: 'the fork-lightning flashed and scintillated from every quarter of the horizon: the thunder broke over the Castle, as if the keep were rocking with artillery: amid the momentary pauses of the explosion, the rain was heard descending like dissolving water-spouts' (p. 409). The first simile underlines the extent to which the storm is a portent: Coningsby and Oswald have united forces in a gesture prefiguring the even more substantial alliance between Coningsby and Edith which eventually prevails despite the hostility of the older generation. The storm symbolises the fracturing of the old order. Disraeli uses a similar device in the opening chapter of *Sybil*, in which the storm would relate more closely, within the scheme of the novel, to the coming of Chartism.

The main event of book eight is the confrontation between Coningsby and Lord Monmouth, who invites, and indeed expects, Coningsby to stand for the Conservatives at Darlford, in opposition to Mr Millbank.

Coningsby mulls over his position: 'what sympathy could there exist between Coningsby and the "great Conservative Party," that for ten years in an age of revolution had never promulgated a principle . . . ; and who were at this moment, when Coningsby was formally solicited to join their ranks, in open insurrection against the prerogatives of the English Monarchy!' (p. 428). Arguing with Monmouth, Coningsby states that he seeks, 'political faith . . . instead of political infidelity', adding, 'before I support Conservative principles . . . I merely wish to be informed what those principles aim to conserve' (p. 431). This is Disraeli's covert attack on his own party. Disraeli was 'testing the water' with *Coningsby* and *Sybil*, exposing his arguments from a creative distance, prior to their open presentation in Parliament when he defiantly stood against Peel. At the end of Coningsby's argument with Monmouth, he clarifies his position: 'what we want, sir, is not to fashion new dukes and furbish up old baronies, but to establish great principles which may maintain the realm and secure the happiness of the people. Let me see authority once more honoured; a solemn reverence again the habit of our lives; let me see property acknowledging, as in the old days of faith, that labour is his twin brother' (p. 434). The identification of a common feeling and purpose between a territorial aristocracy and the working classes, voiced here as a general principle, is at the centre of *Sybil* and is therefore developed to a far greater extent. By the end of book eight of *Coningsby*, the hero's enemies, Rigby and Lucretia Colonna (now Lady Monmouth) are conspiring against him. The movement from political formulation into prospective political action places Coningsby into adversarial relationships and, as Coningsby's creator had himself discovered, practical ability matters as well as political platitudes.

In the opening to the final book of *Coningsby* we are presented with another ideal relationship, as Christmas prompts a burst of munificence: 'all day long, carts laden with fuel and warm raiment were traversing the various districts, distributing comfort and dispensing cheer. For a Christian gentleman of high degree was Eustace Lyle' (p. 463). The behaviour of Eustace Lyle is an example of the principle held by Lord Henry Sydney: 'that a mere mechanical mitigation of the material necessities of the humbler classes, a mitigation which must inevitably be limited, can never alone avail sufficiently to ameliorate their condition; that their condition is not merely "a knife and fork question," to use the coarse and shallow phrase of the Utilitarian school; that a simple satisfaction of the grosser necessities of our nature will not make a happy people; that you must cultivate the heart as well as seek to content the belly; and that the surest means to elevate the character of the people is to appeal to their affections' (p. 464). Disraeli's hostility to utilitarianism is based on an open questioning of the importance of economics. Romanticism becomes the celebrated cause of party politics, suggesting that communication on an emotional level is more likely to improve the nation than measures designed to alleviate poverty. Again we bear witness to the selective analysis practised by Disraeli in *Coningsby*. The redistribution of political power within English history is explored, yet the economic organisation of society is relegated to a dull encumbrance, while individual generosity is posited as a serious basis on which to ensure pleasant subsistence and harmonious relations within society as a whole. This may have been a workable principle within a very small community, but it is an unsatisfactory and naïve template for a nation in the throes of an industrial revolution. The politics of *Coningsby* is a reaction to the uncertainties of industrialisation; Disraeli offered the nostalgic suggestion that a simpler, less regulated mode of living was still possible.

By the end of the novel Coningsby's political apprenticeship is complete. Walking the streets of London, he feels that he understands the power and the purpose of leadership:

> Well had Sidonia taught him, view everything in its relation to the rest. 'Tis the secret of all wisdom. Here was the mightiest of modern cities; the rival even of the most celebrated of the ancient. Whether he inherited or forfeited fortunes, what was it to the passing throng? They would not share his splendour, or his luxury, or his comfort. But a word from his lip, a thought from his brain, expressed at the right time, at the right place, might turn their hearts, might influence their passions, might change their opinions, might affect their destiny. Nothing is great but the personal. As civilisation advances, the accidents of life become each day less important. The power of man, his greatness and his glory, depend on essential qualities. Brains every day become more precious than blood. You must give men new ideas, you must teach them new words, you must modify their manners, you must change their laws, you must root out prejudices, subvert convictions, if you wish to be great. (p. 480)

With Sidonia as his guru, Coningsby achieves a sense of his own potential. Having shed any class identification he aspires to be like Sidonia, pursuing a superior, disconnected position which allows him to assume a vantage point over everyone and everything. The populace is represented as dormant and indifferent, yet capable of being galvanised by the correct application of charisma. The influence of Disraeli's earlier fictional heroes is also noteworthy, as the isolated, aloof, melancholic Coningsby experiences his epiphany. The conclusion to Coningsby's thoughts is breathtaking in its scope and confidence: 'the greatness of this city destroys my misery . . . and my genius shall conquer its greatness!' (p. 480).

Coningsby is victorious in the Darlford election. His subsequent arrival in the town is messianic in its imagery, recalling the similarly exuberant reception given to Aubrey Bohun or Alroy: 'they were met by an anxious deputation, who received Coningsby as if he were a prophet. . . Triumphant music sounded; banners waved; the multitude were marshalled' (p. 499). The novel ends on a challenging question, asking whether Coningsby and his cohorts will 'denounce to a perplexed and disheartened world the frigid theories of a generalising age that have destroyed the individuality of man, and restore the happiness of their country by believing in their own energies, and daring to be great?' (p. 503). The novel as a whole has traced the political maturation of the hero, guided primarily by Sidonia yet also informed by representatives of industry and the aristocracy. Thus equipped, the Disraelian hero is now in a position to challenge the oligarchy held responsible for national moribundity. It was to be left to Disraeli's next hero to contribute to the destruction of corruption and the restoration of a true, territorial nobility.

SYBIL

'. . . it is the past alone that can explain the present, and it is youth that alone can mould the remedial future.'

If *Coningsby* details the development of a cohesive political philosophy, then *Sybil*, published in May 1845, is more about final honing and the subsequent application of that philosophy in order to halt national decline and create a more benign future.[31] Furthermore, in some of its depictions of working-class life it is tied closely to reality, drawing upon reports to Parliament, most notably the First Report of the Children's Employment Commission (1843). *Sybil* was responding to real problems and anxieties; in 1842 there were one and a half million paupers in receipt of poor relief, among a total national population of sixteen million, or nearly ten percent of the population. *Sybil* was, moreover, written at a time of agricultural riots and Chartist agitation.[32]

There are also literary influences at work in *Sybil*, most notably that of Thomas Carlyle, whose publication of *Sartor Resartus* (which first appeared in *Fraser's Magazine* in 1833–4) had helped to kill off the fashionable novel. *Sartor Resartus* also presented the idea of 'two nations' before Disraeli: 'two sects will one day part England between them', before further defining the sects as, 'two contradictory, uncommunicating masses'.[33] Carlyle's *Chartism* (1839) and *Past and Present* (1843) are both also relevant to the theme of *Sybil*. *Chartism* lamented a perceived decline in religion and read dire prospects into the French Revolution, in which a downtrodden lower class had turned upon their irresponsible aristocratic rulers. For both Carlyle and Disraeli, the English upper classes in the first half of the nineteenth century were being similarly, dangerously neglectful. *Past and Present* looks back with nostalgic fondness at the Medieval period. It is not certain whether Disraeli read Carlyle; certainly, Carlyle was not sympathetic to Young England, stating that it would be better off by 'honestly recognising what was dead'.[34] However, Carlyle was at the height of his fame in the 1840s and Disraeli's exposure to his ideas is highly likely.

Works by Disraeli's father, Isaac Disraeli, may also have influenced the trilogy, with *Commentaries on the Life and Reign of Charles I* (1828–30) inspiring, to a degree, *Coningsby* and *Sybil,* and *Genius of Judaism* (1833) influencing *Tancred.* According to Blake, Disraeli claimed that his theories of history had been formed by reading in his father's library, and thus it is possible to see how the Royalist and Judaistic sympathies of the elder Disraeli's works would have fed through into Benjamin Disraeli's writing.[35] It has also been claimed that William Cobbett was an influence on both *Coningsby* and *Sybil*, as Cobbett's *History of the Protestant Reformation in England and Ireland* (1829) argues, as does *Sybil*, that the dissolution of the monasteries had an adverse impact upon society. Cobbett also came strikingly close to coining the two nations phrase, as he wrote that there are 'but two classes of people in a community, masters and slaves, a very few enjoying the extreme of luxury and millions doomed to the extreme of misery'.[36] There is, in addition, intellectual continuity between *Coningsby* and *Sybil*. In a speech in the Great Free-Trade Hall, Manchester, on 3 October 1844, Disraeli spoke on the theme, 'Knowledge is Power.' In line with the thinking of *Coningsby* he addressed the youth of the nation as 'the trustees of Posterity' and encouraged them to 'aspire'. Anticipating the central concerns of *Sybil*, he issued a call to 'emancipate this country from the degrading thraldom of faction'. The speech links the two novels: identifying the group within society in which hope principally rests, and presenting them with a clear aspiration, though not with a specific programme. Conversely, while there is an intellectual connection between *Coningsby* and *Sybil*, the latter can be read politically as signifying a slight yet significant departure from the principles of Young England. *Coningsby* is clearly rooted in Young England, right down to many of the central characters being modelled on leading figures from the movement. *Sybil*, dedicated by Disraeli to his wife, is a more personal vision, despite the plethora of data, and the appropriation of testimony given to parliamentary committees. The ideas developed in *Sybil*, therefore, are more central to Disraeli's political philosophy than those explored under the banner heading of Young England in *Coningsby*.

The first book of *Sybil*, set in 1837, assesses the present state of the nation. After its despondent conclusions, it offers the prospect of a better future through the ascendancy of the new queen. In an extended metaphor running through the opening two chapters, Disraeli uses the fanatical gambling of the aristocracy to signify their degradation. In an exclusive club, on the eve of the Epsom Derby, a sense of lethargy prevails on every subject except gambling: 'the seats on each side of the table were occupied by persons consuming, with a heedless air, delicacies for which they had no appetite' (p. 2). The degradation and appalling excesses are total; as Alfred Mountchesney declares, extolling the virtues of eating in bad, suburban restaurants: '"I rather like bad wine," said Mr Mountchesney: "one gets so bored with good wine"' (p. 3). Therefore, *Sybil* begins as a fashionable novel before rejecting the genre abruptly in favour of a more empirical and serious procedure.[37] The mood of soporific calm in *Sybil* is disrupted by a sudden storm. The sombre response of the club members is caused primarily by the likely effect of heavy rain on the race course, yet, on a metaphorical level, *Sybil* will bring down a colossal and destructive political storm by the end of the novel.

The events at the race course itself are a synoptic representation of Disraeli's bleakest feelings about the shape that democracy had taken in the 1830s and '40s. Among the bookmakers present are Hump Chippendale and Captain Spruce. The latter 'had a weakness for the aristocracy, who knowing his graceful infirmity patronised him with condescending dexterity, acknowledged his existence in Pall Mall as well as Tattersall's, and thus occasionally got a point more than the betting out of him'. Spruce's admiration for the aristocracy leads to him being exploited (despite the fact that he is recognised in social as well as gambling arenas), in a relationship which, for the narrator, degrades both parties. Chippendale, however, 'was a democratic leg, who loved to fleece a noble and thought all men were born equal – a consoling creed that was a hedge for his hump'. He is less accommodating to aristocrats, and, declining a bet, 'turned with malignant abruptness from the heir apparent of an English earldom' (pp. 6–7). For Disraeli, the absorption of the aristocracy into a wider melding of classes has resulted in a breakdown of social relations. The malignancy of Chippendale, expressed in his appearance as well as his behaviour, is no longer impeded by any class boundaries and he is free to practise his parasitism. Applying Disraeli's imaginary confrontation in a wider context, political conflict is similarly motivated by personal grudges and weaknesses as much as matters of principle. The image of a gambling aristocracy encapsulates Disraeli's ideas concerning the abrogation of social responsibility by the upper classes, and the need for them to take a new direction.

In chapter three Disraeli presents his objections to the current composition of Parliament and the balance of power therein: 'power had been transferred from the crown to a parliament, the members of which were appointed by a limited and exclusive class, who owned no responsibility to the country, who debated and voted in secret, and who were regularly paid by the small knot of great families that by this machinery had secured the permanent possession of the king's treasury' (p. 15). In a subsequent chapter, Disraeli is more specific in directing blame not at Parliament as a whole, but at the House of Commons:

> One house of Parliament has been irremediably degraded into the decaying position of a mere court of registry, possessing great privileges, on condition that it never exercises them; while the other chamber, that, at the first blush, and to the superficial, exhibits symptoms of almost unnatural vitality, engrossing in its orbit all the business of the country, assumes on a more studious inspection somewhat of the character of a select vestry, fulfilling municipal rather than imperial offices, and beleaguered by critical and clamorous millions, who cannot comprehend why a privileged and exclusive senate is requisite to perform functions which immediately concern all, which most personally comprehend, and which many in their civic spheres believe they could accomplish in a manner not less satisfactory, though certainly less ostentatious. (p. 35)

The increase in influence of the House of Commons, arising from the fact that, post-1832, it was now representative of a wider cross-section of the community is, to Disraeli, a malevolent conjuring trick whereby power has been appropriated from its natural resting place. Disraeli further argues that the Reform Act has been a retrograde step because it has effected a change in the values of the country, with the pursuit of profit now being the determining principle of government: 'since the passing of the Reform Act the altar of mammon has blazed with triple worship. To acquire, to accumulate, to plunder each other by virtue of philosophic phrases, to propose a Utopia to consist only of WEALTH and TOIL, this has been the breathless business of enfranchised England for the last twelve years' (p. 36). For Disraeli, this calamitous state of affairs is worse than a recipe for national decline because it constitutes a betrayal of a glorious history, with the superior qualities of preceding generations having been lost, succeeded by an uncharismatic, economically rapacious cabal: 'O! England, glorious and ancient realm, the fortunes of thy polity are indeed strange! The wisdom of the Saxons, Norman valour, the statecraft of the Tudors, the national sympathies of the Stuarts, the spirit of the latter Guelphs struggling against their enslaved sovereignty, these are the high qualities, that for a thousand years have secured thy national development. And now all thy memorial dynasties end in the huckstering rule of some thirty unknown and anonymous jobbers' (p. 43). The tone of impassioned despair that runs through the passage underlines the extent to which the state of contemporary politics is, for Disraeli, a matter of national disgrace.

Against this general overview of misery, the final paragraph of book one offers the tentative prospect of national renewal through the intercession of the new monarch, ruler of the nation 'which at this moment looks to her with anxiety, with affection, perhaps with hope. Fair and serene, she has the blood and beauty of the Saxon. Will it be her proud destiny at length to bear relief to suffering millions, and with that soft hand which might inspire troubadours and guerdon knights, break the last links in the chain of Saxon thraldom?' (p. 48). In common with the general analytical procedure adopted in book one, Disraeli places his opinion in a historical context. Furthermore, the standpoint of Young England is also admitted into Disraeli's vision, suggesting by implication that the movement has the potential to be part of the process of national restoration.

Book two introduces Lord Marney, who represents the utilitarian, Whiggist values embodied by Lord Everingham in *Coningsby*. His political standpoint forms an echo of Everingham in *Coningsby*, as 'he eulogised the new poor-law' (p. 53). However, the area over which he presides is squalid, neglected and downtrodden. Disraeli uses the local geography to imply the falsity of Lord Marney's confidence.

> The situation of the rural town of Marney was one of the most delightful easily to be imagined. In a spreading dale, contiguous to the margin of a clear and lively stream, surrounded by meadows and gardens, and backed by lofty hills, undulating and richly wooded, the traveller on opposite heights of the dale would often stop to admire the merry prospect, that recalled to him the traditional epithet of his country.
>
> Beautiful illusion! For behind that laughing landscape, penury and disease fed upon the vitals of a miserable population! (p. 60)

Thus far in Disraeli's novels we have been accustomed to the pastoral signifying the beneficent and the symbiotic. Here, however, Disraeli presents an ideal with a dark and sinister aspect, exposing the tumult and degradation underpinning the notion of smooth progress. Furthermore, the description of Marney anticipates the 'Two Nations' dictum, with radically contrasting living conditions co-existing in the same social space. Disraeli focuses graphically on the extent of the poverty and misery in Marney, taking the symbol of cosy, rural living – the thatched cottage –

before subverting its pleasant connotations: 'the gaping chinks admitted every blast; the leaning chimneys had lost half their original height; the rotten rafters were evidently misplaced; while in many instances the thatch, yawning in some parts to admit the wind and wet, and in all utterly unfit for its original purpose of giving protection from the weather, looked more like the top of a dunghill than a cottage' (pp. 60–1). It is inevitable that the inhabitants of these near-derelict cottages reflect their immediate environment: 'the bold British peasant, returned to encounter the worst of diseases, with a frame the least qualified to oppose them' (p. 63). By beginning with a description of the material community and then reflecting that portrayal in individual characters, Disraeli suggests implicitly the determining effect of environment upon character. The condition of the locality also provides an explanation for the violence and incendiarism with which Marney is afflicted.

It is into this context of conflict that the hero, Charles Egremont, Lord Marney's younger brother, is placed. A local farmer provides him with an illustration of the severity of the problem: 'do you know, sir, there were two or three score of them here, and, except my own farm servants, not one of them would lend a helping hand to put out the flames' (p. 65). Looking further into the matter, Egremont questions an agricultural labourer: '"and what do you think of this fire?" said Egremont to the hind. "I think 'tis hard times for the poor, sir." "But rick-burning will not make the times easier, my man." The man made no reply, but with a dogged look led away the horse to his stable' (p. 66). Rick-burning was a feature of the agricultural disturbances in the early 1830s and early '40s; Disraeli is therefore aligning his novel with a contemporary social problem. Following these encounters, Egremont is brought to consider the state of the nation. Melding the character's experience with the reader's, it can be seen how Disraeli has arranged book two, moving chronologically from Lord Marney to the general character of his neighbourhood, to specific dwellings, to the inhabitants and to their conduct. This development encourages us to look back down the line analytically, and to attribute the dire plight of Marney to the ignorance and negligence of its proprietor.

Standing in the ruins of an abbey, in the shadows of the remnants of a supposedly less corrupted past, Egremont considers the condition of England: 'why was England not the same land as in the days of his light-hearted youth? Why were these hard times for the poor?. . . . New orders of men had arisen in the county, new sources of wealth had opened, new dispositions of power to which that wealth had necessarily led.' His thoughts conclude on another question: 'were there any rick-burners in the times of the lord abbots. And if not, why not?' (pp. 69–70). There is a correlation here between Egremont's anguished questioning and Sidonia's analysis of English history in *Coningsby*, to the extent that both acknowledge the transference over time of power from one class to another. However, while Sidonia's argument refutes economic determinism, Egremont recognises it through the implicit acknowledgement that the creation of new wealth has altered social relations. Egremont feels himself to be besieged by the pressure of history itself as much as the agitation of any particular section of society, and he sees that the wealth gap has increased between rich and poor. His thoughts lead to more questions, yet by the end of the passage they are practically rhetorical as his analysis promotes the view that profound economic changes have taken place in society without regard to the social consequences.

Egremont's musings precede the catalytic moment when he meets Stephen Morley, Walter Gerard and Sybil herself. In the early stages of Egremont's conversation with Gerard, the latter is identified only as 'the stranger' and thus he acquires briefly the oracular tone which prevails in many of the character-forming conversations undertaken by Disraeli's heroes. One of Gerard's earliest statements clarifies the point that he is not a revolutionary: 'I am not one who would object to the lord, provided he were a gentle one.' In the same speech he claims that the more elaborate hierarchy of the pre-reformation era was preferable to the class polarisation of the present: 'there were yeomen then, sir: the country was not divided into two classes, masters and slaves; there was some resting place between luxury and misery'. He further argues that the people appreciated continuity of land ownership, positing a hypothetical speaker saying, 'we held under him, and his father and his grandfather before him' (pp. 71–2). Despite his status within the novel as a leading figure within the Chartist movement, Disraeli presents Gerard (at least in the first half of the novel) as somebody content to argue for class deference or even servitude. Gerard is thus, at the point of his introduction, a contained reformer, articulating the grievances of the working class yet seeking nothing more radical than a reversion to an earlier mode of government. Indeed, he petitions for the merits of a clericy: 'the monks were in short a point of refuge for all who needed succour, counsel, and protection; a body of individuals having no cares of their own, with wisdom to guide the inexperienced, with wealth to relieve the suffering, and often with power to protect the oppressed'. Even the nobility, within Gerard's view of history, are seen to be under the monks' care: 'the aristocracy had their share, no more. They, like all other classes, were benefited by the monasteries' (pp. 72–3). By presenting a benign clericy as a transcendent force, elevated spiritually above all considerations of class, Disraeli anticipates the concerns of *Tancred*, which sees religious belief as the foundation of a good and truly progressive society: Disraeli's assessment of society, grounded in history and (less explicitly) economics, shifts (or lapses) into metaphysics, the belief that a more fundamental and not immediately discernible principle underpins human existence. However, the paradoxes in Disraeli's analysis continue as he then argues in favour of a form of dialectical tension. Gerard, describing visitors to the abbey, states, 'travellers come and stare at these ruins, and think themselves very wise to moralise over time. They are the children of violence, not of time' (p. 74). History is represented as a series of jolting disruptions rather than a smooth continuity. Movement arises from conflict rather than consensus.

The introduction of Stephen Morley into the conversation is significant, as the defects in his appearance have an unsettling effect and anticipate the narrative crisis that Morley subsequently brings about: 'his pale countenance, slightly marked with the small-pox, was redeemed from absolute ugliness by a highly intellectual brow. . . . Though young, he was already a little bald; he was dressed entirely in black' (p. 75). His appearance separates him from Gerard: his lack of physical appeal parallels the distaste felt for his Socialist politics by the narrator. However, there are levels of political correspondence between Morley and Disraeli himself; the author's task is to show how analyses that commence from the same empirical basis may veer in different directions depending upon the ingrained political outlook of the observer. Disraeli is hostile to Morley's politics, which offer further disruption in the name of a greater diffusion of political power, whilst Disraeli's own politics offered, he believed, the restoration of peaceful symbiosis between the classes.

Morley's contributions to this first conversation could have come from Disraeli himself, or from the heroes of any of his novels: 'it is a community of purpose that constitutes society. . . . In great cities men are brought together by the desire of gain. They are not in a state of co-operation, but of isolation, as to the making of fortunes; and for all the rest they are careless of neighbours' (pp. 75–6). Morley argues for the alienating effects of industrialisation and the morally corrosive nature of the blind pursuit of profit. When Morley replies to Egremont's observation that 'we live in strange times', stating, 'when the infant begins to walk, it also thinks that it lives in strange times', (p. 76) the reader could be forgiven for thinking of Sidonia. Morley's address concludes with the most well-known passage in the whole of Disraeli's fiction.

> 'Well, society may be in its infancy,' said Egremont, slightly smiling; 'but, say what you like, our Queen reigns over the greatest nation that ever existed.'
> 'Which nation?' asked the younger stranger, 'for she reigns over two.'

The stranger paused; Egremont was silent but looked inquiringly.

'Yes,' resumed the younger stranger after a moment's interval. 'Two nations; between whom there is no intercourse and no sympathy; who are as ignorant of each other's habits, thoughts, and feelings, as if they were dwellers in different zones, or inhabitants of different planets; who are formed by a different breeding, are fed by a different food, are ordered by different manners, and are not governed by the same laws.'

'You speak of——' said Egremont, hesitatingly.

'THE RICH AND THE POOR.' (pp. 76–7)

The formula, attributed generally to Disraeli (but as has been shown, originally constructed in essence by Carlyle), caught on: 'the "two nations" became a household word, perhaps the most famous of all Disraeli's inventions' according to Blake.[38] Furthermore, Disraeli utilised the image again in a speech in Lady Londonderry's grounds in 1848, using an architectural metonym to convey the same principle: 'the palace is not safe when the cottage is not happy'.[39] Moreover, Disraeli's dualistic formulation had (according to Kathleen Tillotson) a considerable influence throughout the novel genre: 'this then came more and more to occupy novelists in the forties. Most novel-readers belonged to the other nation; the novelists were scouts who had crossed the frontier or penetrated the iron curtain and brought back their reports.'[40] In this sense, prior to the exotic geographical journey described in *Tancred*, Disraeli had undertaken a similarly thrilling political journey in *Sybil*, bringing to his middle- and upper-class readers an insight into the strange and dangerous world which threatened to destroy their sense of stability. 'Two nations' implied antagonism, suggesting that society was in a perilous condition.

In creating Morley, Disraeli constructed a character whose narrative role would be primarily that of a villain, not least in his unwanted amorous attentions towards the heroine. However, Disraeli also created a very significant overlap between Morley's Chartist allegiance and Socialist politics on the one hand, and Disraeli's own status as a Conservative parliamentarian and leader of the Young England movement on the other. This moment, therefore, is a potential point of crisis in *Sybil*: we have an aporia in which Morley's rhetoric threatens to overpower Disraeli's hostility towards his (Morley's) political ends beyond the short-term. Disraeli's answer to the problem is to veer once more into the spiritual, achieved through the revelation of the eponymous heroine: 'from the Lady's chapel there rose the evening hymn to the Virgin. A single voice; but tones of almost supernatural sweetness; tender and solemn, yet flexible and thrilling.' Sybil's voice paves the way for her appearance and her unearthly presence.

She was apparently in the habit of a Religious, yet scarcely could be a nun, for her veil, if indeed it were a veil, had fallen on her shoulders, and revealed her thick tresses of long fair hair. The blush of deep emotion lingered on a countenance which, though extremely young, was impressed with a character of almost divine majesty; while her dark eyes and long dark lashes, contrasting with the brightness of her complexion and the luxuriance of her radiant locks, combined to produce a beauty as rare as it is choice; and so strange, that Egremont might for a moment have been pardoned for believing her a seraph, who had lighted on this sphere, or the fair phantom of some saint haunting the sacred ruins of her desecrated fane. (pp. 77–8)

Disraeli concludes his chapter with this image, thereby adding to its importance. The sensual language used to describe Sybil is undercut by the chastity of her overall appearance. Disraeli's spiritual response to political complexity is embodied in a character who will resolve conflict through moral force in conjunction with a long-suppressed aristocratic lineage.

The following two chapters comprise a return to mundane reality, in the form of a conversation between Egremont and Lord Marney, followed by a narrative commentary on social progress in the industrial age. Through a change in narrative focus Disraeli is able to sidestep many of the issues raised in the triangular conversation between Egremont, Gerard and Morley. Marney's utilitarian perspective degrades instinct and the imagination: 'everything in this world is calculation; there is no such thing as luck, depend upon it; and if you go on calculating with equal exactness, you must succeed in life'. His assessment of rural incendiarism is similarly arithmetical; when Egremont enquires into the cause of rickburning, his reply is unequivocal: '"because there is a surplus population in the kingdom," said Lord Marney, "and no rural police in the county"' (pp. 78–9). However, while the utilitarian spirit predominates, the narrator argues that a more historically grounded principle of English government leads to the absorption of new wealth into an existing system, rather than its replacement by a new one: 'the application of science to industry developed the Manufacturer, who in turn aspires to be "large acred," and always will, so long as we have a territorial constitution; a better security for the preponderance of the landed interest than any cornlaw, fixed or fluctuating' (p. 88). Disraeli's dismissal of the main political controversy of the day stands in stark contrast to the tenacity with which he hounded Peel over the same issue. His stance on this particular issue in *Sybil* supports the argument for Disraeli's political insincerity, yet a belief in the territorial aristocracy was part of the bedrock of Disraeli's politics, an enduring principle which absorbed temporary dilemmas. His dispute with Peel was not rooted in the Corn Laws *per se*, but in the extent to which agricultural reform signified a more general shift in power and a reformulation of the British constitution.

Sybil's idiom is archaic, not to say pompous, though it has been argued by Arthur Pollard that her status in the text is deliberately allegorical, signifying Disraeli's perception of the divine and inspirational Middle Ages; she is an 'angel of light'.[41] She tells her father, 'I have drank of the spring of the Holy Abbey, . . . and none other must touch my lips this eve'. In addition to establishing her spiritual credentials, Disraeli also takes an early opportunity to associate her with a pre-industrial age: 'think you not it would be a fairer lot to bide this night at some kind monastery, than to be hastening now to that least picturesque of all creations, a railway station?' (pp. 95–6). Morley responds by asserting the merits of the railways, thereby establishing his own modernity, a quality which the novel constantly seeks to discredit. On the basis of Sybil's early remarks it is difficult to form any conclusions concerning her character; it is more accurate to think of her as the personification of the uncorrupted distant past as perceived by Disraeli.

However, *Sybil* is intensely preoccupied by the problems of the present. Two working-class characters are introduced: Dandy Mick and Devilsdust. The latter has survived a childhood of neglect, leading Disraeli, who had previously, in *England and France: or a Cure for Ministerial Gallomania*, summarised his politics in one word, 'England', to make a barbed point about the distribution of Christian charity: 'infanticide is practised as extensively and as legally in England, as it is on the banks of the Ganges; a circumstance which apparently has not yet engaged the attention of the Society for the Propagation of the Gospel in Foreign Parts' (p. 113). However, Devilsdust has since thrived: 'he was a first-rate workman, and received high wages; he had availed himself of the advantages of the factory school; he had soon learned to read and write with facility' (pp. 114–15). At the end of the chapter the words that he exchanges with Dandy Mick signify the eruption of a phase of militancy: '"labour may be weak, but capital is weaker," said Devilsdust. "Their capital is all paper." "I tell you what," said Mick, with a knowing look, and in a lowered tone, "the only thing, my hearties, that can save this here nation is a – good strike"' (p. 117). A modest amount of education has generated, among some of the workers, an awareness of their own oppression. They have also identified the weak spot of capitalism, which lies in their own political potential in the workplace. At first glance, and not for the first time, Disraeli's sympathies appear to lie with aspects of Socialist thought, yet it is important to remember that Disraeli insisted upon aristocratic leadership for the efficacy of any transformative movement. Furthermore, comparatively few working-class characters in *Sybil* are presented with any depth; unlike the aristocrats they tend to remain one largely homogeneous, anonymous, mass. When a mob of workers descends upon Marney's home towards the end of *Sybil*, they are anarchic and brutal.

Lord Marney is also depicted as an opportunist, sacrificing principle in the name of profit. He resists the expansion of the railways across his land until the compensation is to his satisfaction. Apart from his younger brother, he meets no resistance in his household until the emergence of Aubrey St Lys, vicar of Mowbray. St Lys may be based upon Frederick William Faber, though he and Disraeli probably never met. Faber was the author of *Sights and Thoughts in Foreign Churches and among Foreign Peoples* (1842), which Disraeli sought, unsuccessfully, to borrow from John Jones Robert Manners (7th Duke of Rutland).[42] Faber was also a keen advocate of Young England; Disraeli's presentation of the character of St Lys, therefore, signifies the socially ameliorative possibilities of the adoption of Young England principles, without committing the novel in its entirety to the movement's position. St Lys's spirited opposition to Lord Marney underlines the latter character's cold implacability. When the two characters converse, each represents a distinct point of view: Marney's utilitarianism makes it difficult for him to think in any terms other than cause and effect, while St Lys espouses a more humanitarian position which clearly enjoys the narrator's sympathy. Marney argues in favour of low pay: 'I have generally found the higher the wages the worse the workman. They only spend their money in the beer-shops. *They* are the curse of this country.' St Lys's more considered reply sees alcohol as a symptom rather than a cause.

> 'But what is a poor man to do,' said Mr St Lys; 'after his day's work if he returns to his own roof and finds no home: his fire extinguished, his food unprepared; the partner of his life, wearied with labour in the field or the factory, still absent, or perhaps in bed from exhaustion, or because she has returned wet to the skin, and has no change of raiment for her relief. We have removed woman from her sphere; we may have reduced wages by her introduction into the market of labour; but under these circumstances what we call domestic life is a condition impossible to be realized for the people of this country; and we must not therefore be surprised that they seek solace or rather refuge in the beer-shop.' (p. 127)

St Lys's analysis demonstrates a clear understanding of the determining effect of economics. Poverty is shown to have a direct impact on behaviour, and the extension of female employment is condemned both economically and in terms of nineteenth-century orthodox Christian morality. St Lys concludes his remarks by accusing Marney of declaring war on the cottage. Given how Disraeli has already utilised the significa-tion of the cottage in his first description of Marney's estate, St Lys's comment suggests, metonymically, that Marney and his ilk are destroying established modes of living in the name of a theoretical progress that ignores the social impact of its own decisions. It is surely no coincidence that Walter Gerard lives in a pleasant cottage, the garden of which 'teemed with cultivation' (p. 155).

St Lys, established as a character of moral depth and seriousness, then becomes a vehicle to present Disraeli's views on faith, which are an offshoot of Sidonia's. St Lys's remarks concerning the spiritual validity of Catholicism facilitate the advocacy of Judaism, suggesting that Disraeli arrived at his own commitment to Judaism (as a cultural and historical phenomenon, if not as an organised religion) via his appreciation of Catholic ritual: 'the Church of Rome is to be respected as the only Hebraeo-christian church extant; all other churches established by the Hebrew apostles have disappeared, but Rome remains; and we must never permit the exaggerated position which it assumed in the middle centuries to make us forget its early and apostolical character'. The conclusion he draws is that, 'Christianity is completed Judaism, or it is nothing. Christianity is incomprehensible without Judaism, as Judaism is incom-plete without Christianity' (pp. 129–31). The analysis here is historical, while the relationship between the faiths is viewed as complementary; there is a clear similarity to be noted between the attitude to politics and the attitude to religion in *Sybil*. In both cases a reductive, though not necessarily invalid, historical overview is employed in order to demon-strate the value of continuity (in faith) and the perils of discontinuity (in society). Furthermore, while the mutual sympathy and support of the aris-tocracy and workers is posited as having socially ameliorative possibilities, an equally organic relationship between Judaism and Christianity facilitates the full realisation and value of both faiths. In addi-tion, St Lys's position on the relationship between Judaism and Christianity is very similar to that adopted by Disraeli in the House of Commons in December 1847 (see below).

To underline the fact that there is no doubt regarding Disraeli's own sympathies in the debate between Lord Marney and St Lys, the action of *Sybil* then shifts to give a specific illustration of working-class poverty and its effects. Warner is the impoverished hand-loom weaver. Disraeli's char-acterisation of him is not wholly an act of the imagination, as Disraeli had visited the North of England in 1844 and had been moved by what he saw of the living conditions of hand-loom workers.[43] Subsequently, in a House of Commons debate in 1845, Disraeli said, 'the people of England are the hardest worked and the worst fed, the most miserable and degraded population in the world'.[44] In *Sybil,* Warner's statements comprise a vigorous anti-capitalist manifesto, presenting one of the most challenging aspects of Disraeli's own thoughts. Initially, Warner's recollection of former happiness accords with Young England's perspective: 'I was born to labour and I was ready to labour. I loved my loom and my loom loved me. It gave me a cottage in my native village. . . . It gave me for a wife the maiden that I had ever loved; and it gathered my children round my hearth with plenteousness and peace. I was content: I sought no other lot.' He then questions how this pastoral bliss succumbed to degradation: 'why are we driven from our innocent and happy homes, our country cottages that we loved, first to bide in close towns without comforts, and gradually to crouch into cellars, or find a squalid lair like this'. The conclusion he comes to is unambiguous: 'it is that the Capitalist has found a slave that has supplanted the labour and ingenuity of man. . . . The capitalist flourishes, he amasses immense wealth; we sink, lower and lower.' Warner's most serious grievance, exceeding his resentment of the fact that machinery has superseded labour, is that the State has not sought to redeem the workers, and he is acutely conscious of class prejudice when he assesses his own situation in relation to the aftermath of the French Revolution: 'when the class of the Nobility were supplanted in France, they did not amount in number to one-third of us Hand-Loom weavers; yet all Europe went to war to avenge their wrongs. . . . Who cares for us? Yet we have lost our estates. Who raises a voice for us?' (pp. 133–4). The case for working-class people in industrial economies could not be pleaded with greater eloquence.

A remedy arrives in the form of Sybil, accompanied by her dog, 'a young bloodhound of the ancient breed, such as are now found but in a few old halls and granges in the north of England'. The dog symbolises history and nobility, aspects of Sybil that only become manifest when her true ancestry is revealed. He is an ongoing symbol of noble English indomitability throughout the text, standing by Sybil as the final crisis at Mowbray takes place. The dog's name, Harold, carries monarchic connotations, and is a reliable barometer of character in the novel: he likes Egremont but dislikes Morley.

In conversation with Warner, Sybil gives a reason for her conduct which deflates Warner's anger into an argument for charity and mutual support: 'when the people support the people, the Divine blessing will not be wanting' (p. 141). Warner's class-based analysis is transformed into spirituality. The working classes in *Sybil* are not urged to act collectively for their own benefit; instead, they are encouraged to act together for no other purpose than to await a benign solution arising out of metaphysics. At the end of the chapter it becomes clear that Sybil's perspective is nostalgic: 'when I remember what this English people once was; the truest, the freest, and the bravest, the best-natured and the best-looking, the happiest and most religious race upon the surface of this globe; and think of them now, with all their crimes and all their slavish sufferings, their soured spirits and their stunted forms; their lives without enjoyment, and their deaths without hope' (p. 144). Paradoxically, Disraeli's analysis is frequently teleological when he presents his understanding of society's present condition, yet it becomes nostalgic when he anticipates the best that the future may have to offer. Sybil works for the restoration of a nonexistent utopia. For all of its careful anatomisation of a contemporary crisis, grounded frequently in the testimony given to parliamentary committees, *Sybil* regularly withdraws into amorphous spiritualism, embodying aspirations in an enigmatic character who eludes systematic analysis.

One of the most graphic illustrations in *Sybil* of the brutality of working-class life is to be found in the description of the tommy-shop in chapter three of book three. Tommy-shops were general stores run by an employer, where goods were provided for labour instead of wages. Disraeli's description of the tommy-shop is Dickensian in the sense that he caricatures the shopkeeper in order to emphasise his villainy: 'behind the substantial counter, which was an impregnable fortification, was his popular son, Master Joseph; a short, ill-favoured cur, with a spirit of vulgar oppression and malicious mischief stamped on his visage. His black, greasy lank hair, his pug nose, his coarse red face, and his projecting tusks, contrasted with the mild and lengthened countenance of his father, who looked very much like a wolf in sheep's clothing' (pp. 183–4). At the height of his villainy Master Joseph puts out a baby's eye; the shop scene as a whole suggests that Disraeli has moved beyond depicting an industrial economy as merely exploitative: here it becomes blatantly sadistic.

Book three also provides a lengthy, set-piece conversation between Gerard and Sybil. Within their exchange, Gerard frequently voices the thoughts of Morley, and thus the debate is essentially between Morley's militancy and Sybil's moral force. Disraeli expresses his own belief in the importance of charismatic leaders through Sybil.

> 'Ah! Why have we not such a man now,' said Sybil, 'to protect the people! Were I a prince I know no career that I should deem so great.'
>
> 'But Stephen says no,' said Gerard; 'he says that these great men have never made use of us but as tools; and that the people never can have their rights until they produce competent champions from their own order.'
>
> 'But then Stephen does not want to recall the past,' said Sybil with a kind of sigh; 'he wishes to create the future.'

'The past is a dream,' said Gerard.
'And what is the future?' inquired Sybil. (p. 196)

Sybil's nostalgia, viewed objectively, seems less coherent than Morley's confident assertion, via Gerard, of working-class autonomy. However, in the context of the 1840s the views voiced by Sybil are a good deal less unrealistic, at least in relation to the popular imagination of the time. Young England was not the only cultural manifestation of popular medievalism in England: from Lord Eglinton's tournament (jousting included) of 1839 through to re-workings of Arthurian myths in litera-ture and the visual arts, nostalgia was a popular and pervasive strategy for dealing with the anxieties generated within the context of a rapidly expanding industrial economy. As their conversation develops and they are joined by Egremont, Gerard continues with his empirical approach, but this makes little impact on Sybil's spiritual platitudes. Gerard recites sociological data, 'the average term of life in this district among the work-ing classes is seventeen. What think you of that? Of the infants born in Mowbray, more than a moiety die before the age of five.' A more typical contribution from Sybil is 'to see the people once more kneel before our blessed Lady'. Morley's contribution, through Gerard, is that 'God will help those who help themselves' (p. 201). Egremont, the aristocrat, is exposed to the varying arguments, and though the chapter does not end with him forming any evaluation of what he has heard, his developing attraction to Sybil determines that she will exert the greatest influence over him.

Gerard works for Mr Trafford, giving Disraeli another opportunity to show how the factory system might work harmoniously. As with Mr Millbank in *Coningsby*, Trafford is portrayed as a philanthropist first and businessman thereafter, holding 'a correct conception of the relations which should subsist between the employer and the employed. He felt that between them there should be other ties than the payment and the receipt of wages.' He is preoccupied by 'the health and content of his workpeople'. Disraeli argues that the benevolent conditions of employ-ment established by Trafford improve greatly the 'morals and manners' of his workforce: 'the connexion of a labourer with his place of work, whether agricultural or manufacturing, is itself a vast advantage' (pp. 210–12). The obvious contrast is with Warner's alienating and poverty-stricken situation. Trafford, when he speaks, is presented more as a generous patriarch than a businessman, though his removed, observa-tional perspective also identifies him as a political experimenter: 'they say we all have our hobbies; and it was ever mine to improve the condition of my workpeople, to see what good tenements, and good schools, and just wages paid in a fair manner, and the encouragement of civilizing pursuits, would do to elevate their character'. As for the economic implications of this approach, 'the investment of capital has been one of the most profitable I ever made' (p. 217). No rigorous assessment is offered of the profitability of Trafford's factory, and none is strictly necessary, as Disraeli creates in his imagination an ideal system of factory production which has more to do with a microcosmic representation of ideal government than it does with discourses of profit and loss. However, a more troubling idea implicit in Trafford's statement is that the working classes are almost tantamount to a different species. They are presented *en masse* as the passive recipients of generosity. Disraeli's ideas of good government, here presented within the context of a factory, involve a handing-down from above rather than a meaningful exchange across the classes.

In the next chapter, an exchange between Morley and Gerard creates a gap between their two perspectives. On this occasion Egremont participates as well as listening, offering some encouragement to Gerard, who laments that 'the domestic feeling is fast vanishing among the working classes of this country', adding 'the home no longer exists'. Egremont, fresh from his exposure to Trafford's factory, states, 'if all men acted like Mr Trafford, the condition of the people would soon be changed'. However, as Morley swiftly reminds him, 'all men will not act like Mr Trafford'. Thereafter he flatly contradicts the essential Disraelian argument by stating, 'it is not individual influence that can renovate society; it is some new principle that must reconstruct it'. Morley is divorced from narrative sympathy with statements such as these, in which he reaches towards the new rather than embracing the old; Disraeli places him beyond the main, didactic thrust of the novel. Instead, Morley represents a dangerous strand of militancy that finds its extreme political expression through the rampaging mob that appears in the name of Chartism near the end of the novel. Morley's conclusion is entirely antithetical to Disraeli's ideal, as he states, 'Home is a dangerous thing.' The last words of the chapter, spoken by Gerard, provide Disraeli with a perfect retort: '"it's all very fine," said Gerard, "and I dare say you are right, Stephen; but I like stretching my feet on my own hearth"' (pp. 224–5). Disraeli's belief in the territorial aristocracy extends here to a wider, pervading sense of territory and ownership across society.

Disraeli's fondness for the mysterious and the exotic is featured in *Sybil* through the Trades Union initiation ceremony involving Dandy Mick in the early stages of book four. A sinister aura surrounds unionism, as its rituals render it akin to necromancy: 'the shadowy concourse increased, the dim circle of the nocturnal assemblage each moment spread and widened' (p. 251). The scene in which Dandy Mick prepares for initiation is almost excessively dark, even pagan, in terms of its description: 'enveloped in dark cloaks and wearing black masks, a conical cap of the same colour adding to their considerable height, each held a torch. They stood in silence – two awful sentries' (p. 254). The subsequent vow sworn by Dandy Mick forges a clear link between the sinister and the revolutionary, as he is asked to undertake 'every task and injunction that the majority of your brethren, testified by the mandate of this grand committee, shall impose upon you, in furtherance of our common welfare, of which they are the sole judges'. Duties include 'the assassination of oppressive and tyrannical masters', or the destruction of workplaces deemed 'incorrigible' by the union hierarchy (p. 257). The suggestion that Mick is to be a passive foot soldier serving the interests of a murderous union elite which is closed off and thus oligarchical in its composition, condemns Trades Unions as a power structure no less damaging to the nation than the post-Reform Act government that Disraeli attacked so vigorously. Furthermore, while the Whig government may have been, in Disraeli's eyes, conspiratorial, the union is downright seditious. In addition, Disraeli ignores the fact that the Unions were operating within a prohibitive legislative climate; as Sheila M. Smith states, he makes 'melodramatic hocus-pocus' out of their need for secrecy.[45] It appears as though sinister cabals are everywhere, countered only by inspirational upper-class leaders and their worshipful followers. Another effect of the description of the Trades Union initiation ceremony is that it undermines the following chapter's account of a discussion between a Chartist delegation and an aristocrat broadly sympathetic to their cause, as we have already been made aware of the threatening forces underpinning their respectable exterior personified through Gerard. Behind every well-meaning Gerard is a Morley pulling the political strings, and behind *him* is a belligerent mass.

The conversation between the Chartist delegation and Lord Valentine is used to signify the common ground between the two camps. Lord Valentine points out that 'the finest trees in England were planted by my family; they raised several of your most beautiful churches; they have built bridges, made roads, dug mines, and constructed canals, and drained a marsh of a million of acres which bears our name to this day, and is now one of the most flourishing portions of the country. You talk of our taxation and our wars; and of your inventions and your industry. Our wars converted an island into an empire.' The delegate, in response, draws attention to the fact that all of these achievements are predicated on the fact of working-class labour: 'and the people, have not they shed their blood in battle, though they may have commanded fleets less often

107

than your lordship's relatives? And these mines and canals that you have
excavated and constructed, these woods you have planted, these waters
you have drained – had the people no hand in these creations?' (pp.
262–3). The sense of class antagonism here is muted by the good terms
under which the parties separate. The incident is used to illustrate a
sense of creative, often passionate, interdependency more than a sense of
animosity.

Egremont's next meeting with Sybil is prefaced by another mystical
apparition. He sees a woman standing in a church and notices that 'the
light, pouring through the western window, suffused the body of the
church with a soft radiance, just touching the head of the unknown with
a kind of halo'. When she is identified as Sybil and then speaks, her religious qualities are reinforced as she aspires to a condition of martyrdom:
'I should die content if the people were only free, and a Gerard had freed
them.' Her ambition is nominally political, yet the structure of the entire
passage makes it spiritual. Narrative favour is bestowed upon working-
class aspirations in *Sybil* when they are articulated spiritually. When a
more explicitly political analysis is offered through Morley, Disraeli is a
good deal less supportive of his character. Sybil informs Egremont that
'all the People want is justice; that Labour should be as much respected
by law and society as Property'. At this point her complaint threatens to
become more overtly political; the text therefore withdraws into a
symbolic restoration of pre-industrial harmony as Egremont and Sybil
continue walking.

> While they thus conversed they passed through several clean, still streets,
> that had rather the appearance of streets in a very quiet country town, than
> of abodes in the greatest city in the world, and in the vicinity of palaces and
> parliaments. Rarely was a shop to be remarked among the neat little tene-
> ments, many of them built of curious old brick, and all of them raised
> without any regard to symmetry or proportion. Not the sound of a single
> wheel was heard; sometimes not a single individual was visible or stirring.
> (pp. 270–3)

The sudden relocation of the passage from the industrial to the pastoral,
the removal of commerce and signs of mechanistic and industrial progress,
in fact the removal of all machinery, suggests that the hero and heroine
have momentarily absented themselves from the complexities of modern
society and are drawn closer together within a rarefied environment.

The narrator steps forward on several occasions to offer more explicit
political commentary. In particular, at the end of chapter fourteen of book
four, Disraeli laments the state of the current Conservative Party even
while maintaining total faith in the institution itself. Disraeli even uses the

first person to state his creed as the chapter rises to a symphonic conclusion: 'I will believe that it [the Conservative Party] still lives in the thought and sentiment and consecrated memory of the English nation. It has its origin in great principles and in noble instincts; it sympathises with the lowly, it looks up to the Most High.' Having stressed its socially unifying nature, Disraeli then uses a telling metaphor with industrial connotations when he refers to the realignment of power in the Whigs' favour after the Reform Act, as he talks of 'the iron progress of oligarchical supremacy'. At one point Disraeli's diction becomes archaic, even biblical, as he refers metaphorically to the state of the party: 'even now it is not dead, but sleepeth'. The reader may be reminded here of the hero's first experience of Parliament in *The Young Duke* (1831), when he found the members temporarily listless yet intrinsically powerful. In *Sybil*, Disraeli's conclusion to the chapter relies upon history to deliver justice: 'toryism will yet rise from the tomb . . . to bring back strength to the Crown, liberty to the Subject, and to announce that power has only one duty: to secure the social welfare of the PEOPLE' (pp. 317–18). In this personal manifesto, Disraeli was committing himself to an agenda of social welfare, which he subsequently enacted during his second spell as Prime Minister. Although it would be far too reductive to draw a simple line between a statement made in a novel of 1845 and the complexities of a legislative programme in the second half of the 1870s, yet it would be equally untrue to say that the Acts of the 1870s were without precedent in Disraeli's thoughts. In the 1840s he envisaged the Conservative Party as a socially ameliorative organisation, even if this aspiration was expressed as a platitude rather than a finely detailed programme.

In the latter stages of book four and the whole of book five, Sybil becomes an increasingly important actor. She has a unifying function, linking the separate arguments of her father, Egremont and Morley. From her position of moral supremacy she also exposes what Disraeli perceived as the more nefarious and conspiratorial aspects of Chartism. Initially she entertains Egremont's claim to be included in the scheme for national renewal. However, it becomes clear that he does not envisage mere participation in a national movement: 'there is a dayspring in the history of this nation, which perhaps those only who are on the mountain tops can as yet recognise. You deem you are in darkness, and I see a dawn. The new generation of the aristocracy of England are not tyrants, not oppressors, Sybil, as you persist in believing. . . . They are the natural leaders of the People, Sybil; believe me, they are the only ones.' Egremont's metaphor presupposes an unchanging hierarchy with himself and his ilk at the top. Sybil has a retort: 'the leaders of the People are those whom the People trust'; yet Egremont is able to counter with the accusation that those same people, 'may betray them' (pp. 321–2). The narrative of *Sybil* validates Egremont's perspective on two counts: first, as his fears concerning the Chartist leadership are proved to be correct, and secondly, as Sybil transpires to be an aristocrat herself, and thus a fit character to be a leading figure for national, moral renewal.

Later Sybil is re-examining her political beliefs, partly as a result of Egremont's performance in Parliament ('there was one voice that had sounded in that proud Parliament, that free from the slang of faction, had dared to express immortal truths'). Egremont is thus more active in directing the political thrust of the novel, while Sybil continues to inhabit the moral centre of the text. The rudimentary socialism of Sybil's previous conversation is slowly mutating into a position in which class conflict is dissolved within a perception of common national interest. She has formerly held, 'one profound and gloomy conviction that the world was divided only between the oppressors and the oppressed'. However, 'the experience of the last few months had operated a great change in these impressions. She had seen enough to suspect that the world was a more complicated system than she had preconceived.' Moreover, Egremont's suspicions of the Chartist leaders are proving to be correct: 'these delegates of their choice turned out to be a plebian senate of wild ambitions and sinister and selfish ends'. A combination of Egremont's influence and disillusionment with her own movement leads her to a new conviction: 'she would ascribe rather the want of sympathy that unquestionably exists between Wealth and Work in England, to mutual ignorance between the classes which possess these two great elements of national prosperity' (pp. 337–9). Disraeli brings his character gradually, grudgingly around to his own position: Chartism is over-simplistic and irresponsibly led; only the new aristocracy can harness discontent into a socially unifying programme for national restoration.

If Chartism in *Sybil* is disreputable, as the author inevitably intended it to be, then this places Walter Gerard, a character of previously high repute, in an anomalous position. Disraeli's strategy is to present him as the unwitting dupe of nefarious interests, in a passage in which Sybil is still reluctant to accept the implications of the failings of her movement's leadership. She tells Egremont, 'I am anxious about my father. I fear that he is surrounded by men unworthy of his confidence.' She is also adamant that the Chartists would never accept Egremont: 'the lion and the lamb will not lie down together; and the conquerors will never rescue the conquered'. However, Egremont has the last and decisive words in their argument: 'those opinions which you have been educated to dread and mistrust, are opinions that are dying away. . . . The future principle of English politics will not be a levelling principle; not a principle adverse to

110

privileges, but favourable to their extension. It will seek to ensure equality, not by levelling the Few, but by elevating the Many.' The complacent assumption of upper-class munificence diffusing voluntarily the wealth of the nation is, to say the least, open to question. However, Disraeli deals with the unresolved issues arising out of this argument by employing his standard technique in *Sybil*: withdrawal into the realms of the spiritual. The final words of the chapter are spoken by Egremont, to Sybil: '"heaven will guard over you!" said Egremont, "for you are a celestial charge"' (pp. 341–3).

Fresh from her conversation with Egremont, Sybil now confronts her father, whose 'customary good-tempered placidity' signifies implicitly his gullibility. Sybil complains that, 'these are riots in which you are involved, not revolutions', thereby degrading political dissent and transforming it into thuggery. Gerard defends his position, but in so doing voices his doubts about the absent Morley: 'he is a visionary, indulging in impossible dreams, and if possible, little desirable. He knows nothing of the feeling of the country or the character of his countrymen.' He also identifies the crucial difference between Morley and himself: 'Stephen is a scholar; I have no pretensions that way; but I can feel the pulse of a people.' Disraeli's belief in the territorial aristocracy is reiterated: Gerard can boast supremacy as a character over Morley, because he has a sense of belonging to his community, conjoined with an instinctive perception of brotherhood. However, the argument between Sybil and her father ends acrimoniously, as he reasserts his allegiance to the Chartist cause: 'if the people will struggle, I will struggle with them; and die, if need be, in the front. Nor will I be deterred from my purpose by the tears of a girl' (pp. 345–8). Although the end of the chapter features a reunion between father and daughter, Disraeli has used the argument to illustrate the morally corrosive effect of a political philosophy which seeks to further disrupt what is, for Disraeli, an already fractured nation. Gerard's goodness, like many a decent working man's, is compromised temporarily by his affiliation with the more seditious elements of Chartism.

The depiction of Morley as a villain is confirmed when he attempts to seduce Sybil, in chapter four of book three. Sybil has been thinking of Egremont ('he was what man should be to woman ever: gentle, and yet a guide', p. 349) when she is interrupted by Morley. He tells her that Gerard is to be arrested for conspiring against the state, adding that he will prevent this if Sybil will be his. The full and final unseating of his dubious politics occurs in this incident, when he tells Sybil that it is only to be in proximity to her that he has espoused 'a cause in which I have little sympathy, and which can meet with no success' (p. 354). Sybil considers the emotional blackmail to which she is being subjected: 'this bargaining of blood, and shall I call it love? But that was ever between the oppressors and the oppressed. This is the first time that a child of the people has been so assailed by one of her own class' (p. 357). Morley, reinvented as a tyrant, forfeits his egalitarianism. He turns into the exploiter rather than the defender of the exploited. Disraeli thus discredits Morley's political creed, which, hereafter, is represented predominantly as a violent force devoid of intellectual content, especially when the Liberator of the People heads the rampaging mob at Mowbray.

Sybil heads off to rescue her father, bringing her into direct contact with the lower classes, from whom she has been largely insulated thus far. The incident is one of the most disturbing passages in *Sybil*, as the lower classes are presented as violent, immoral, opportunistic parasites. The neighbourhood is 'where the dog-stealer and the pick-pocket, the burglar and the assassin, found a sympathetic multitude of all ages'. After Sybil's cab crashes she escapes, but 'a group immediately formed round the cab, a knot of young thieves, almost young enough for infant schools, a dustman, a woman nearly naked and very drunk, and two unshorn ruffians with brutality stamped on every feature' (p. 365). Sybil's innocent nature is placed amidst predatory criminals; she is only saved thanks to the intervention of respectable society in the form of a policeman. She continues to seek out her father, and is brought by a young man to 'a glass illuminated door, covered with a red curtain' (p. 367). The building is not identified explicitly by Disraeli as a brothel, but 'an inner door was violently thrown open, and Sybil moving aside, two girls, still beautiful in spite of gin and paint, stepped into the street'. Sybil is only saved from violation by an Irishman who hears Sybil cry, 'Holy Virgin, aid me!' (p. 368). The incident encourages fear of the lower classes, a threatening mass demarcated only by their degrees of criminality and baseness. The crucial intercession of the Irishman connects with Disraeli's wider perspective concerning Catholicism, as the Irishman has moral depths which may be appealed to. In this specific sense Disraeli is castigating industrial society itself and its social consequences rather than the working classes *per se*: they do not have the Irishman's spiritual roots and therefore there is no moral restraint operating upon their conduct. However, the graphic nature of Disraeli's description of Sybil's near downfall degrades lower-class Londoners into animalistic despoilers of youth and innocence.

As book six, set in 1842, commences, there is a growing sense of imminent conflict brewing in society. As a Trades Unionist, Devilsdust insists that 'we must have a struggle', believing that the soldiers will 'stick their bayonets into the Capitalists who have hired them to cut the throats of the working-classes' (p. 414). For the Chartists, Gerard insists, 'there will be no leaders this time, at least no visible ones. The people will do it themselves. All the children of Labour are to rise on the same day, and to toil no more, till they have their rights. No violence, no bloodshed; but toil halts, and then our oppressors will learn the great economical truth as well as moral lesson, that when Toil plays, Wealth ceases' (p. 427). At the most militant end of the political spectrum, the people of Wodgate, a brutal industrial settlement based upon testimony given to a Parliamentary committee concerning Willenhall, have formed themselves as the Hell-cats, and 'halt at every town and offer fifty pounds for a live policeman' (p. 434). The only defence against imminent strikes, bloodshed and anarchy (phenomena which, from the narrative point of view, are interconnected within a maelstrom of violence) comes from Sybil. She tells her father that, 'when Toil ceases the People suffer', and declares her intention to 'pray that all this is wild talk' (pp. 427–8), maintaining the moral high ground that will ultimately triumph.

As the rival forces prepare for combat, Disraeli steps forward again and offers an account of a strike in Lancashire, during which, according to the author, two thousand people visited a local squire to seek food. The squire's wife, in her husband's absence, fed 'the multitude', whose behaviour was orderly throughout the episode. The people then visited the gardens of the house in an equally respectful fashion, giving 'three cheers for the fair castellan' upon their departure (pp. 437–8). Irrespective of the extent to which this account is true, its placement in *Sybil* is significant because, prior to the final conflagration, it provides an image of how things might be organised differently, with reason and restraint prevailing between a squierarchy and striking workers. The account also provides the sternest of contrasts with the destruction that an unorganised working-class rabble is about to inflict on Mowbray.

Disraeli also dedicates space in this section of *Sybil* for a discussion among working-class women. The arguments range from political apathy – 'they bayn't in a manner of business for our sex' – to engagement – 'ayn't we as much concerned in the cause of good government as the men?' – through to class grievance, 'why are we not to interfere with politics as much as the swell ladies in London?' and acquiescence to the *status quo*: 'I don't grudge the Queen her throne, nor the nobleman and gentlemen their good things' (pp. 443–4). This last serious point made in the argument is in accord with Disraeli's own views. However, prior to the mob's attack, Disraeli goes to the trouble to tease out political divisions within the working classes, which is as much a sign of intellectual fertility as disunity. We get some sense of working-class characters as individuals, prior to them being grouped together in the novel's final, large-scale conflict.

Chapter nine of book six sees the introduction of the Liberator of the

People: 'a very thick-set man, rather under the middle size, with a brutal and grimy countenance, wearing the unbuttoned coat of a police serjeant conquered in fight, a cocked hat, with a white plume, which was also a trophy of war, a pair of leather breeches and topped boots, which from their antiquity had the appearance of being his authentic property' (p. 454). His clothing signifies his brutal usurpation of reliable institutions (the police having proved their credentials by rescuing Sybil and arresting seditious Chartists) and the large hammer which he carries suggests both his industrial background and his primitive belligerence. The Liberator's decision to attack Trafford's factory underlines his commitment to havoc rather than reform: autonomous working-class action is presented unambiguously as ignorant brutality. Disraeli uses the Liberator to signify the characteristic traits of all despots and revolutionaries: 'like all great revolutionary characters and military leaders, the only foundation of his power was constant employment for his troops and constant excitement for the populace, he determined to place himself at the head of the chastising force, and make a great example, which should establish his awful reputation, and spread the terror of his name throughout the district' (p. 458). Disraeli discredits working-class action by locating it within the context of political and military tyranny. Furthermore, as Sheila M. Smith has noted, 'to describe the Other Nation as savages . . . creates a curiosity that distances these people, emphasizes their strangeness and separateness'.[46] The Liberator of the People, the inhabitants of Wodgate and the Londoners eager to accost Sybil are all 'savages' within the English nation. While Disraeli certainly urged compassion and material sustenance for the lower orders, he also viewed them frequently as a separate and inferior species (this is especially true when we consider Disraeli's views on race and his belief in the leadership qualities inherent in noble blood).

In the ensuing chaos in *Sybil*, a form of biblical justice is meted out: Lord Marney is stoned to death, leaving Egremont to assume his title. This, in conjunction with Sybil's discovery of her noble ancestry, facilitates an aristocratic restoration. The death of Stephen Morley underlines the impression that all encumbrances to genuine progress are being removed, in an orgy of destruction which is paradoxically purgatorial. One may also recall that the first act of violence in *Sybil*, the rick-burning in book two, provided the catalyst for Egremont to start questioning the state of the nation. Therefore, while *Sybil* is fearful of the prospect of violence, on a narrative level violent incidents propel the characters towards a workable solution. Despite Disraeli's nostalgic perspective, dialectical tension between the haves and the have-nots in *Sybil* is the means by which restoration is effected. The exception to this principle is the violence intended against Sybil, perpetrated by the lower classes, which is unambiguously malign. Violence in *Sybil* therefore clarifies the nature of characters and societies. It is not condoned, yet it exposes important truths within the confines of the narrative, removing encumbrances, allowing good or evil to present itself in explicit terms.

The conclusion to the novel, in which Disraeli's voice again features prominently, makes the message of *Sybil* explicit. He links *Sybil* to *Coningsby*, thus highlighting the intellectual continuity between the two works. Furthermore, he declares his wider creed, that 'the elements of national welfare' depend upon 'the energies of heroic youth' in conjunction with a reappraisal of history. Elaborating upon this principle, he states, 'it is the past alone that can explain the present, and it is youth that alone can mould the remedial future'. He reduces national problems to an ultimate determining instance, the severance of a connection between the monarchy and the people: 'in the selfish strife of factions, two great existences have been blotted out of the history of England, the Monarch and the Multitude; as the power of the Crown has diminished, the Privileges of the People have disappeared; till at length the sceptre has become a pageant, and its subject has degenerated again into a serf'. His outlook suggests that society is an organic entity and that, therefore, damage inflicted upon one section of society necessarily percolates down to affect other areas. The final paragraph begins with an aspiration: 'that we may live to see England once more possess a free Monarchy and a privileged and prosperous People, is my prayer' (pp. 490–2). *Sybil* has already suggested that the two hopes are interdependent, that monarchic revival is a necessary ingredient for national renewal, and subsequently, in a House of Commons debate of 1846, Disraeli spoke of the monarchy having 'its roots in the hearts of the people',[47] signifying his belief in a fundamentally symbiotic relationship between the crown and the populace. Disraeli's formula in *Sybil* is as interesting for what it excludes as for what it includes: the middle class is written out of Disraeli's hoped-for future. Industrialists like Trafford are welcomed, but Trafford is a businessman in name only; the bulk of his characterisation focuses on his warm philanthropy and he is akin to a little monarch in his own kingdom, playing out Disraeli's ideal national formula within a smaller context. This is not to suggest that *Sybil* is without contradictions; lower-class, violent rebellion has a paradoxically cleansing effect, ridding the novel of Lord Marney, Morley and the Liberator and thus paving the way for Sybil and Egremont's ascension (though as the working classes are the principle instigators of the rebellion such violent acts may ultimately be seen as self-destructive). Despite this, however, the novel can claim a general consistency of vision, as a revivified past conquers a corrupted present, to heal the wounds effected by industrial and political transformation.

There is a notable similarity between the analysis of England in the 1830s and '40s offered by Disraeli in *Coningsby* and *Sybil*, and the observations made of English society at approximately the same time by Karl Marx and Friedrich Engels. The comparison is relevant not only because of the similarity of their complaints regarding the plight of working people (which suggests that anxiety about the social consequences of industrialisation spanned the entire political spectrum), but also because their wider theories of history differ totally, leading them to propose strikingly contrasting solutions; the vast difference demonstrates how bedrock principles which pervaded Disraeli's thinking had a conditioning effect on his perceptions of his society, whilst also supporting the view that Disraeli held firm beliefs, thereby discrediting the suggestion that he was solely an opportunist.

In *The Condition of the Working Class in England*, Engels states: 'population becomes centralized just as capital does; and, very naturally, since the human being, the worker, is regarded in manufacture simply as a piece of capital for the use of which the manufacturer pays interest under the name of wages'. In *Sybil* this situation is personified through Warner, who is degraded personally as a result of industrialisation. Conversely, Disraeli (who, like Engels, had seen working-class poverty in England at first hand in the 1840s) also presents ideal industry at Mr Trafford's factory, just as he had with the philanthropic businessman Mr Millbank in *Coningsby*. The degradation suffered by the inhabitants of Marney in *Sybil* is again given more general expression by Engels: 'the end of it all is, that the stronger treads the weaker under foot, and that the powerful few, the capitalists, seize everything for themselves, while to the weak many, the poor, scarcely a bare existence remains'. Where Engels writes, concerning the living conditions of agricultural labourers: 'their dwellings cramped and desolate, small, wretched huts, with no comforts whatsoever', Disraeli (utilising the descriptive tools used in the novel) creates a more specific image, talking of a thatched roof 'looking more like the top of a dunghill than a cottage'. Similarly, the sense of indignant compassion felt by Disraeli for the victims of industrial society (thinking, for example, of the blinding of a baby in the tommy-shop in *Sybil*) is also felt by Engels: 'fine freedom, where the proletarian has no other choice than that of either accepting the conditions which the bourgeoisie offers him, or of starving, of freezing to death, of sleeping naked among the beasts of the forest!' Nor is Engels without a touch of nostalgia: 'in the patriarchal time, the hands and their families lived on the farm, and their children grew up there, the farmer trying to find occupation on the spot for the oncoming generation'. There is, however, a significant difference in the way that the two writers respond to the clergy. For Disraeli they offer hope; St Lys in *Sybil* is the counterpoint to the callous utilitarianism of Lord Marney. But, for Engels the clergy in rural districts are a feature of oppression, not an antidote to it. Citing a *Morning Chronicle* correspondent, Engels reports agricultural workers saying, 'I never knew a parson but what was begging for this or the other', and, 'see the rich vagabonds with whom the parsons eat and drink'. The conclusion drawn is 'that the condition of these people, their poverty, their hatred of the church, their external submission and inward bitterness against the ecclesiastical dignitaries, is the rule among the country parishes of England, and its opposite is the exception'.[48] It is difficult to account for the striking contrast between the two writers in this respect; though, as Engels' approach was consistently journalistic and empirical, his account is probably closer to reality than Disraeli's vision. However, St Lys's function in *Sybil* is to present an embodiment of a principle of local care and succour. In *Sybil* St Lys pleads for the politically voiceless. Disraeli certainly saw religion as a force for change in the nation, but part of the purpose of *Tancred* was to demonstrate a process of spiritual rejuvenation. Like the House of Lords in *The Young Duke*, Disraeli saw heroic potential in the church, whatever its present lethargy and corruption.

Although Engels is credited as co-author of *The Communist Manifesto*, the first copies of which were printed (in German) in London in 1848, the text itself was written solely by Karl Marx. Despite this, *The Communist Manifesto* can be read as representative of both men's opinions. The opening section of the manifesto shares Disraeli's 'Two Nations' perspective: 'our epoch, the epoch of the bourgeoisie, possesses, however, this distinctive feature: it has simplified the class antagonisms. Society as a whole is more and more splitting up into two great hostile camps, into two great classes directly facing each other'. However, while for Disraeli the opposing camps are the rich and the poor, Marx has the more explicitly political formulation, 'Bourgeoisie and proletariat'. Another significant similarity between Marx and Disraeli is that both recognise how new forms of economic and political organisation have been socially destructive: 'the bourgeoisie, wherever it has got the upper hand, has put an end to all feudal, patriarchal, idyllic relations'. It is difficult to draw much distinction between this critique of industrial capitalism and that offered by Disraeli and the Young England movement. Even some of Marx's language would not look out of place in Disraeli's trilogy: the bourgeoisie 'has drowned the most heavenly ecstasies of religious fervour, of chivalrous enthusiasm, of philistine sentimentalism, in the icy water of egotistical calculation'.

However, in a section headed 'Feudal Socialism', Marx also attacks the nostalgic thinking characteristic of Disraeli and Young England: 'half lamentation, half lampoon; half echo of the past, half menace of the future'. Marx goes on to claim that 'what they upbraid the bourgeoisie with is not so much that it creates a proletariat, as that it creates a *revolutionary* proletariat'.[49] Therefore, Marx and Engels, witnessing similar phenomena to Disraeli at around the same time and in some of the same places, arrived at a radically different conclusion. *The Communist Manifesto* adopts a strictly teleological outlook, while Disraeli withdraws into nostalgia, retreating from the complexities and conflicts of his own epoch. We must not forget that the destruction at the end of *Sybil* is enacted by a working-class mob. Disraeli did not want to convert the working class into the governing class; his primary concern was that the working class remain *nurtured* and *sustained* working class, governed by the aristocracy. This perspective is entirely consistent with Disraeli's core political belief in the importance of the territorial aristocracy. Like Marx and Engels, Disraeli is interested in the material conditions of society. Unlike the Communists, however, Disraeli believed that a solution was available, not by adjustment or revolutionary upheaval on the economic level of society, but through the intercession of a geographically and historically embedded aristocracy. *Tancred* adds complexity to Disraeli's analysis by suggesting that spirituality was also an important aspect of the nation's health; not, perhaps, an opiate of the people, but a template, directing the limits of behaviour and determining the (non-commercial) values which should inhere in human intercourse. Disraeli was no Marxist, and no proto-Marxist, yet he shared Marx's and Engels' dismay at the living conditions of working-class people in early-Victorian England, and he also applied his thoughts to the means by which their liberation might be effected.

TANCRED

'I am guided by angels.'

While mysticism is implicit in *Coningsby* and *Sybil*, it is very much to the fore in the final part of the Young England trilogy, *Tancred*, set in 1845 and first published in March 1847.[50] For the second half of the novel the action relocates from England to the Middle East, and thus the exotic becomes a feature of narrative, character and environment. Disraeli had travelled through the region in 1831 and some of his memories of this experience feed through into *Tancred*. However, *Tancred* does deviate from the conventions of the realist novel and uses a lengthy journey as a conceit for a process of self-exploration.[51] Although it has been argued by Clyde J. Lewis that 'the original intention of *Tancred* was to popularise the Anglican Church by a re-examination of its Hebrew origins',[52] the process of religious examining in *Tancred* works through to far more fundamental levels, exploring the foundations and nature of belief itself.

In common with a number of his previous novels, Disraeli offers satirical observations on the middle-class ascendancy. Referring to a dearth of chefs, Leander (himself a chef), observes: 'the cooks are like the civil engineers: since the middle class have taken to giving dinners, the demand exceeds the supply' (p. 6). Later in book one, Leander is used again to illustrate a more general principle: 'Leander, then, like other eminent men, had duties to perform as well as rights to enjoy; he had a right to fame, but it was also his duty to form and direct public taste' (p. 39). Disraeli has used his ideal mode of aristocratic behaviour as a template, to be replicated through society for the benefit of a wider cross-section of classes. Even the description of the kitchen within which Leander works is significant: 'the kitchen of Montacute Castle was of the old style, fitted for baronial feasts. It covered a great space, and was very lofty' (p. 37). In common with Millbank's factory and its environs in *Coningsby*, design signifies concern for the welfare of the inhabitants and respect for the values of a previous era.

In the opening book of *Tancred*, Disraeli is less interested in criticising the new than he is in extolling the old. The reader is introduced, in chapter two, to the Duke of Bellamont: 'he had a lofty idea of his duty to his sovereign and his country. . . . Next to his domestic hearth, all his being was concentrated in his duties as a great proprietor of the soil. On these he had long pondered, and these he attempted to fulfil. That performance, indeed, was as much a source of delight to him as of obligation' (pp. 14–15). Focusing his attentions on home, neighbourhood and nation, the Duke embodies all the qualities of Disraeli's perfect aristocrat. Moreover, his wife extends this ideal image: 'while the duke, at the head of the magistracy, in the management of his estates, and in the sports of which he was fond, found ample occupation, his wife gave an impulse to the charity of the county, founded schools, endowed churches, received their neighbours, read her books, and amused herself in the creation of beautiful gardens, for which she had a passion' (p. 17). Inevitably, given the historical context, the duchess's activities tend towards the compassionate and ornamental rather than the governmentally serious. However, there is a sense of beneficence that emanates from the aristocratic household. The duke's patronage of sport is note-worthy within an historical context in which popular recreation had become a matter of political concern, as any recreational activity which contained within it the potential to compromise the attendance or disci-pline of the workforce within an industrial economy was perceived as a threat. The duke's fondness for sport therefore signifies his adherence to the values of a pre-industrial era, in which aristocrat and commoner shared recreational preferences.[53]

The duke's environment is afforded similarly generous treatment. The Forest of Montacute spreads 'over a wide expanse, the eye ranges on corn-fields and rich hedgerows, many a sparkling spire, and many a merry windmill'. All the signs of economic activity are characteristically pre-industrial, and the individual dwellings present stereotypical pastoral values to a hypothetical traveller: 'he finds himself by the homestead of a forest farm, and remarks the buildings, distinguished not only by their neatness, but the propriety of their rustic architecture'. The duke's local-ity, therefore, remains rooted in a sort of unreal two-dimensional utopianism. All forms of conflict are dissolved within a pastoral idyll which challenges the very existence of the wider economic context. It thus (unlike the initial account of the town of Marney in *Sybil*) has the tendency to come across as a hermetically sealed geographical relic of an idealised former age.

We first meet Tancred at his twenty-first birthday party. The enter-tainment at the party, especially the Morris dancing, has a nostalgic tone, and Disraeli's description of the event underlines his fondness for medievalism: 'the frequent cheers and laughter of the multitude, combined with the brilliancy of the sun and the brightness of the ale to make a right gladsome scene' (p. 34). The purity of Tancred's blood is also noteworthy, as it signifies his undiluted belonging to the nobility. His mother and father are cousins, and in chapter six a guest at the party states that 'the duchess suckled him herself, which shows her heart is very true; for they may say what they like, but if another's milk is in your child's veins, he seems, in a sort of way, as much her bairn as your own' (p. 35). Tancred's purity of blood also promotes, implicitly, the theory of race presented in *Coningsby* yet, at this early point in *Tancred*, Disraeli does not use these narrative details as a springboard for a theory of racial supremacy. Immediately prior to Tancred's introduction, his aristocratic credentials are further underlined by the fact of his ancestor's service in the Crusades: 'a Montacute had been one of the most distinguished knights in that great adventure, and had saved the life of Coeur de Lion at the siege of Ascalon' (p. 42). With such a heroic build-up, the introduction of Tancred himself does not disappoint:

His dark brown hair, in those hyacinthine curls which Greek poets have celebrated, and which Grecian sculptors have immortalised, clustered over his brow, which, however, they only partially concealed. It was pale, as was his whole countenance, but the liquid richness of the dark brown eye, and the colour of the lip, denoted anything but a languid circulation. The features were regular, and inclined rather to a refinement which might have imparted to the countenance a character of too much delicacy, had it not been for the deep meditation of the brow, and for the lower part of the visage, which intimated indomitable will and an iron resolution. (p. 43)

His classical bearing, refined breeding and inner strength of purpose are all evident. From the description, it is clear that Tancred will play the role of the Disraelian hero, driving the narrative on through the next five books.

In book two, Tancred's complaints are typical of the Disraelian hero in the Young England trilogy: 'I see nothing in this fresh development of material industry, but fresh causes of moral deterioration' (p. 52). However, while Coningsby and Egremont seek spiritual guidance (through Sidonia and Sybil, respectively) as one aspect of their wider pursuit of either a coherent political programme or a specific political rejuvenation, Tancred places spiritual aspiration at the heart of his personal quest. In an early conversation with his father he states, 'I obey an impulse that I believe comes from above' (p. 53). Dissatisfied with contemporary existence, Tancred looks to the metaphysical. The narrator shares the hero's complaint, identifying the Church of England as a feature of the spiritual malaise in the nation: 'the Church of England, mainly from its deficiency of oriental knowledge, and from a misconception of the priestly character which has been the consequence of that want, has fallen of late years into great straits' (p. 72). At an early stage in the novel, Disraeli's analysis foreshadows Tancred's quest to reclaim, through personal experience, eastern wisdom. *Tancred* also suggests that the exclusion of the eastern world-view from western thought has fostered the spiritual degradation of England. Renewal, therefore, will arise from an opening-up of western society to eastern influence.

Tancred treats London as a metonym for the mechanistic and dull nature of England and English society as a whole: 'London is not grand. It possesses only one of the qualifications of a grand city, size; but it wants the equally important one, beauty. . . . Grand cities are unknown since the beautiful ceased to be the principle of invention.' From Disraeli's perspective, beauty suggests both the imaginative and (given the novel's subsequent preoccupation with the aesthetic qualities and values of the East) the exotic. The practical priorities of utilitarianism are, in London, realised in architectural form and expression. Disraeli delivers a scathing

121

assessment of the capital's visual style: 'though London is vast, it is very monotonous. All those new districts that have sprung up within the last half-century, the creatures of our commercial and colonial wealth, it is impossible to conceive anything more tame, more insipid, more uniform.' Most seriously of all, degradation has not spared the class that Disraeli most esteems, the aristocracy: 'in our own days we have witnessed the rapid creation of a new metropolitan quarter, built solely for the aristocracy by an aristocrat. The Belgrave district is as monotonous as Mary-le-bone; and is so contrived as to be at the same time insipid and tawdry' (pp. 115–17). The maltreatment of the aristocracy, expressed architecturally here, is consistent with Disraeli's broader analysis, namely that economic progress has had unwelcome social consequences, depriving society of its natural leaders, who have been complicit in their own downfall.

Within this squalid metropolitan landscape, one old house stands out, possessing 'something of the classic repose of a college' (p. 118). Unsurprisingly, this turns out to be the business premises of Sidonia from *Coningsby*, reintroduced to give specific direction to the hero. The interior of the building is similarly impressive, as Tancred notes: 'he looked round at the old oak hall, on the walls of which were hung several portraits, and from which ascended one of those noble staircases never found in a modern London mansion'. Ushered into Sidonia's apartment, Tancred sees it is 'panelled with old oak up to the white coved ceiling, which was richly ornamented. Four windows looked upon the fountain and the plane tree.' The furnishings include 'a Turkey carpet, curtains of crimson damask' (pp. 122–4). The aggregate effect of these images is to suggest erudition, antiquity and seniority, yet there is also a suggestion of the exotic. These impressions define Sidonia's character.

In conversation, Sidonia continues to espouse the importance of Judaistic tradition. He points out, concerning Moses and Jesus, that 'both were, at least carnally, children of Israel' (p. 126). He further bestows some spiritual credit upon Catholicism: 'that Church was founded by a Hebrew, and the magnetic influence lingers'. Having thus laid his claim for the value of the Jewish faith and identified its residual presence in Catholicism, Sidonia then proceeds to argue that a different mindset is required for spiritual learning than that which is appropriate for engaging with an industrial society: 'you cannot get on with theology as you do with chemistry and mechanics'. There is a base-superstructure analysis here, implying that modern society creates particular modes of thinking. However, a shift from the material to the metaphysical subsequently occurs, with Sidonia's suggestion that religious study requires a more substantial yet less clearly defined approach: 'trust me, there is something deeper in it' (p. 129). There is a structural correlation between *Tancred* and *Sybil* in this sense, as both texts avoid the complexities of sustained political analysis and opt instead for metaphysics, though the privileging of the imagination over the analysing intellect is, broadly speaking, a convention of the novel genre. Sidonia's view of Tancred is telling, given the level of credibility established thus far by Sidonia in the trilogy: 'he recognised in this youth not a vain and vague visionary, but a being in whom the faculties of reason and imagination were both of the highest class, and both equally developed. . . . He perceived that though, at this moment, Tancred was as ignorant of the world as a young monk, he possessed all the latent qualities which in future would qualify him to control society' (p. 127). Sidonia's reference is thus a reliable appraisal of both Tancred's abilities and potential, and leads us to expect that he will achieve greatness of some form within the novel.

Tancred also provides, in chapter thirteen of book four, a roll call of some of the most significant figures to have appeared in the previous two volumes of the trilogy. It is a valedictory address to the political heroes of the first two novels, prior to Tancred's departure for territory which will ultimately move beyond the realm of the material and into an unambiguous spiritual quest, whereas, in both *Coningsby* and *Sybil*, the spiritual is a mode of representation for the political, though it can also comprise an evasion of political complexity. Tancred meets with Lord Henry Sydney, whose 'object of his public life, namely to elevate the condition of the people', is an echo of Disraeli's ambition for the Conservative Party as a whole (as voiced in book four of *Sybil*, see above). Sydney's belief, 'that labour had its rights as well as its duties', (pp. 138–9) is part of the staple diet of the Young England trilogy, and has already been prefigured in *Tancred* by the creed of the chef, Leander. Sybil appears in a predictably munificent role: 'devoted to the improvement of the condition of the people, she was the moving spring of the charitable development of this great city'. Yet Egremont (now Lord Marney) has acquired a slightly misanthropic cast: 'he held that the state of England, notwithstanding the superficies of a material prosperity, was one of impending doom, unless it were timely arrested by those who were in high places. A man of fine mind rather than of brilliant talents, Lord Marney found, in the more vivid and impassioned intelligence of Coningsby, the directing sympathy which he required' (pp. 142–3). One can only speculate on what Disraeli thought had happened to Egremont in the three years since the conclusion of the narrative in *Sybil*. Conviction and purpose has been taken over by gloom and comparative inaction. However, given that Coningsby now appears to have galvanised his thought into political practice, Disraeli's purpose may have been to amalgamate the two characters into one principled politician, a process which also ensures (in conjunction with their brief presence in the text) that Tancred's status as the novel's hero and central character remains unchallenged.

In the build up to Tancred's departure for the east, he has a further conversation with Sidonia. Tancred complains that 'individuality is dead; there is a want of inward and personal energy in man; and that is what people feel and mean when they go about complaining there is no faith'. In this way Tancred manages to link utilitarianism with a perceived crisis of faith; the unqualified application of reason degrades the imagination and thus compromises the faculty that enables people to accept something beyond the empirical. Sidonia, contradicting Tancred, draws the issue round to his favourite dogma, race: 'is it the universal development of the faculties of man that has rendered an island, almost unknown to the ancients, the arbiter of the world? Clearly not. It is her inhabitants that have done this; it is an affair of race.' Sidonia's reduction of history to an ultimately determining instance produces its own conclusion: 'all is race; there is no other truth', and to a gloomy prognosis for the future, in which absolute separatism offers the only prospect of salvation: 'the decay of a race is an inevitable necessity, unless it lives in deserts and never mixes its blood' (pp. 152–4). The creed of race discussed in *Coningsby* is here presented synoptically. Sidonia's formula passes unchallenged and thus it attracts narrative approval. It is further noteworthy that this doctrine is relatively muted in *Sybil*; in the context of a novel in which empirical data is used widely, Sidonia's racial theory would be conspicuous by its absence of factual data or statistical support, beyond the eccentric and anecdotal accounts which he provides. In *Sybil*, though, the analytical gives way to the mystical; in *Tancred* the spiritual is overwhelmingly dominant. Therefore, Sidonia's creed, articulated as a blunt truism, and despite all the evidence to the contrary both in the text and the wider world, becomes admissible in the final volume of the trilogy by virtue of its phrasing as a spiritual truth.

Book three of *Tancred* relocates to the east, though there is still time at the end of book two for Tancred to react with horror at the prospect of there being a railroad to Jerusalem (tantamount to an act of sacrilege for the hero as it involves the corruption of the ancient by the modern), and for Tancred, perhaps under Sidonia's influence, to dwell on the 'good old days, when the magnetic power of Western Asia on the Gothic races had been more puissant' (p. 163). Book three also sees the introduction of Besso, whose presence allows Disraeli to make a further intertextual reference, as 'he is the same Besso who was the friend at Jerusalem of Contarini Fleming' (p. 184). Disraeli's former literary creations disappear from *Tancred* after this, reinforcing the idea that the final text in the trilogy will be a departure from previous literary strategies both narratively and thematically.

However, when the heroine of *Tancred*, Eva, is introduced in book three, she conforms to the typical template for the Disraelian muse and love interest, as her spiritual, ethereal qualities are foregrounded, not least because Tancred first sees her as he awakens from a sleep, during which his own appearance is described as 'angelic'. Eva appears, and is immediately seen as precious, exotic and opulent: 'she wore an amber vest of gold-embroidered silk, fitting closely to her shape, and fastening with buttons of precious stones from the bosom to the waist' (pp. 191–2). In their ensuing conversation, Eva, who is at this stage unknown and therefore, like Sidonia (or Walter Gerard in his first conversation with Egremont in *Sybil*), has an enigmatic, oracular quality, espouses the merits of the Jewish faith, employing some of the arguments used in *Coningsby*. Her views are clearly also Disraeli's: first, because they are enunciated throughout Disraeli's published writing in the 1840s and '50s; and secondly, because, on 16 December 1847, Disraeli spoke in Parliament on behalf of Jewish emancipation. This was a brave decision; given the casual, man-in-the-street anti-Semitism, such an act could have been potentially harmful in the face of his political ambitions. The measure was considered necessary in order for Baron Lionel de Rothschild to be able to take the seat for which he had been elected, the City of London (he had refused to swear an oath on the New Testament). Disraeli had not previously been a forthright parliamentary advocate of Jewish emancipation, but in the December 1847 debate his principled support of Jewish history and culture overcame any political expediency. Disraeli repeated the concerns expressed in his fiction when he asked the House, 'where is your Christianity if you do not believe in their Judaism?' Like his literary creations, Disraeli drew attention to the connections between Judaism and Christianity: 'it is as a Christian that I will not take upon me the awful responsibility of excluding from the legislature those who are of the religion of which my Lord and Saviour was born'.[54]

In *Tancred*, Eva says of Jesus, 'he was born a Jew, lived a Jew, and died a Jew'. She even launches an argument for Jewish superiority, claiming that Jehovah has performed his duty to the Jews by 'endowing them with faculties superior to those of the nations among whom they dwell'. Concerning injustice against Jews, she states, 'we have saved the human race, and you persecute us for doing it'. To Tancred she says: '"we agree that half Christendom worships a Jewess, and the other half a Jew. Now let me ask you one more question. Which do you think should be the superior race, the worshipped or the worshippers?" Tancred looked up to reply, but the lady had disappeared' (pp. 195–202). The chapter ends here, thus imbuing the moment with additional significance. In common with both *Coningsby* and *Sybil*, *Tancred* presents us with a central character who, dissatisfied with his society and receptive to new ideas, is challenged by a different world-view to which he ultimately becomes a convert. This is the fate of all of Disraeli's central characters in the Young England trilogy. They are confronted by unorthodox ideas which unseat the ingrained attitudes of the characters themselves, whilst simultaneously offering an implied challenge to England in the 1840s by refuting received opinion concerning the state of the nation, the conduct of its politicians and its assumptions about religion. These defining conversations for the central characters function as narrative prophecies and also provide outlets for views held by Disraeli which ran counter to the governmental priorities of both the Whigs and Peel's Tories.

One of the more unorthodox characters in *Tancred* is Fakredeen. Given his uneasy relationship with Tancred and the ultimate necessity for the hero to break from him, he may be compared with the characters of Lord Monmouth in *Coningsby* or Stephen Morley in *Sybil*. However, Fakredeen's impulsiveness, mercurial nature and grand ambition mark him out as being more similar to the protagonists in Disraeli's earlier novels, especially *Vivian Grey*, *Contarini Fleming* and *Alroy*. Tancred develops a close relationship with Fakredeen but he comes to realise the temperamental inadequacies of his friend, and thereafter removes himself from his influence. Turning his back on Fakredeen, Disraeli recognises the shortcomings, not merely of his earlier fictional heroes but also of his own persona. Through his extraordinary zeal, Disraeli had elevated himself to Parliament but not to high office, something he had quite clearly sought from Peel in 1841. In a letter to Peel of 5 September he wrote of the efforts he had made on the Party's behalf, and of the dismay he felt at being rejected, in language reminiscent of The Young Duke or Coningsby when thwarted in love: 'I will not say that I have fought since 1834 four contests for your party, that I have expended great sums, have exerted my intelligence to the utmost for the propagation of your policy. . . . I have had to struggle against a storm of political hate and malice, which few men ever experienced. . . . I confess to be unrecognised at this moment by you appears to me to be overwhelming; and I appeal to your own heart – to that justice and that magnanimity, which I feel are your characteristics – to save me from an intolerable humiliation.'[55] After this Disraeli was no longer so supplicating towards Peel, adopting a fundamentally different parliamentary identity as he turned against his party leader. *Tancred* also traces a chameleonic process whereby previous literary incarnations are shed, leaving a new, fledgling persona in their place. Disraeli bids farewell to Contarini Fleming, Coningsby, Sybil and Egremont: confronted with an Asiatic Contarini or Vivian in the form of Fakredeen, he listens, engages, probes and evaluates, but ultimately rejects a figure whose ambitions could never be reinforced by a coherent strategy. It has also been argued by Richard Faber that Fakredeen has 'Smythe-like qualities', which is compatible with my analysis, as Disraeli had by now left the moribund Young England movement some way behind him.[56] *Tancred* bears a close analogous relationship to Disraeli's political career.

The first description of Fakredeen establishes significant aspects of his personality. We learn that, 'at ten years of age he was initiated in all the mysteries of political intrigue'. With this background it is not hard to see how he has developed into a character who revels in the intricacies of politics:

> To dissemble and to simulate; to conduct confidential negotiations with contending powers and parties at the same time; to be ready to adopt any opinion and possess none; to fall into the public humour of the moment, and to evade the impending catastrophe; to look upon every man as a tool, and never to do anything which had not a definite though circuitous purpose; these were his political accomplishments; and, while he recognised them as the best means of success, he found in their exercise excitement and delight. (p. 220)

This portrayal has echoes of Vivian Grey seeking to found a new political party and, if the episode from *Vivian Grey* is read autobiographically, a definition also of Disraeli himself during his involvement with *The Representative*: an ambitious figure deals with contending parties, having grand ambitions of his own yet, simultaneously, revelling in the process of intrigue. However, the description of Fakredeen is critical rather than complimentary; his fickleness, hypocrisy and egotism alienate rather than entice the reader. The narcissistic idealist chasing glory is discredited, left in exile: *Tancred* demonstrates a more serious level of self-enquiry as the hero tries to understand what underpins societies and the individuals that comprise them. The remoter the territory penetrated by Tancred, the deeper the enquiry goes.

From the vantage point of Syria, Tancred assesses the culture that he has left behind: 'enlightened Europe is not happy. Its existence is a fever, which it calls progress. Progress to what?' Shortly thereafter the question is picked up by the narrator: 'progress to what, and from whence? Amid empires shrivelled into deserts, amid the wrecks of great cities, . . . the European talks of progress, because, by an ingenious application of some scientific acquirements, he has established a society which has mistaken

comfort for civilisation' (pp. 231–3). Underpinning the general denunciation of European culture rests Disraeli's hostility to utilitarianism and a
profound discomfort with the disregard given to the social impact of
economic policies. Although industrialisation has effected cultural movement, for Disraeli this process lacks principle and direction. When
Fakredeen states that he wishes to raise a loan, Tancred refers to this as
'the poison of modern liberalism', underlining his belief that the improvement of nations was not primarily an economic affair. The location of
Syria is significant, because, geopolitically, the Holy Land was at that time
part of Turkish Syria.[57] Tancred has reached the spot from which he
expects to derive personal fulfilment. His arrival at a spiritually profound
place paves the way for his metaphorical exploration of the religious
essence of human civilisation.

In a conversation with Fakredeen in chapter three of book four,
Tancred elaborates his critique of western society: 'I do not believe that
anything great is ever effected by management', adding, 'to free a nation
you require something more vigorous and more simple'. Despite its
apparent simplicity, however, no explicit solution is offered. There is a
suggestion of hope when Tancred states, 'there are popular sympathies,
however imperfect, to appeal to', yet in the concluding part of his statement to Fakredeen he emphasises the scale of the problem: 'if you wish to
free your country, and make the Syrians a nation, it is not to be done by
sending secret envoys to Paris or London, cities themselves which are
perhaps both doomed to fall; you must act like Moses and Mahomet
(Muhammed)' (p. 266). The call for a messiah demands a crucial follow-
up by Tancred, complete (ideally) with identification of the saviour.
However, he is able to do nothing other than emphasise the confusion of
nineteenth-century western society: 'amid the wreck of creeds, the crash
of empires, French revolutions, English reforms, Catholicism in agony,
and Protestantism in convulsions, discordant Europe demands the keynote, which none can sound. If Asia be in decay, Europe is in confusion.
Your repose may be death, but our life is anarchy' (p. 267).

Anarchy in the above context radically misrepresents and over-empha-
sises the situation in England, though arguably not on the Continent.
Significant redistributions of political power, and realignments of faiths
to suit or challenge the new economic and political power structures in
society were sufficient cause for Disraeli to claim the existence of chaos.
However, despite the overt violence of the French Revolution and social
pressures in Britain which often took confrontational form, political overhaul in Britain was less traumatic than that witnessed in mainland Europe.
Moreover, while hostility to Catholicism endured, even after 1829, and
Protestantism was characterised by internal disaffection, religious contro-

versies never erupted into street fighting. Britain navigated its way through its own industrial revolution both competently and fortuitously. The anarchic society perceived by Disraeli was, in practice, less disorderly than he feared. Disraeli sought a keynote principle, and saw himself as the very individual to commence national restoration. However, his analysis was flawed to the extent that he mistook the anxieties of a revolutionary epoch for lawless anarchy.

Within the same conversation, Fakredeen offers a solution which has, by some critics, been regarded as prophetic of Disraeli's decision in the 1870s to make Queen Victoria, Empress of India:[58] 'let the Queen of the English collect a great fleet, let her stow away all her treasure, bullion, gold plate, and precious arms; be accompanied by all her court and chief people, and transfer the seat of her empire from London to Delhi' (p. 271). At first sight this may be regarded as an anticipation in literature of Disraeli's romantic construction of Imperialism when he held high office. Following the Indian Mutiny of 1857, Disraeli argued that the people of India and Queen Victoria should be drawn closer together, a sentiment anticipated in a purely English context in *Sybil*. However, Disraeli had not always held the fact of the colonies in such high regard; in 1866 he had written to Derby advocating withdrawal from West Africa. As Robert Blake notes: 'Disraeli's imperialism was a later development, and essentially concerned with India, which appealed to something in his imagination in a sense that the "colonies" did not.'[59] *Tancred* is not interested in colonialism, a political phenomenon, because the hero is pursuing an uncorrupted source of political truth. Colonialism carried too many connotations, too many concerns and was therefore, in Disraeli's eyes, a 'smeared' philosophy.

More importantly, the remarks in *Tancred* are voiced by a character who does not enjoy narrative approval. *Tancred* demonstrates a modification of the procedure adopted in *Sybil*; in the earlier novel, profound discussions mutate into amorphous spiritual platitudes. In *Tancred*, where a serious assessment of the spiritual is so central to the text, this is not a strategy which can be used by the narrator to sidestep or, more charitably, phrase imagistically, the issues raised by a conversation between characters. Therefore, in *Tancred*, this manoeuvre is effected by a deliberately fatuous observation which dissolves into a wild comment made by a hopeless dreamer. *Tancred*'s suggestion that the British Empire should be relocated to the East is playful, teasing the political establishment, carrying an undercurrent of seriousness, which is also evident in the conclusion to the novel, in which Tancred's parents arrive, suggesting some meaningful relationship (itself unresolved in the text) between East and West.

Tancred has turned away completely from the superficiality of western culture, personifying it as 'the growing melancholy of enlightened Europe, veiled, as it may be, with sometimes a conceited bustle, sometimes a desperate shipwreck gaiety, sometimes with all the exciting empiricism of science'. Instead, the narrator speaks of Tancred's 'passionate desire to penetrate the mystery of the elder world, and share its celestial privileges and divine prerogative' (pp. 278–9). His ambition attracts comment from Baroni, Sidonia's servant, who travels with Tancred: 'he thinks as much as M. de Sidonia, and feels more. There is his weakness. The strength of my master is his superiority to all sentiment' (p. 291). Armed with a cocktail of emotion and intellect Tancred ascends the spiritually significant location of Mount Sinai where he experiences a vision. In Disraeli's other novels figures appear to the hero in visionary terms, yet the characters themselves are real within the boundaries of the novel. In *Tancred*, however, the secular is swept away and the hero's experience is unambiguously religious; the only Disraeli novel to have adopted this strategy previously is *Alroy*, the implication is that Tancred is aspiring to similarly elevated heights.

Disraeli phrases the incident in *Tancred* in biblical terms, commencing with 'and there appeared to him a form'. The male 'angel of Arabia' addresses Tancred as 'child of Christendom' and tells him, 'power is neither the sword nor the shield, for these pass away, but ideas, which are divine'. In similar language, the angel recognises the seismic shift in western society in the first half of the nineteenth century: 'Europe is in the throes of a great birth. The multitudes again are brooding; but they are not now in the forest, they are in the cities and the fertile plains. Since the first sun of this century rose, the intellectual colony of Arabia, once called Christendom, has been in a state of partial and blind revolt.' The solution, for the angel, involves submission to a patriarchal leader: 'the longing for fraternity can never be satisfied but under the sway of a common father' (pp. 298–300).

The angel's formula is a spiritual rendition of Disraeli's fundamental, secular, political principles: industrial revolution has thrown social relations into chaos; true, visionary leadership is required to reconstruct symbiotic relations between the classes. However, despite this hitherto materialistic analysis of society, Disraeli asserts that the principles informing visionary leadership will be metaphysical, as he draws a distinction between material effort ('the sword and the shield', p. 299) and intellectual inspiration. The Angel stresses the importance of the imagination and the need for leadership; in so doing he reflects Disraeli's hostility to utilitarianism in politics and his belief in benign, paternalistic government.

130

Book four of *Tancred* also features a separate sub-section of the narrative which tells the story, through a series of brief chapters, of the circumstances by which Baroni came to be a servant of Sidonia. Baroni's father ran a family theatrical company, based on firm principles: 'I have no rebels in my company, no traitors. With one mind and heart we get on' (p. 334). Of his children he states, 'I have taught them to obey God and to honour their parents. These two principles have made them a religious and a moral family. They have kept us united, and sustained us under severe trials' (p. 337). The family symbolises the main tenets of Disraeli's ethos; as a theatre company, they occupy a metaphorical centre stage in the novel. His own principles are expressed within a small unit, contained performatively on the stage, and thus their common and harmonious sense of purpose can be witnessed both by their observer within the novel, Sidonia, and by the reader. To make the family's function within the text explicit, it is interpreted by Sidonia: 'these youthful vagabonds, struggling for life, have received a perfect education. . . . A sublime religious principle sustains their souls; a tender morality regulates their lives; and with the heart and the spirit thus developed, they are brought up in the pursuit and production of the beautiful. It is the complete culture of philosophic dreams' (p. 342). The Baroni family, therefore, enacts microcosmically the principles advocated by Disraeli as the basis for proper government. He envisaged a political model replicating the family structure, with benign leadership from above reinforced by enthusiastic co-operation from below. The sense of unity and common identity promoted in relation to the family structure was also held by Disraeli to be the ideal mode of national identity. Moving back from the Baroni chapters into the main narrative of the novel, Tancred observes 'there is something most interesting . . . in this idea of a single family issuing from obscurity, and disseminating their genius through the world, charming mankind with so many spells' (p. 346). The principles of the Baroni family – and, by extension, Disraeli's – are magical in their implications, producing transformative results well beyond their own boundaries.

In book five, the narrator intervenes, drawing the novel back from its spiritual effusions and offering cynical observations concerning the insincerity of western society: 'a man may have friends, but then, are they sincere ones? Do not they abuse you behind your back, and blackball you at societies where they have had the honour to propose you?'. Disraeli had experienced the rejection of many clubs, and thus the bitterness of his comment may have been rooted in personal experience.[60] The paragraph concludes, 'generally speaking, among sensible persons, it would seem that a rich man deems his friend a sincere one who does not want to borrow his money; while, among the less favoured with fortune's gifts, the sincere friend is generally esteemed to be the individual who is ready to lend it' (p. 352). Epigrammatic wit is not in general a feature of *Tancred*; its presence here demonstrates both a measure of continuity with regard to Disraeli's literary style from *Vivian Grey* onwards, and a continuing focus on English society in Disraeli's work, despite the narrative relocation of *Tancred* to the east. The condition of England is expressed differently in *Tancred* than in *Coningsby* and *Sybil*, yet it remains a highly significant aspect of the novel's purpose, as evidenced in Disraeli's manifesto-style statement concerning the trilogy as a whole (quoted at the outset of this chapter). The narrator in *Tancred* also offers comment on the political condition of Syria, drawing attention to its feudal character and the emergence in 1844 of a Young Syria movement; by these means Disraeli constructs a broadly parallel relationship between the terrain in which the action of the novel is played out and the political situation in which Disraeli was writing, featuring nostalgia for feudalism articulated through the Young England movement, though the group itself was effectively obsolete, having ceased to function as a unified body in Parliament by 1845.

As book five progresses Tancred becomes more involved with Fakredeen and his intrigues. Again one is reminded of Disraeli's involvement with *The Representative* in 1825, as grandiose schemes are formulated without the means to bring them to fruition. Tancred speaks in global generalisations: Europe is 'a forest not yet cleared', while Asia is 'a ruin about to tumble' (p. 405). He wants to begin a 'movement' in the desert, and envisages only success in his scheme, predicting that they will soon be, 'overrunning the Babylonian and Assyrian monarchies' (p. 380). It is hard to read this without thinking of Disraeli's letters to Murray in 1825 when, instead of merely founding a paper to rival *The Times*, Disraeli envisaged the formation of a new political party. Furthermore, Tancred's ambition does not carry any real credibility. Disraeli, in the composition of *Tancred*, would have been aware of this fact; the author is reviewing imaginatively one of his earlier real-life failures, acknowledging the unrealistic nature of his ambitions at that time. *Tancred* thus reintroduces the personal into a trilogy hitherto dominated by social concerns. The novel revisits earlier characters and, underpinning them, an earlier persona, impressive in its youthful idealism but woefully lacking in pragmatism.

In order to move on Tancred must explore the east more deeply, a process which, symbolically, is the extension of a sustained act of self-examination. He is introduced to another enigmatic guide, the Queen of the Ansarey. In common with previous guides she utters amorphous wisdom, though at times her comments lapse into truism: 'there are things to be said, and there are things not to be said' (p. 432). When Tancred speaks to her it becomes clear that he now views Asia as the final and imperilled realm of spiritual truth: 'Asia is the only portion of the world which the Creator of that world has deigned to visit, and in which he has ever conferred with man.' Tancred now intends using the wisdom of the east as the base upon which he will construct and launch a force for overwhelming political renewal: 'we wish to conquer that world, with angels at our head, in order that we may establish the happiness of man by a divine dominion, and, crushing the political atheism that is now desolating existence, utterly extinguish the grovelling tyranny of self-government' (p. 434). What is envisaged here is not any formal structural union between religion and politics, but the *subsuming* of the latter to the former. Tancred's own imagined role is both submissive and profoundly egotistical, as he is simultaneously the committed disciple of an unnamed deity and its privileged ambassador facilitating the expression of divine will. Only at the end of the extract does Disraeli return to a familiar theme, with the assumption that democracy in its present form limits rather than expresses the will of the people. By seeking to destroy 'political atheism' it appears as though Disraeli desires synthesis between the secular and the spiritual, yet he envisages a hierarchy which conforms to his main theory of an ideal governmental structure: wisdom and leadership comes from above; the enactment of the leader's wisdom is the responsibility of the lower tier.

Just when it appears as though *Tancred* has moved into an allegorical, narrative section in which characters and incidents serve as a means of expressing the pursuit, revelation and enactment of spiritual truth, the Jewish question reappears. Tancred claims that, 'Christianity is Judaism for the multitude', adding that Gentiles are 'sprung from a horde of Baltic pirates' (pp. 439–40). In the presence of ancient deities (Tancred sees the impressions of Greek Gods sculpted into the mountains, thereby incorporating classical civilisation into his grand mythical scheme), newer religions are rendered superfluous. The spiritual beliefs of *Tancred* parallel Disraeli's political principles: both are atavistic, involving deep and narrow historical penetration in order to unearth a kernel of uncorrupted truth, upon which may be constructed a programme for restoration in defiance of a troubled present. Even Fakredeen seems to be imbued with a sense of contemplative gravity in the mountains, wondering if the misery of Europeans had been caused, 'by their deserting those divinities who had once made them so happy' (p. 445).

However, Tancred's experience of spiritual serenity becomes complex, even soured. The two immediate causes are the prospect of an Ottoman invasion of the Ansarey, and the taking prisoner of Eva, who has arrived in search of Tancred. Prior to his confrontation with the Queen on this latter point, Tancred witnesses her in her most holy form, kneeling before a statue: 'he beheld the fair Queen of the Ansarey, motionless and speechless, her arms crossed upon her breast, and her eyes fixed upon her divinity, in a dream of ecstatic devotion. The splendour of the ascending sun fell full upon the statue, suffusing the ethereal form with radiancy, and spreading around it for some space a broad and golden halo.' Like Sybil before her, the halo signifies a privileged spiritual position. However, when Tancred brings up the subject of Eva's captivity there is a notable change: 'she was quite pale, almost livid; her features, of exquisite shape, had become hard and even distorted; all the bad passions of our nature seemed suddenly to have concentrated in that face which usually combined perfect beauty of form with an expression the most gentle, and in truth most lovely' (pp. 473–5). The passage expresses the unavoidable contamination of the spiritual by the physical. The Queen, possibly inspired by envy, has herself become corrupted. She offers her fortress to Tancred, 'for your head-quarters until you conquer that world which you are born to command', but he resists temptation: '"I have been the unconscious agent in petty machinations," said Tancred. "I must return to the Desert to recover the purity of my mind. It is Arabia alone that can regenerate the world"' (p. 479). Tancred's response signifies an ascetic, even messianic nature as he, like Christ in the wilderness, declines the prospect of material reward. The incident also signifies a failure of nerve on Tancred's part, undermining the fervour of his quest so far. Furthermore, there is a despondent undertone within the passage as a whole, with the suggestion that the pursuit of spiritual truth is ultimately in vain, because the demarcation between the material and the spiritual cannot be maintained. Tancred believes that he is merely in the wrong place and that his mission remains valid, yet he declines the opportunity to put his spiritual conviction into practice.

The Ottoman invasion force displaces the spiritual peace that Tancred seeks. On this occasion, however, realising the scale of the threat, Tancred rises to the challenge: 'this invasion of the Ottomans may lead to results of which none can dream. I will meet them at the head of your warriors!' (p. 480). The main tension here exists between corruption and integrity, focusing on Tancred's efforts to resist the temptation-laden offer until a greater threat looms, whereafter he acquiesces. The passage also demonstrates the tension between principle and pragmatism; Tancred holds out for principle until practical considerations dictate a different form of action. Disraeli is working through conflicting ideas of his own, using his characters to articulate different sides of the corruption–integrity argument. Having to evaluate constantly in his political life the conflicting demands of expediency and vision, *Tancred* facilitated the projection of these anxieties and, ideally, their clarification.

Given the religious preoccupations of *Tancred*, and a narrative procedure which implies that the hero is getting closer to the heart of the matter, the novel promises a large-scale, final revelation. A political conclusion is offered, though (in line with both *Coningsby* and *Sybil*) it is more of a challenge than a solution: 'the most energetic men in Europe are mere busybodies. Empires are now governed like parishes, and a great statesman is only a select vestryman. And they are right: unless we bring man nearer to heaven, unless government become again divine, the insignificance of the human scheme must paralyse all effort' (p. 496). Aside from the spiritual plea that lies at the thematic centre of *Tancred*, the quote is problematic because in its attempt to degrade contemporary politics through the reference to Empires being governed like parishes, it ignores the fact that Disraeli's prescription for good government involved local methods applied in a larger context, his political ideal in *Tancred* being expressed microcosmically through the Baroni family.

Aside from politics, the religious conclusion to *Tancred* is even less satisfactory. After riding for three days, an exhausted Tancred, at the end of chapter ten of book six, states, 'the longer I live and the more I think', (p. 491) before promptly passing out. A similar sense of anti-climax is generated when, at the very end of the novel, Tancred's parents arrive unannounced at Jerusalem. For Disraeli, the path to truth and self-realisation is an infinite one; quests are without end, yet they are still worth embarking upon for the personal, political and spiritual self-awakenings they facilitate. He may also have wished to deliberately leave his hero's fate hanging in the air, as had happened to an extent in both *Coningsby* and *Sybil*. More importantly, *Tancred* takes the political principles and programme, gestated through *Coningsby* and *Sybil,* and seeks to forge a relationship between secular politics and religion. The two areas are complementary for Disraeli, as political truth is validated by its spiritual underpinning, and the religious principle requires a political system to organise it and bring it to fruition. Ultimately, however, the spiritual is more important than the secular in *Tancred*; hierarchically it represents the ultimate source of truth from which all other truths follow. It is debatable as to whether *Tancred* adequately defines spiritual truth, which Disraeli associates with eastern antiquity, although it is never made wholly manifest in the text. Paradoxically, when spiritual principles *do* find secular expression in *Tancred* they do achieve a coherent viewpoint, but this comprises a critique of the political direction of western Europe rather than a clear blueprint for the ameliorative treatment of the spiritual and social ills of contemporary society.

Regarding the trilogy as a whole, Blake states that its main purpose was to 'puncture the balloon of early Victorian complacency'. This is certainly a sustainable point of view when applied to *Coningsby* and *Sybil*, but it over-simplifies *Tancred*, if only in the sense that the final part of the trilogy is interested in the roots of all civilisation, and not just Victorian society. Blake also states that, 'the novel was the ideal form in which to air his anti-liberal anti-progressive opinions without being personally too much associated with them'.[61] Fiction provided a disguise, a structure within which Disraeli could articulate imaginatively his aspirations and anxieties, voicing his most controversial opinions through characters from whom he could withdraw personally. Sheila M. Smith states that the Young England trilogy is 'the fruit of his [Disraeli's] practical experience in politics';[62] this is also apt in the sense that the trilogy takes the aspirations of Disraeli's earlier heroes and translates them into clear political action (though, again, *Tancred* is problematic text because the ambitions of Tancred, both spiritual and political, never seem capable of realisation and thus they remain aspirational).

A structural principle of the three books, especially *Sybil*, is repeated in the organisation of the trilogy as a whole. We have seen how material analysis frequently veers into mysticism in Disraeli: in, for example, Egremont's first conversation with Gerard and Morley in *Sybil*, their discussion arrives at no clear resolution because the focus shifts to the first description (presented as a religious revelation) of the heroine. A wealth of empirical data and serious political argument exist in both *Coningsby* and *Sybil*. This is translated into a quest for religious truth in *Tancred*, the seriousness and urgency of which (from the hero's point of view) enables the irresolution of many of the main points raised in the first two books. A further structural feature of all three novels, as noted by Kathleen Tillotson, is that 'for the first half of the book the aristocratic hero is shown in fashionable society, in the second half in flight from it'.[63] His disassociation from his environment signifies a fault in his natural milieu; his own character remains impeccable. Withdrawal from the corruption of fashionable society is necessary to achieve perspective. Having been a participant in the life of the nation, the Disraelian hero becomes a commentator on its weaknesses and an advocate of a political and indeed spiritual change of direction. With specific regard to *Lord George Bentinck* (see below), Disraeli again appropriates his genre in order to voice his own views, especially controversial or innovative ones. Given that he was on the Opposition front bench in the House of Commons by the time *Tancred* came out, he had reasons for treading carefully.

LORD GEORGE BENTINCK

'The first duty of an aristocracy is to lead, to guide, and to enlighten; to soften vulgar prejudices and to dare to encounter popular passion.'

Lord George Bentinck: A Political Biography purports to record posthumously the life and times of the leading figure, aside from Disraeli himself, in the movement against Peel within the Conservative Party in the mid-1840s, a movement which brought about Peel's political downfall.[64] Bentinck (1802–48) was Conservative M.P. for Lyme Regis from 1826 to his death. He was also a well-known figure in horse racing circles and renowned for his integrity. However, after it had become clear that Peel intended reforming the Corn Laws, Bentinck became one of Peel's most formidable opponents. Commencing with the Conservative Party election victory in 1841, *Lord George Bentinck* (first published in December 1851) records, sometimes in great detail, the parliamentary combat and off-stage manoeuvrings which characterised the political struggle of the period. However, despite the narrative focus on Bentinck the book also examines Disraeli's own contribution to political life in the 1840s. In addition, it presents many of Disraeli's political principles, occasionally through the character of Bentinck but without the mediating process of fiction.

As early as chapter one, Disraeli quotes with approval an unattributed speech delivered in the House of Commons: 'true it is, that towards the end of the session of '45, a solitary voice from the tory benches had presumed to prophesy that protection then was in about the same condition as Protestantism was in 1828, and amid tumultuous sympathy a conservative government had been denounced as "an organised hypocrisy"; but the cheers of mutual sensibility were in a great degree furnished by the voices opposite, and the tory gentlemen beneath the gangway who swelled the chorus did so with downcast eyes, as if they yet hesitated to give utterance to feelings too long and too painfully suppressed' (pp. 7–8). It comes as no surprise to know that the speech was made by Disraeli himself, on 17 March. Therefore, Disraeli registers as a significant political presence within *Lord George Bentinck*. In one sense this is wholly merited, as the two worked together in Parliament in opposition to Peel. However, there are whole chapters of the book where Bentinck is not mentioned at all, and thus Disraeli's own views and analysis unambiguously take centre stage. Furthermore, when Bentinck's own principles are expressed they are inevitably in accord with Disraeli's. In chapter two we learn of Bentinck's 'great sympathy' for 'the condition of the Roman catholic portion of the Irish population' (p. 37), when we already know that Disraeli's own instinctive support for Catholicism had been amply recorded in his fictional works. In chapter nine, Disraeli quotes selectively from a speech given in Parliament by Bentinck on 6/7 April 1846: 'I believe that the first ingredient in the happiness of a people is, that the gentry should reside on their native soil, and spend their rents among those from whom they receive them' (pp. 166–7). Bentinck's observation was not altogether remarkable; the belief in the merits of a territorial aristocracy formed a part of the Young England philosophy and the idea was thus in the public domain. However, it is significant that the maintenance of the territorial aristocracy was at the heart of Disraeli's own political principles, demonstrated, for example, by a Parliamentary speech made by Disraeli in 1846;[65] the promotion of this view within *Lord George Bentinck* is therefore an advocacy of Disraeli's politics as well. As Disraeli himself wrote to Lord Stanley, Conservative Party leader, at the end of 1848: 'the office of leader of the Conservative Party in the H. of C., at the present day, is to uphold the aristocratic settlement of this country'.[66] While Disraeli was conscious that he was writing to his leader, and therefore wished to present a responsible and thoughtful façade, his belief in the aristocracy and its right to govern was a constant theme throughout his career.

While Bentinck frequently functions as a cipher in the text, behind which lies the presentation of Disraeli's own politics and strategies in Parliament in the 1840s, his adversary, Sir Robert Peel, is a rounded character whose voice is ostensibly his own. There is something gladiatorial in the descriptions of Parliamentary combat in *Lord George Bentinck*. Peel is presented as a champion in the House; he 'was the readiest, easiest, most flexible and adroit of men. He played upon the house of commons as on an old fiddle' (p. 69). Before the battle begins in earnest, Disraeli offers an analysis of Peel's downfall – 'the fall of Sir Robert Peel was perhaps occasioned not so much by his repeal of the corn laws as by the mistake in tactics which this adroit and experienced parliamentary commander so strangely committed' (p. 157) – and some barbed observations: 'his practical mind, more clear-sighted than foreseeing' (p. 133). The accumulative effect of both the commentary and the structure of the book as a whole is that Disraeli's personal involvement and indeed centrality in Peel's downfall becomes muted. Partially concealed behind Bentinck, he is not Peel's adversary. Disraeli's attempt at self-justification flies in the face of his comments in a debate in the House of Commons in 1845, during which he attacked Peel's 'arrogant silence', and 'haughty frigidity'.[67] Moreover, making Peel active in his own downfall further lessens Disraeli's role in the conflict. Therefore, *Lord George Bentinck* is an attempt to make Disraeli more acceptable to mainstream Conservatives. Far from being Peel's upstart nemesis he becomes the sage voice of reason, the 'solitary voice' who gradually brings popular opinion around to his position. It is further noteworthy that Lord Stanley is hardly mentioned in the book: Disraeli comes across as a dominant figure in the Conservative Party. Accuracy is subsumed to ambition in *Lord George Bentinck*, with Disraeli emphasising his own contribution to political life in order to enhance his reputation within his own party and the country at large, though it also fair to point out that, as Stanley sat in the House of Lords, he was unlikely to be as central to the narrative of *Lord George Bentinck* as Peel, Disraeli or Bentinck himself.

By chapter twelve, the Parliamentary conflict with Peel has become the main narrative focus. Peel is shown to be arrogant: 'elate with long success, haughty with court favour, continental influence and parliamentary sway', believing his position to be 'impregnable' (pp. 215–16). Conversely, in chapter fifteen, his Conservative opponents are seen as tyrannised and oppressed: 'every influence that existed or that could be created was now used and devised to break up the protectionist party' (p. 261). Following a Parliamentary defeat for the government we are told that 'Sir Robert Peel was still first minister of England, as Napoleon remained emperor for a while after Moscow' (p. 301). The effect of these observations is to direct the reader's sympathies towards Bentinck and Disraeli: Peel is the aloof autocrat, while his opponents are ranged against him like David against Goliath. Bentinck is described in very different terms to Peel: 'he shook his head with a sort of suppressed smile, a faint blush, and an air of proud humility that was natural to him' (p. 81). The above description, in its innate warmth, recalls Tancred looking 'angelic' while sleeping. Peel is shown as the aggressor, while his opponents have only their innate decency.

It would, however, be an error to think there is no subtlety at all in Disraeli's presentation of Peel. He records assiduously Peel's good points: 'he was gifted with the faculty of method in the highest degree'. This can also be read as an article of criticism as Peel is praised for pragmatism, not vision, which, within Disraeli's conception of politics, was a quality of the highest importance. Disraeli goes on to expose Peel's main weakness: 'he was without imagination' (pp. 303–5). In addition, after accusing Peel of destroying the Tory party in 1846, Disraeli castigates him as an orator: 'his speeches will afford no sentiment of surpassing grandeur or beauty that will linger in the ears of coming generations. He embalmed no great political truth in immortal words. His flights were ponderous; he soared with the wing of the vulture rather than the plume of the eagle; and his perorations, when most elaborate, were most unwieldy' (p. 315).

Peel thus emerges as a pedestrian figure, an impression alleviated only at the end of chapter eleven, when Disraeli describes a solitary Peel sitting alone in the chamber following a defeat. Disraeli's portrayal of Peel in *Lord George Bentinck* was rendered problematic by the fact that Peel had recently died, in 1850. Disraeli was obliged, in effect, to construct a valedictory epitaph, in order not to appear callous, a position which would certainly have further besmirched his reputation within Conservative circles. Chapter seventeen thus concludes: 'peace to his ashes! His name will often be appealed to in that scene which he loved so well, and never without homage even by his opponents.' Even here, however, Disraeli's praise is muted because, after stating that 'Peel was a very good-looking man', Disraeli adds, 'the eye was not good; it was sly, and he had an awkward habit of looking askance' (pp. 319–20). Therefore, *Lord George Bentinck* gives a superficially measured appraisal of Peel and his achievements, yet the overall evaluation is clearly critical. His appearance and mode of speech are caricatured in order to alienate the reader, and his political gift degraded from the visionary to the merely administrative. In the House of Commons, on 11 April 1845, Disraeli had attacked Peel as 'a great Parliamentary middleman'.[68] *Lord George Bentinck* does not deviate from this position.

With Peel having now departed, the following chapter allows Disraeli to present some of his core beliefs. He states, 'the first duty of an aristocracy is to lead, to guide and to enlighten; to soften vulgar prejudices and to dare to encounter popular passion' (p. 325). Furthermore, a number of these qualities are embodied in Disraeli's characterisation of Lord George Bentinck: 'there never was a man so scrupulously polite to his inferiors as Lord George Bentinck'. Bentinck is utterly without mercenary motive: 'no one perhaps ever cared less for money' (p. 348). Bentinck thus lives up the aristocrat's duties, being a selfless and courteous patrician, though Disraeli may equally have said that a lack of anxiety about money is the consequence of having a surplus amount of it in the first place. More worryingly, *Lord George Bentinck* repeats the dictum, 'all is race'. The justification for this statement within the text rests on the attribution of current political orthodoxy to 'the influence of the Saxon population' and the decline in 'the Norman element' (p. 331), leading to the cultural prioritisation of practicality over imagination. Leaving to one side the grossly reductive nature of Disraeli's argument, it is a major flaw in Disraeli's writings that, rather than assessing the material conditions of contemporary society, he travels far back into history, making crude, extreme generalisations about eras whose simplicity in Disraeli's imagination is inaccurate and deceiving. As in the Young England trilogy, analysis gives way to simplifications based on assumptions concerning history and racial characteristics, though the spiritual flights of the novels (thinking, for example, of *Sybil*'s interweaving of politics and religion) find no place in the biography.

Lord George Bentinck offers a definition of good business practice compatible with Disraeli's belief in a territorial aristocracy: 'commerce is not a mere affair of gross purchase; it is a pursuit of skill; of traditionary means, of local knowledge and organised connection' (p. 361). The relocation of commerce from discourses of profit and loss to a significant place in an intricate system of class symbiosis is effected briskly, forming part of a general political overview in the chapters following the death of Peel. However, chapter twenty-four in its entirety is devoted to Judaism. It is clear at this point that Disraeli is utilising the biography in order to present his personal philosophy. After the chapter has concluded, chapter twenty-five commences: 'the views expressed in the preceding chapter were not those which influenced Lord George Bentinck in forming his opinion that the civil disabilities of those subjects of her majesty who profess that limited belief in divine revelation which is commonly called the Jewish religion, should be removed' (p. 508). It is therefore apparent that chapter twenty-four is less part of a biography (though Bentinck was a supporter of Jewish emancipation) than an extended interjection, enabling Disraeli to present a sustained case for the merits of Judaism.

In the early part of the chapter Disraeli claims that, 'the first preachers of the gospel were Jews, and none else; the historians of the gospel were Jews, and none else' (p. 485); the Jewish faith is therefore responsible for the spread of Christianity. Disraeli's logic is not always compelling ('the degradation of the Jewish race is alone a striking evidence of its excellence, for none but one of the great races could have survived the trials which it has endured'), yet his claim for Jewish supremacy is enunciated with brisk confidence: 'we hesitate not to say that there is no race at this present, and following in this only the example of a long period, that so much delights, and fascinates, and elevates, and ennobles Europe, as the Jewish' (pp. 490–2). From these opening assertions Disraeli moves on to locate his view of Judaism within his wider theories of history and race. He cites 'the inexorable law of nature which has decreed that a superior race should never be destroyed or absorbed by an inferior', and claims that Judaism's long history imbues it axiomatically with spiritual authenticity: 'the Jewish race connects the modern populations with the early ages of the world, when the relations of the Creator with the created were more intimate than in these days, when angels visited the earth, and God himself even spoke with man' (pp. 495–6). Using his historically based assessment of Judaism, Disraeli brings his analysis up to the present, stating that the Jews, 'are a living and the most striking evidence of the falsity of that pernicious doctrine of modern times, the natural equality of man'. From this Disraeli projects a dystopian future in which racial mixing has irredeemably corrupted western society. The general principle here presents Disraeli's views at their most ill-thought out:

> What would be the consequence on the great Anglo-Saxon republic, for example, were its citizens to secede from their sound principle for reserve, and mingle with their negro and coloured populations? In the course of time they would become so deteriorated that their states would probably be reconquered and regained by the aborigines whom they have expelled, and who would then be their superiors. (p. 496)

Disraeli's comments focus on the debate surrounding slavery in America (which would go to war with itself in a little over a decade over this very issue), yet his specific illustration is of less concern than the thought that underpins it. In one sense Disraeli is being consistent, as his thinking repeatedly identifies wellsprings: the medieval period socio-politically, and Judaism spiritually. His pursuit of racial purity is thus part of his methodology.

Abhorrent though his views appear to us now they need to be qualified by a recognition of mainstream views on race in the Victorian era. It was a period during which, as Christine Bolt has remarked, 'race became far more than a biological concept: race and culture were dangerously linked'.[69] In 1850 Robert Knox had published *The Races of Men* in which he used language remarkably similar to Disraeli's, stating, 'in human history race is everything'.[70] Therefore, when Disraeli alludes to race he is not being a supremacist in the modern sense of the term. The ideas that he expressed were in public circulation and were considered respectable. However, an evaluation of Disraeli's contribution to political theory, whether approached through his literary output or by other means, must surely recognise the fundamental deficiencies and dangers in Disraeli's views on race, though it may be going too far to suggest, as Cecil Roth has done, that Disraeli was among the 'spiritual ancestors of Nazism'.[71] Critical views regarding Disraeli's theories of race were aired in his own time. Writing in the *Edinburgh Review* in 1847, in a lengthy article which attacked Disraeli as a novelist, Monckton Milnes (himself unflatteringly characterised by Disraeli as Vavasour Firebrace) pointed out that 'the religious attitudes expressed in the trilogy are undermined by racism, hero-worship and the desire for a new aristocracy'.[72] Therefore, while Disraeli was part of a culture which regarded race as a significant determinant of character, alternative perspectives were also available, yet Disraeli gave them little or no attention. Disraeli is also maltreating the biography genre by using it as a platform to present his own, individual

viewpoint. The views expressed are Disraeli's own and bear little relationship to the life of Lord George Bentinck. *Lord George Bentinck* enabled
Disraeli to voice his own views with an added gloss of gravity and reverence, as he was nominally extolling the virtues of his erstwhile
Parliamentary colleague.

Lord George Bentinck also features another of Disraeli's long-standing
preoccupations, namely his belief in secret societies and their influence.
The idea is brought to the fore in chapter twenty-seven, with Disraeli
offering one single cause for the French Revolution: 'the throne was
surprised by the secret societies, ever prepared to ravage Europe' (p. 553).
He goes on to summarise the history, defining features and future potential of the societies: 'the origin of the secret societies that prevail in Europe
is very remote. . . . The two characteristics of these confederations, which
now cover Europe like network, are war against property and hatred of
the Semitic revelation. . . . Alone, the secret societies can disturb, but they
cannot control, Europe. Acting in unison with a great popular movement
they may destroy society, as they did at the end of the last century' (pp.
553–4). In one sense it is characteristic of Disraeli to offer a mystical rather
than material analysis of pan-European political influence and government. *Sybil*, for example, followed a broadly similar procedure, with
empiricism yielding to spirituality. However, Disraeli's belief in secret
societies is remarkable in view of the fact that most of his life was spent
in the front line of politics, nationally and internationally, the experience
of which would, common sense dictates, militate against superstitious
theories relating to government. Perhaps Disraeli's dogged adherence to
a belief in secret societies signifies a structural feature of his thinking,
namely the conviction that facts and cold reason were less likely to supply
answers to the problems of life and government than the imagination.

While this discussion of *Lord George Bentinck* has focused on the political ideas it expresses (an emphasis reflecting the purpose of this study as
a whole) it would be an error to think that the text does not display some
of the orthodox features of a biography. It dwells upon Bentinck's love of
horse racing, notes Peel's appreciation of Bentinck's work on the
Committee on Sugar and Coffee Planting, and describes his death in
respectful detail. However, as the book concludes Disraeli ties in the work
once again with his own political ethos, arguing in the opening paragraph
of the final chapter that 'the great contention between the patriotic and
the cosmopolitan principle' (p. 583), is the defining conflict of the day. It
is customary of Disraeli to construct dualisms: Whig versus Tory, the rich
and the poor, rationality versus the imagination. To present a similar
structure in the final chapter of *Lord George Bentinck* is to impose his
own world-view on the biography of a senior colleague. However, it is

fair to say that Bentinck would have approved of the model, perceiving of himself as part of the 'patriotic principle' in opposition to the 'cosmopolitan' reform of the Corn Laws, which were cosmopolitan in the sense that reform demonstrated a shifting balance of economic priorities, with the agricultural fraternity yielding some privileges in the context of a perceived wider national interest. Clyde J. Lewis maintains that Disraeli sensed a seditious intent underpinning the campaign for reform: 'behind the popular unrest was a middle-class bid for supremacy and a plan for using the common people to destroy the aristocratic system',[73] an analysis which would explain Disraeli's vigorous opposition to Peel in Parliament, and it is further possible to understand Disraeli's defence of the landed interest given that, for him, land was far more than geographical terrain: it signified belonging, proprietorship and an obligation to undertake benign government. However, his standpoint over agricultural reform was brusquely unseated by his subsequent defenestration of his earlier principles once he became leader of the Conservatives in the House of Commons. The *volte face* lends itself to accusations of political insincerity on Disraeli's part, yet, by now the pragmatist as well as the visionary, he recognised that there was no turning back the clock with regard to agricultural reform, and that the Party would have to move on from the issue in order to make progress nationally. The decision to acquiesce to the Corn Laws reform does not necessarily constitute a betrayal of principle because the change in the law did not, in itself, effect a change in the distribution of power within the nation as a whole. In symbolic terms, Corn Law reform signified a decline in the political influence of agriculture, but it did not result in Disraeli reneging on his principled commitment to aristocratic power.[74]

Generically, *Lord George Bentinck* is distinct from the Young England trilogy, yet thematically there are consistencies to be found. *Lord George Bentinck* does present aspects of Disraeli's developed political philosophy.[75] Removed from the guise of fiction, his comments on race are more disconcerting than in the earlier works, and the fact that they are presented over the course of a whole chapter that digresses from Bentinck's life story, shows that the matter was of serious concern to Disraeli and formed a significant element in his social and political thinking. The reader gleans a vivid sense of Disraeli's politics in the early 1850s from a reading of *Lord George Bentinck* yet, to Disraeli's credit, he also presents a lucid portrait of his subject. Following a description of a parliamentary victory we are told that 'his eye sparkled with fire, his nostril dilated with triumph, his brow was elate like a conqueror' (p. 540), a description which is also illustrative of the fervour and energy with which Disraeli describes Parliamentary debates, converting them into jousts or other forms of displaced masculine combat. Disraeli's evocative language reflects his own fondness for debate in the House of Commons, an arena in which he came to excel in the 1840s.

Cabinet office finally came to Disraeli in February 1852, when he was appointed Chancellor of the Exchequer in the Earl of Derby's (formerly Lord Stanley) Conservative government. However, the government fell in December 1852 when Disraeli's budget Bill was rejected by Parliament. In literature, Disraeli's solid reputation was underlined in 1853 when his collected works were published. Disraeli made a number of revisions to his earlier novels, especially *Vivian Grey* and *The Young Duke,* in order to distance himself as narrator from some of his protagonists. For example, in *The Young Duke* phrases such as, 'I use the word advisedly' in the 1831 text is altered to 'we use the word advisedly' in the 1853 text, and 'let me say' in 1831 is adjusted to 'let us say' in 1853.[76] This renders such sentences as general observations or statements rather than personal beliefs. Given that he had, in effect, been the leading Conservative in the House of Commons since 1849, subservient only to Stanley in the Lords, Disraeli was reluctant to be too closely associated with any of the more indecorous words and acts of his literary creations, a view which supports the idea that Disraeli had offered a developed and comparatively honest appraisal of his personality and philosophy through his literary output from the 1820s to the 1840s.

The 1840s represents the most important phase in Disraeli's life as a writer. Although he produced fewer works in the forties than in the thirties, the trilogy that he did write both cemented his reputation as a novelist and raised his profile as a politician, as Paul Smith stated: 'his return to novel-writing was his means of bypassing a Conservative Party and a House of Commons too slow to recognise his pre-eminence and appealing directly to a public opinion conceived as more powerful than an effete aristocratic elite'.[77] Moreover, the Young England trilogy developed his philosophy and, especially in the case of *Coningsby* and *Sybil*, located and refined his ideas in an explicitly political context. Disraeli undertook a vivid survey of his own epoch, examining, in turn, the state of the political parties, the state of the nation and the crisis of faith. His approach was both macrocosmic and microcosmic as he spoke about the nation at large and also illustrated his ideas and anxieties through particular characters and their circumstances. Furthermore, he did not rely solely upon his imagination; in *Sybil* he used his own experiences when visiting the North of England, as well as the testimony given to parliamentary committees, and in *Tancred* his descriptions of the East can be related back to his own travels at the beginning of the 1830s.

Disraeli's findings in the Young England trilogy are paradoxical:

although he made countless bleak observations about economics, politics and religion he also identified the potential for restoration. However, salvation, from Disraeli's point of view, was going to be effected by the inspired work of certain uniquely gifted individuals rather than through the conscious actions of any given class or, more obliquely, through a complex interplay of material factors which would make seismic change in the country more likely. Disraeli's heroes in the Young England trilogy undertake journeys and experience epiphanies, enabling them to assume an authoritative perspective over the societies they survey. Therefore, while Disraeli is often capable in the trilogy of conducting a rigorous examination of his own circumstances and that of others, he could not foresee restoration occurring without inspirational leadership. Moreover, Disraeli believed that the leaders were available. Like Disraeli's conception of the Conservative Party, they were not dead, but sleeping.

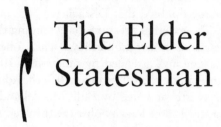

Chapter Three

The Elder Statesman

'You are a man born for power and high condition, whose name in time
ought to ring with those of the great statesmen of the continent,
the true lords of Europe.'

Endymion

The Conservatives returned to power in 1866, with Disraeli as Chancellor
of the Exchequer. Within a brief period, however, he was entering the
House of Commons as Prime Minster, on 5 March 1868, following the
retirement of Lord Derby on the grounds of ill health. Despite this
personal and political triumph, Disraeli's government was unstable,
falling in a General Election of November 1868 when the Liberals were
returned with a House of Commons majority of 110.

The Conservative government, during its stay in office, passed progressive legislation. The Corrupt Practices Bill sought to end electoral bribery,
and there were also measures to improve public schools, railways and the
Scottish legal system. Public executions were abolished, and the first
measure of nationalisation was enacted when the government enabled the
Post Office to buy up telegraph companies. In addition, a Royal
Commission was established on the Sanitary Laws.[1] Most importantly,
the Conservative government under Derby and Disraeli had overseen the
passing of the 1867 Reform Act, which gave the vote to sections of the
urban working class.

On the surface, it appears as though Disraeli brought about, through
legislation, the social compassion he had urged throughout his literary
career, and especially in the Young England trilogy; as early as 1836
Disraeli had claimed that, 'the wider the popular suffrage the more
powerful would be the natural aristocracy'.[2] However, this explanation
ignores the inevitably collaborative nature of government and the fact that
the gestation period for legislation was such that an Act passed by one
government was often the ideological product of its opponent. For
example, the Liberal government under Russell had produced its own bill

for parliamentary reform in 1866. Disraeli and Derby then introduced their bill in February 1867, but according to Edgar Feuchtwanger, 'neither friend nor foe doubted that Disraeli was the prime mover in getting it through'.[3] The external pressure for extending the franchise was considerable; a large demonstration in Hyde Park, one of a series called by the Reform League and attended by more than 100,000 people (despite a government ban on the rally), compelled the administration to deal with the matter swiftly as noted by Hall, McClelland and Rendall: 'they [the demonstrations] came to symbolise the threatening power of the working men's movement to Liberal and Conservative politicians alike'.[4] The subsequent legislation extended the franchise further than was originally intended (bringing about the resignation of three Cabinet ministers in the process), a fact which supports the idea that Disraeli was indeed acting upon the principle of consideration and concession to the lower orders espoused in his fiction. Furthermore, in the House of Commons in 1866, Disraeli suggested that women (albeit upper-class women only) should be given the vote.[5] However, it can also be argued that the government realised that the withholding of parliamentary reform would only drive the population towards Radicalism, and from this perspective the 1867 Act had more to do with expediency than principle; Paul Adelman has gone so far as to remark that, 'Disraeli's attitude during the Reform Crisis was purely opportunist.'[6] Furthermore, the final shape of the Bill was in part determined by a successful parliamentary amendment from Hodgkinson, a Liberal. Introducing the Bill in Parliament, Disraeli voiced his hope that it would 'never be the fate of this country to live under a democracy'.[7] Therefore, Disraeli's role in the passage of reform in 1867 was consistent with principles enunciated in his literary works, yet it was also determined by practical considerations emerging out of the political exigencies of the moment. Even though Disraeli was driven to take action by external pressures, the tactics he adopted were rooted in the philanthropic ideas explored in his earlier fiction.

LOTHAIR

'I perceive that life is not so simple an affair as I once supposed.'

In the period that followed the defeat of Disraeli's government, it seemed unlikely that Disraeli would devote time and energy to another novel, especially as more than twenty years had elapsed since *Tancred*. He was no longer dependent on literature for his fame and fortune. Yet this is precisely what happened; Disraeli wrote *Lothair* in 1869.[8] He never explained why he returned to novel-writing. Perhaps it was because the novel format allowed him to explore ideas and anxieties that preoccupied him. His earlier literary works had always performed this function to a greater or lesser extent, and certainly *Lothair* facilitated a consideration of international political tension, to which Disraeli would only have been fully exposed during periods in which he held high office. However, where the Young England trilogy is the presentation of a philosophy, in which the central characters explore inquisitively their geographical, political and spiritual surroundings, the character of Lothair is more reactive, dealing with events as they come along, attempting to steer paths between competing factions.

While the publication of a novel by a former Prime Minister was unexpected, it was also highly successful as noted by Robert Blake: 'the name christened a ship, a new scent, a song and a street, while Baron Rothschild named his famous filly which was to win the Cesarewitch, Corisande'.[9] The interest generated in Disraeli's literary works by the success of *Lothair* (it also sold spectacularly well in the United States) led to the publication of a collected edition of Disraeli's works later in 1870. The triumph of *Lothair* is no doubt attributable largely to the fact that its author occupied such a prominent position in society: celebrity novelists remain popular today, and Prime Ministers enjoy, or endure, a unique form of fame. However, there are also artistic reasons for the novel's success. It is a well-polished literary work, in which the hero explores a sinister plot with factions competing against each other. There is also a pleasing and reassuring narrative pattern, as Lothair voyages into exotic and dangerous territories, both literal and metaphorical, before returning to safety, if not 'a sadder and a wiser man,' then at least a more worldly-wise individual.

Lothair is closely engaged with the anxieties of its time, yet its focus is more on competing ideologies than political detail as Daniel Schwarz has written: 'while *Lothair* covers the period from August 1866 to August 1868, it ostentatiously omits reference to the Reform Bill and to political activity during the period when Disraeli played such a prominent role'.[10] Furthermore, there is no reference to the two Prime Ministers of the period, Lord Derby, and Disraeli himself. The shift of focus away from the *minutiae* of British political life is, however, a narrative necessity in the context of a novel which is interested in exploring broad-based, European political currents and their impact.

Lothair's hostility to Catholicism, a clear departure from Disraeli's earlier works, is linked to a growing fear of Catholic expansion in British society in the late 1860s. Catholic emancipation in 1829, which had allowed offices of state in Ireland to be held by Catholics, had been welcomed by Disraeli, but the restoration of the Catholic hierarchy in 1850 (in which Catholic bishops assumed territorial titles denoting their dioceses) provoked widespread anxiety, leading to its popular renaming as the Papal Aggression. Furthermore, the political violence of Fenians in England in the late-1860s hardened popular opinion against Catholicism; the strategist within Disraeli recognised that support, of any kind, for the Catholic church would be a political liability hereafter. Therefore, when the young Marquess of Bute converted to Catholicism in December 1868, the suspicion that the Catholic church was seeking to regain prominence, even dominance, in English society rose to alarming proportions. Disraeli's long-standing attraction to Catholic ritual was thus obliterated by the conduct of the Catholic church as an institution; it now became, within Disraeli's imaginative conception, a facet of the furtive network of interest groups determined to uproot English society.

At the outset of *Lothair* we are made aware that the eponymous hero's father, a Duke, 'had a high sense of duty, and strong domestic feelings' (p. 2). Lothair is also an orphan, whose guardians represent two starkly conflicting views of the world. On the one hand is Culloden, 'a Scotch noble, a Presbyterian and a Whig'. He is 'honourable and just, but with no softness of heart or manner' (p. 4). Lothair's other guardian is a former clergyman. However, 'unhappily, shortly after Lothair became an orphan, this distinguished man seceded from the Anglican communion, and entered the Church of Rome' (p. 5). Therefore, religious controversy is inscribed in *Lothair* from the outset as two contending ideologies battle for the hero's support beneath the mask of civility. Furthermore, Lothair enters society from a position of relative ignorance, having been brought up in the comparative isolation of Scotland and only exposed to London for brief intervals. Upon his entry to fashionable society, Lothair is bombarded with temptations and influences, a process all the more traumatic because, according to an observer, 'he seemed what is called an earnest young man' (p. 11).

Unlike Disraeli's early literary heroes, Lothair is uncomfortable in high society, stating of a party, 'it seemed to me a mass of affectation, falsehood, and malice'. He holds to his own creed: 'my opinion is, you cannot have too much education, provided it be founded on a religious basis'. He further identifies a female ally, stating, 'Lady Corisande would sympathise with me' (p. 15). Lothair is voicing these views to Corisande's mother, in the process of asking for her daughter's hand in marriage. Given the brief nature of their acquaintance at this stage, the request is declined. However, the incident allows Lothair to be incorporated within the broader body of Disraelian heroes, as the novel traces his individual learning curve. While this is hardly an innovatory structural pattern within the Victorian novel, *Lothair* differs from most of Disraeli's novels in the sense that the hero's journey is circular: Lothair will be exposed to the influence of other significant female characters before returning to Corisande. The only other example of this narrative pattern occurs in *The Young Duke*, though in that earlier novel the hero has to develop, personally, into an appropriate suitor for his beloved, whereas in *Lothair* the main character is as much object as subject, as his allegiance is pursued by contending parties.

The debate concerning Catholicism assumes a prominent position in *Lothair* from an early stage. On the one hand we hear of Lothair's solicitor's wife that 'her principal mission was to destroy the Papacy and to secure Italian unity' (pp. 22–3), yet, conversely, Catholic clergymen within the novel are planning the rapid expansion of their influence. Moreover, their strategy absorbs the impact of wider political events, as Monsignore Berwick notes: 'now that the civil war in America is over, the Irish soldiery are resolved to employ their experience and their weapons in their own land; but they have no thought for the interest of the Holy See, or the welfare of our Holy religion' (p. 38). The clash of ideas is then complicated by General Bruges, a military leader purportedly based on General Cluseret, a prominent military commander in the Paris Commune.[11] Bruges, who later in the novel spearheads a campaign in Italy, states, 'I am not fond of Irish affairs: whatever may be said, and however plausible things may look, in an Irish business there is always a priest at the bottom of it' (p. 46). The complex nature of antagonisms in *Lothair* is a departure from the dualistic tension which characterises many of Disraeli's earlier novels, and particularly the Young England trilogy. There are more than two sides to every conflict in *Lothair*, as a plethora of organisations seek to expand their power.

There is no doubt that Disraeli utilises contemporary fears about the Catholic church in *Lothair*. In particular, the character of Cardinal Grandison is based on the real-life figure of Cardinal Manning, against whom Disraeli bore a grudge, following the former's switching of his political allegiances to Gladstone in 1868.[12] In a conversation which concludes chapter nine of the novel, Grandison and Monsignore Berwick discuss the future: '"We must all pray, as I pray every morn and every night," said the Cardinal, "for the conversion of England." "Or the conquest," murmured Berwick' (p. 41). However, while this exchange depicts the Catholic church as a seditious organisation, Disraeli's long-standing attraction to Catholic ritual remains, evident in a description of the *Tenebrae* service during Holy Week.

The altar was desolate, the choir was dumb; and while the services proceeded in hushed tones of subdued sorrow, and sometimes even of suppressed anguish, gradually, with each psalm and canticle, a light of the altar was extinguished, till at length the Miserere was muttered, and all became darkness. A sound as of a distant and rising wind was heard, and a crash, as it were the fall of trees in a storm. The earth is covered with darkness, and the veil of the temple is rent. But just at this moment of extreme woe, when all human voices are silent, and when it is forbidden even to breathe 'Amen'; when everything is symbolical of the confusion and despair of the Church at the loss of her expiring Lord, a priest brings forth a concealed light of silvery flame from a corner of the altar. This is the light of the world, and announces the resurrection, and then all rise up and depart in silence. (p. 57)

The condensed and abbreviated, ritualistic playing through of the death and resurrection is presented in tones of awe. The power of the Catholic priest as spiritual intermediary is reinforced by his restoring light to the darkness. Both Lothair and his creator delectate in the details of the ritual. Catholicism is presented evocatively as a redemptive agency within a desolate world. However, in *Lothair* a line is drawn between ritual and institution. The intoxicating nature of the former is undercut by the cold calculation of the latter. Catholicism in *Lothair* is much more structured and hierarchical than in Disraeli's previous novels; its deep historical roots are not foregrounded, rather the Church is characterised by its avaricious institutional designs on the immediate future.

Catholicism also provides Lothair with his second important female influence, after the rejection of his proposal to Lady Corisande. Clare Arundel shares Lothair's philanthropic streak, though hers is aligned with a distinct, theological perspective: 'I would purchase some of those squalid streets in Westminster, which are the shame of the metropolis, and clear a great space and build a real cathedral, where the worship of heaven should be perpetually conducted in the full spirit of the ordinances of the Church. I believe, were this done, even this country might be saved' (pp. 61–2). Her ideas appeal to Lothair, and his fabulous wealth creates the conditions in which he can realise her dream: 'Lothair found himself frequently in a reverie over Miss Arundel's ideal fane; and feeling that he had the power of buying up a district in forlorn Westminster, and raising there a temple to the living God, which might influence the future welfare of millions, and even effect the salvation of his country, he began to ask himself, whether he could incur the responsibility of shrinking from the fulfilment of this great duty.' In their next conversation Clare Arundel tells him that the times they live in are suitable for 'new crusades' (p. 63). Both her character and Lothair's, at this stage in the novel, are better suited to

Tancred than to *Lothair*. Both adopt the earlier novel's position of seeing religion as a means of national rejuvenation. However, while the pursuit of spiritual truth becomes Tancred's *raison d'être*, Lothair has more diverse choices to make before finding his own course in life. While Tancred's mission draws him further and further away from English society, prior to the unexpected arrival of his parents in Jerusalem at the end of the novel, Lothair will travel in order to return, finally embracing the comparative stability of England in opposition to more exotic yet more hazardous options elsewhere.

In Lothair's first conversation with Grandison, the Cardinal subtly attempts to harness Lothair's philanthropic impulses for his own purposes. His opening move is to steer Lothair's social conscience towards religion generally: "'it seems to me that a sense of duty is natural to man,'" said Lothair, "and that there can be no satisfaction in life without attempting to fulfil it." "Noble words, my dear young friend; noble and true. And the highest duty of man, especially in this age, is to vindicate the principles of religion, without which the world must soon become a scene of universal desolation.'" Thereafter, the Cardinal criticises politics, 'the world is wearied of statesmen, whom democracy has degraded into politicians'; science, 'but the pursuit of science leads only to the insoluble'; and, implicitly, the Church of England: 'perplexed churches are churches made by Act of Parliament, not by God' (pp. 67–8). It is further apparent that Lothair is being targeted by the Catholic church, as the Cardinal tells him, 'I perceive in you great qualities: qualities so great . . . that, properly guided, they may considerably affect the history of this country, and perhaps even have a wider range' (p. 69). As Lothair is being groomed, so the reader is being alienated; Disraeli replaces sensory delight in Catholic ritual with rational disconcertion at the revelation of a hidden agenda.

Lothair continues to gain valuable experiences and meet opinionated individuals. Each of these encounters exerts, to a greater or lesser extent, a deterministic effect on his perception. He encounters club-life at White's, finding only 'a group of grey-headed men,' regarding Lothair with 'cynical nonchalance' (p. 72). Having thus dismissed the previous generation, Lothair goes on to engage with the tumult of the present, both intellectual and political. An Oxford professor astounds Lothair by saying, 'I would get rid of the religion' (p. 97). Thereafter, Lothair stumbles into a Fenian meeting, from which he is extricated by Bruges, who tells him, 'their treason is a fairy tale, and their sedition a child talking in its sleep' (p. 112). As a high-profile politician it suited Disraeli professionally to be sanguine about the Fenians who had carried out attacks in Manchester and London in 1867–8. Had Disraeli emphasised the destructive potential rather than the limitations of the Fenians, he would have been acknowledging implicitly their power, an unlikely strategy for a high-ranking, mainstream politician to adopt.

Lothair is exposed to the aesthetic philosophy when he meets the painter, Mr Phoebus, to whom art is all important.[13] To the serious hero, this is mere frivolity: 'Lothair had felt an antipathy for Mr Phoebus the moment he saw him' (p. 139). Lothair is a proto-existentialist, in that he is being shaped by the world around him, occasionally rejecting but more often absorbing the stimuli to which he is exposed. However, the two most important influences on Lothair at this stage are both female. On the one hand is Clare Arundel, who draws him closer to Catholicism, while on the other is Theodora, wife of Colonel Campian, first introduced in chapter twenty-three. Her horse-drawn vehicle has met with an accident, in a manner reminiscent of Sybil, though Theodora has far more vivacity as a character than the heroine of Disraeli's earlier novel and, furthermore, the location in which she has come to grief is far less threatening; she is hardly a damsel in distress. Instead, she leads and guides Lothair with greater magnetism than any other character in the novel. From the outset she has a 'singularly distinguished presence'. She is 'serene' with a 'striking countenance' (p. 92). Some of her early comments make her an unlikely Disraelian muse: when she says 'railways have elevated and softened the lot of man' (p. 104), it is hard not to recall Sybil's denunciation of railway stations as 'that least picturesque of all creations' (see chapter two). However, in *Lothair*, the characters and narrative are more multi-faceted and complex than in Disraeli's earlier novels. This is partly a result of the labyrinthine plot of *Lothair*, though it also signifies a development and greater level of sophistication in Disraeli's literary style. Although the central character may appear passive, his exposure to the conflicting discourses of the day enables a lucid portrait of individuals and ideologies.

Lothair's first visit to Theodora's home allows Disraeli to present another pastoral idyll in his fiction:

> He entered a green and winding lane, fringed with tall elms and dim with fragrant shade, and after proceeding about half a mile came to a long low-built lodge with a thatched and shelving roof and surrounded by a rustic colonnade covered with honeysuckle. Passing through the gate at hand, he found himself in a road winding through gently undulating banks of exquisite turf studded with rare shrubs and occasionally rarer trees. Suddenly the confined scene expanded; wide lawns spread out before him, shadowed with the dark forms of many huge cedars and blazing with flower-beds of every hue. (pp. 126–7)

The scenery shifts from the pastoral idyllic to the majestic and striking, yet the outcome is not abrupt or garish, despite the use of the adverb 'suddenly'. Similarly, Lothair's horizons are about to expand under the tutelage of Theodora. In Theodora's presence Lothair is able to articulate a vague ambition, 'I wish I were a hero,' generating a positive response: 'you may yet prove one' (p. 155).

The principal reason for the lack of specificity in Lothair's aspirations is the gentle and not so gentle pressure he is repeatedly placed under by vying factions, most notably the Catholic Church. Clare Arundel continues to fascinate him; at a ball she wears 'a wondrous white robe garlanded with violets, just arrived from Paris, a present from her godmother the Duchess of Lorrain-Schulenbourg' (p. 124). Her blend of purity and nobility guarantees her a dancing partner in Lothair. However, Lothair is also confronted by the less aesthetic, more ideological face of Catholicism in the form of Monsignore Catesby, who posits Catholicism as the last bulwark against the ravages of evolutionism: 'instead of Adam, our ancestry is traced to the most grotesque of creatures; thought is phosphorus, the soul complex nerves, and our moral sense a secretion of sugar. Do you want these views in England? Rest assured they are coming. And how are we to contend against them? Only by Divine truth. And where is Divine truth? In the Church of Christ: in the gospel of order, peace and purity' (p. 145). In the Monsignore's speech, the theory of evolution is attacked because of its dire predicted social consequences. Discourses in *Lothair* are not contained within the realms of abstract debate; they spill over into the lives of the characters and into the societies they inhabit. *Lothair* depicts a febrile world, far removed from the Young England trilogy, where the battleground and the opposing forces were both clearly (and somewhat crudely) visible.

Lothair's plea, 'I wish I had been born in the Middle Ages' is, in essence, a familiar refrain from a Disraelian hero, but Lothair further comments: 'anywhere, or at any time, but in this country and in this age' (p. 145). One cannot say with confidence that the 1860s were any more or less tempestuous than the 1840s or the 1850s, but as the decade neared its end the accumulative effect of continued pressure for further parliamentary reform at home, militant resistance to British rule in Ireland, insurrection in Jamaica in 1865, a financial crisis in 1866, European conflicts between Catholicism and revolutionary nationalism,[14] civil war in America and the widening intellectual impact of evolutionism, all created the conditions in which the age seemed unduly fraught with difficulties. If we add Disraeli's long-standing belief in secret societies and conspiracies (to which, in a speech to his constituents, he erroneously attributed events in Turkey and the Balkans in the 1870s[15]) to the mixture, it is no wonder that the intellectual contest in *Lothair* is fought by such diverse and committed parties.

In chapter thirty-seven Lothair visits his ancestral seat, Muriel Towers. Its historical credentials are made immediately apparent through a description of the surrounding grounds: 'the park, too, was full of life, for there were not only herds of red and fallow deer, but, in its more secret haunts, wandered a race of wild cattle, extremely savage, white and dove-coloured, and said to be of the time of the Romans' (p. 183). The fanfare and devotion with which Lothair is met recalls the arrival of Aubrey Bohun in Hartlebury after his successful election campaign (*A Year at Hartlebury*), yet in *Lothair* the paraphernalia is even more spectacular: 'he was met at the station by five hundred horsemen all well mounted, and some of them gentlemen of high degree. . . . His carriage passed under triumphal arches, and choirs of enthusiastic children, waving parochial banners, hymned his auspicious approach.' Periodically, as he drives through his park, 'his carriage seemed in the heart of an ancient forest' (p. 184). His home contains the beauty of nature and the thrill of exotic orna-mentation, all within an Englishman's castle: 'what charmed Lothair most as he proceeded were the number of courts and quadrangles in the castle, all of bright and fantastic architecture, and each of which was a garden, glowing with brilliant colours, and gay with the voice of fountains or the forms of gorgeous birds' (p. 186). The messianic quality of his reception, more suggestive of Alroy or Iskander (see chapter one) than the secular triumph of Aubrey Bohun, underwritten by history and supported by the gentry, generates a level of narrative expectation concerning Lothair's fate; little short of an apotheosis is expected.

Lothair occasionally makes its overall narrative standpoint more explicit through interjections in the text. For example, in chapter thirty-eight: 'atheism may be consistent with fine taste, and fine taste under certain conditions may for a time regulate a polished society; but ethics with atheism are impossible; and without ethics no human order can be strong or permanent' (p. 191). A clear link is forged between religious morality and government. *Lothair* distils the argument of *Tancred*, arguing for the importance of religion without the spiritual effusions of the earlier novel. In the twenty-three years separating the publication of the two novels, evolutionism had permeated the public consciousness, with the publication of Darwin's *The Origin of Species* in 1859. Intriguingly, when questioned directly on the subject, Disraeli said, 'I am on the side of the angels.'[16] The narrator's comment in *Lothair* engages with one of the chief social consequences of evolutionism, namely the crit-ical questioning of religious belief, and it defends religion not on intrinsic, theological grounds but, instead, in terms of religion being conducive to the maintenance of social cohesion. Aside from the comparatively complex plot of *Lothair*, the novel is still functioning as a vehicle for the expression of the author's philosophy. Spiritual seriousness is Disraeli's bedrock and guarantor of stable government.

Religion continues to be the principal battleground in *Lothair*. Cardinal Grandison recruits converts to Catholicism with conquistadorial skill and panache: 'in the height of her beauty and fame, the most distinguished member of the demi-monde had suddenly thrown up her golden whip and jingling reins, and cast herself at the feet of the Cardinal' (pp. 211–12). Moreover, when Clare Arundel and her mother show respect to Grandison upon his arrival, 'they seemed to sink into the earth, and then slowly and supernaturally to emerge' (p. 205). Like Lothair, Grandison inspires reverence from those who surround him. Unlike Lothair, however, Grandison prompts displays of submissiveness, emphasising his power and influence in the world rather than his innate qualities. Consequently, his asceticism – 'he dined off biscuits and drank only water' (p. 224) – is more akin to pomposity than spirituality. Grandison's effect on Lothair himself is not magical, but the Cardinal's position is strengthened through the intercession of Clare Arundel, who concludes chapter forty-five by saying to Lothair: 'I summon you to meet me at Rome' (p. 233).

Away from the Catholic church, however, religion is still a highly contested territory, prone to conversions, remonstrations and intrigue. The daughters of one of Lothair's guardians, the Earl of Culloden, 'had been secretly converted to the Episcopal Church of Scotland by a governess,' who is branded by Culloden as 'a Jesuit in disguise' (p. 217). Culloden also warns Lothair against Catholicism and reminds him of his national duty: 'you owe the country a great deal, and you should never forget you are born to be a protector of its liberties, civil and religious' (p. 237). His position is also articulated from an English gentlewoman's point of view, as Lady Corisande (the mother of Lothair's eventual bride) criticises Catholicism on political grounds: 'irrespective of all religious considerations, on which I will not presume to touch, it is an abnegation of patriotism; and in this age, when all things are questioned, a love of our country seems to me the one sentiment to cling to' (p. 226). Lady Corisande represents the family within which Lothair eventually finds stability and happiness. As she therefore enjoys the narrator's support, a position underlined by her sensible rejection of Lothair's first, impulsive proposal of marriage to her daughter, her views concur clearly with Disraeli's.

Lady Corisande's argument falls in line with Disraeli's two important speeches of April and June 1872, identified by Blake as 'the major contribution of Disraeli to a new concept of progressive conservatism,'[17] within which he identified patriotism as a national rallying point, transcending sectional interests just as nationalism was beginning to grip the countries of mainland Europe, as witnessed by Otto von Bismarck's unification of Germany. To this end the Royal Family functioned as an all-pervasive embodiment of patriotism, able to 'affect the heart as well as the intelligence of the people,' containing 'the majesty of law, the administration of justice, the fountain of mercy and of honour'.[18] Disraeli also used the concept of empire, in which he had previously shown little interest, as (in the words of Paul Smith) 'a common symbol of national stature, a common source of national prosperity, and a common object of national pride and endeavour'.[19] Through a skilful construction of patriotism Disraeli was able to flesh out the claim, made earlier in *Sybil*, that the Conservative Party was the national party of England. Within Disraeli's vision patriotism becomes a form of religion; the proclaiming of Queen Victoria as Empress of India in 1876 made her, in titular terms at least, more convincing as a figure of esteem, even worship.[20] As religious fanatics practise sedition in *Lothair*, nationhood becomes a more reliable point of reference.

Lothair's coming of age celebration provides another opportunity in *Lothair* for an act of ritualistic worship, culminating in a spectacular display in the darkness, with nature on this occasion providing the altar: 'the sun had set in glory over the broad expanse of waters still glowing in the dying beam; the people were assembled in thousands on the borders of the lake, in the centre of which was an island with a pavilion'. Then, in common with the Catholic ceremony described earlier, light offers the prospect of salvation. At this point, spiritually inebriated Lothair gives way to his infatuation with Theodora: 'as he handed Theodora to her seat the impulse was irresistible: he pressed her hand to his lips'. The light display that follows immediately thereafter signifies both spiritual salvation (given the incident's structural similarities with Disraeli's description of a Catholic act of worship) and a physical awakening:

> Suddenly a rocket rose with a hissing rush from the pavilion. It was instantly responded to from every quarter of the lake. Then the island seemed on fire, and the scene of their late festivity became a brilliant palace, with pediments and columns and statues, bright in the blaze of coloured flame. For half an hour the sky seemed covered with blue lights and the bursting forms of many-coloured stars; golden fountains, like the eruption of a marine volcano, rose from different parts of the water; the statued palace on the island changed and became a forest glowing with green light; and finally a temple of cerulean tint, on which appeared in huge letters of prismatic colour the name of Lothair. (pp. 243–4)

Thus anointed, Lothair now moves on to the next important stage in his life, in which Theodora will be his mentor.

Theodora's first achievement is to draw Lothair away from Catholicism and his plan, inspired by Clare Arundel, to build a church. Instead, he now erects Theodora herself as his object of worship: 'I have long resolved, were I permitted, to devote to you my fortune and my life' (p. 259). His infatuation, however, is problematic on several counts. First, it is born of impulsiveness, signifying a youthful and impetuous character. Secondly, Theodora is married, rendering her ultimately unobtainable. Thirdly, the situation is further complicated by Theodora's strong and active affiliation with revolutionary political and military forces in mainland Europe. Her temporary departure leaves Lothair without his muse, but the void is filled by General Bruges who becomes the wise guru, another Disraelian stock character. General Bruges, possesses 'pure integrity,' and, 'though he was without imagination or sentiment there were occasions on which he had shown he was not deficient in a becoming sympathy, and he had a rapid and correct perception of character' (p. 272). Lothair is therefore not left adrift, yet the return of Theodora brings inspiration to Lothair and his cohorts in battle, beyond the military skill offered by Bruges: 'among these wild warriors, Theodora, delicate and fragile, but with a mien of majesty, moved like the spirit of some other world, and was viewed by them with admiration not unmixed with awe' (p. 275). Less of a character than a mythological deity, Theodora provides Lothair with what he has thus far failed to find: a satisfying object of worship. His eventual fate in the novel signifies an acceptance of rationality, but his formative experiences as an adult are suggestive of a character searching for his purpose in life. This is a typical theme in Disraeli's novels, with direction found through a female character: the Duke of St James has May Dacre, Egremont has Sybil. Tancred engages meaningfully with the Queen of the Ansarey, yet his true muse is undoubtedly Eva. The difference in *Lothair* is that the hero moves through a trio of inspirational female characters: an early proposal to Lady Corisande, an attraction to Clare Arundel and obsession with Theodora. Interestingly, the remainder of the novel will witness him making the same journey in reverse, finally coming back to rest with Lady Corisande. The hero's purpose in *Lothair* is to journey into the realms of the exotic and the hazardous before returning to English stability. Whereas Tancred ventured out into the exotic, Lothair makes the return leg as well, evidently not satisfied with, or disillusioned by, its findings. English society is embraced in spite of (or, quite possibly, because of) its lack of the exotic.

Lothair is preoccupied with secretive, conspiratorial organisations, which in reality were widespread in Europe by the mid-nineteenth century. Sarah Bradford has suggested that novels concerned with secret

societies were 'the Victorian equivalent of the twentieth-century espionage–terrorism genre'.[21] The whole idea of secret societies nagged at
Disraeli throughout his career: *Lothair* allows the creative realisation of
these anxieties through his writing. In chapter fifty we hear that, 'a month
ago, the secret societies in France were only a name; they existed only in
the memory of the place, and almost as a tradition. At present we know
that they are in complete organisation.' The societies are identified as
Republican, suggestive of the First International, and named as 'Mary-
Anne,' explained as 'the red name for the Republic years ago' (p. 264).[22]
Nor is the struggle limited to France. Theodora's battle is being fought in
Italy, where she claims to be involved in 'a struggle between the Church
and the secret societies; and it is a death struggle' (p. 274). The organisation at work in Italy is the 'Madre Natura,' identified by the narrator in
the opening to chapter fifty-four as 'the oldest, the most powerful, and
the most occult of the secret societies of Italy. Its mythic origin reaches
the era of paganism, and it is not impossible that it may have been founded
by some of the despoiled professors of the ancient faith.' Its influence is
measured by the fact that 'one of the most celebrated of the Popes was
admitted to their fraternity as Cardinal dei Medici' (pp. 279–80). *Lothair*
is thus a landscape of conflict beneath a veneer of civility. The book's key
military campaign is underscored by perpetual struggles between faiths,
political parties, even intellectual ideologies.

Running alongside the narrative complexity in *Lothair*, a point of high
drama is reached with the death of Theodora, in a battle described by
Thom Braun as 'a sketchy version of Garibaldi's abortive campaign of
1867'.[23] Her secular, political ambitions are replaced by a death-scene in
which melodramatic spirituality is predominant. As Lothair addresses her
as 'adored being,' her final words, which conclude chapter fifty-nine, are:
'embrace me, for I wish that your spirit should be upon me as mine
departs' (p. 304). Their closing tableau represents a consummation. It is
also a trauma for the Disraelian hero as his muse is withdrawn. Her spiritual presence lingers in the novel, fulfilling her function (like Sybil's) to
inspire and guide the hero.

Lothair himself passes out and regains consciousness in the care, or,
more accurately, the confines of a household of the Catholic church. In
this section of the novel Catholicism is seen at its most dangerous as it
attempts to inveigle Lothair into conversion. The primary agent towards
this end is Clare Arundel, though her motives are broadly honourable,
unlike those of Cardinal Grandison and a priest, Father Coleman. Lothair
appears to Clare Arundel as a figure of beauty, 'his eyes were closed, and
his auburn hair fell in clusters on his white forehead' (p. 309), while he
wakes up to announce, 'I have heard the voice of angels' (p. 311). Again

in *Lothair* we are reminded of *Tancred*, as a period of unconsciousness facilitates an epiphanous exposure to new wisdom. While Tancred, at an early point in his adventures in the East, wakes up in the care of Eva, Lothair's veiled attendant is Clare, though she will ultimately present more perils than pleasures to the hero. Her view is that, 'all things that have happened have tended and been ordained to one end, and that was to make you the champion of the Church of which you are now more than the child' (p. 325). Lothair is being reconstructed as the hero of Catholicism, though his part in the process is conspicuously passive. Lothair is the tool which the Catholic Church intends using to advance its own position. As in the case of the real-life Marquess of Bute, a high-profile conversion will serve to increase the Church's influence on an international scale. The scurrilous activities of Catholicism are high-lighted through a simile describing the constant presence of either Monsignore Catesby (purportedly based on Monsignore Capel, who had converted the Marquess of Bute) or Father Coleman in Lothair's room: 'Father Coleman, who was now on a visit to the family, would look in and pass the evening with him, as men who keep a gaming-table find it discreet occasionally to change the dealer' (pp. 327–8). The Church is presented as a malign conspiracy.

Unbeknown to Lothair, a rumour has circulated in Rome that the peasant woman who rescued him from the battlefield subsequently revealed herself as the Virgin Mary. Furthermore, it is reported that Lothair fought on behalf of Papal forces, not against them. Therefore, Lothair agrees to attend a procession, not knowing that he will be the main object of attention; nor is he aware that a ceremony has also been planned centring around his conversion, at which the Pope will officiate. The Catholic Church is thus a duplicitous organisation; delight at its cere-monies gives way to revulsion at its sly and wilful misrepresentation of events. The combined effect of the sudden withdrawal of Cardinal Manning's political support from Disraeli in 1868, and the Fenian attacks in England, had finally toppled Disraeli's attraction to the symbolism and historical foundation of Catholicism.

At the procession in *Lothair*, some of those present 'rushed forward to kiss the hem of his garment' (p. 340). Grandison finally informs Lothair of his imminent conversion, telling him, 'Christendom will then hail you as its champion and regenerator' (p. 351). Faced with his own reinven-tion as an icon, Lothair is galvanised into a response, less by his own efforts than by a vision he has of Theodora; ironically, he is redeemed from the perils of mysticism by a mystical experience of his own: 'he felt, he saw, he was no longer alone. The moonbeams fell upon a figure that was observing him from the crag of ruin that was near, and as the light clustered and gathered round the form, it became every moment more definite and distinct.' The identity of the vision is not withheld for long: 'now, he could spring forward and throw himself at her feet; but alas! As he reached her, the figure melted into the moonlight, and she was gone: that divine Theodora, who, let us hope, returned at least to those Elysian fields she so well deserved' (p. 357). The ascension of Theodora is a genuine religious phenomenon, starkly contrasting with Lothair's sham procession and falsely-attributed iconic status. The chaste relationship between Theodora and Lothair realizes Disraeli's long-standing attraction to Catholicism, relocated within Theodora Campian and the hero's attraction to her. That is, a devotional object is given a secular identity undermined by her spiritual qualities, while at the same time a spiritual organisation, the Catholic Church, is decidedly worldly in its unprincipled pursuit of power and influence.

Lothair escapes, assisted by a few humble fisherman, a narrative detail which hardly deflates his messianic qualities. He arrives at an Aegean isle occupied by Mr Phoebus, in which pleasure and leisure are the governing principles. Lothair finds himself exposed to a different creed and a different mode of living, while Phoebus is reinvented as a benign patriarch; he 'commanded a large income, and he spent it fairly and fully'. He 'was always beaming with good nature and high spirits' (pp. 367–8). Lothair, previously hostile to Phoebus's immersion in art to the neglect of duty, is now appreciative of Phoebus's eclecticism: 'Mr Phoebus pursued a life in his island partly feudal, partly oriental, partly Venetian, and partly idiosyncratic' (p. 371). Phoebus represents a transitional stage for Lothair; following the doctrinal intensity of Catholicism, and prior to the hero's return to English stability, Lothair is given time to reflect in a world apart from the world, where pleasure and relaxation facilitate rejuvenation.

Phoebus is a Romantic figure who 'looks upon reading and writing as very injurious to education'. However, he draws *Lothair* back to very familiar Disraelian territory through his disquisition on race. He claims that the indigenous islanders are an unmixed race, 'very little changed in anything, even in their religion' (p. 372). This provokes an astonished reaction in Lothair, to whom religion has been relentlessly controversial; yet again in Disraeli's novels, modernity has resulted in confusion rather than progress. However, the islanders' existence, while pleasurable, seems devoid of the powerful sense of social obligation which imbues all of Disraeli's ideal communities: 'they make parties of pleasure; they go in procession to a fountain or grove. They dance and eat fruit, and they return home singing songs.' For Phoebus, 'true religion is the worship of the beautiful. For the beautiful cannot be attained without virtue, if virtue consists, as I believe, in the control of the passions, in the sentiment of repose, and the avoidance in all things of excess' (p. 373). Phoebus's religion, in essence paganistic and devoid of a clear deity, will not gain the ultimate approval of a Disraelian hero, to whom the presence of a guiding figure passing down commandments is indispensable. However, time spent with Phoebus does enable Lothair to explore his own thoughts and feelings, an act which has hitherto been smothered, principally by the Catholic Church.

An important issue for Lothair to revisit is the impact that Theodora has had upon him. During a walk with Phoebus, the elder man points out a contradiction concerning Lucien Campian, Theodora's widower, 'he was fighting for freedom all his life, yet slavery made and slavery destroyed him,' before going on to identify Theodora as 'a divine being, a true Hellenic goddess'. Lothair, ignoring the paradoxes of Lucien Campian's revolutionary activities, reinforces the idea of Theodora's divinity: 'sometimes I think she is always hovering over me' (pp. 378–9). Immediately thereafter 'they entered the sacred circle and beheld a statue raised on a porphyry pedestal. The light fell with magical effect on the face of the statue. It was the statue of Theodora' (p. 380). Lothair's theology is still evolving at this stage yet he has, in effect, his own goddess. The statue of Theodora helps to ensure that her influence upon Lothair is ongoing. Despite this, Phoebus still has a role to play in helping Lothair until he encounters his next guide, the Syrian prince.

Phoebus, accompanied by Lothair, journeys further east to Jerusalem, enabling Disraeli to revisit his own voyage to the east in 1830–1, and to simultaneously extol the virtues of ancient civilisation.

> Time, which changes everything, is changing even the traditionary appearance of forlorn Jerusalem. Not that its mien, after all, was ever very sad. Its airy site, its splendid mosque, its vast monasteries, the bright material of which the whole city is built, its cupolaed houses of freestone, and above all the towers and gates and battlements of its lofty and complete walls, always rendered it a handsome city. Jerusalem has not been sacked so often or so recently as the other two great ancient cities, Rome and Athens. (p. 383)

Comparisons with *Tancred* are again valid; the hero travels further away from western civilisation and consequently understands it with greater lucidity, as distance facilitates perspective. The relatively unspoiled surroundings of Jerusalem imply a state of purity, suggesting in turn that the hero's discoveries here will be authentic. One of Phoebus's last pieces of advice to Lothair is particularly telling: 'man is born to observe, but if he falls into psychology he observes nothing, and then he is astonished that life has no charms for him, or that, never seizing the occasion, his career is a failure' (p. 387). This is a distant echo of Disraeli's claim, 'I wish to act what I write.' Lothair is being urged to turn his gaze outward, to observe the world and then influence it; Tancred, in contrast, tunnelled ever-inward as the landscape around him had become increasingly exotic and other-worldly.

Lothair is introduced to the Syrian, Paraclete, who states, 'I remember also when patriotism was a boast, and now it is a controversy.' Disraeli made good use of patriotism in the 1870s by erecting it as a point of national unification, though he had identified the Conservative Party's potential in this respect as far back as *Sybil*. Paraclete's implicit advocacy of patriotism thus sets him up as a character with whom the narrative voice will sympathise. Paraclete's value is further signified by his origins in 'one of the old Syrian families in the mountain' (p. 391). More specifically he is from 'beyond the Sea of Galilee. My family has dwelt there from time immemorial' (p. 393). Thus, deeply rooted, he becomes the embodiment of much that Disraeli holds dear in his fiction: eastern in origin and characterised by fixity and continuity in an otherwise unstable world. The fact that Paraclete's character is initially without a name enhances his enigmatic status, recalling a narrative strategy Disraeli had employed previously, most notably with regard to Sidonia in *Coningsby*.

Paraclete offers Lothair an alternative to rationalism, the intellectual corollary of utilitarianism in economics and politics. He tells Lothair, 'I know that I have a soul, and I believe that it is immortal.' Paraclete also defends human activity and aspiration in the face of science's post-Darwinian insistence on the inconsequentiality of humankind: 'what is the earth compared with the sun? a molehill by a mountain; yet the inhabitants of this earth can discover the elements of which the great orb consists, and will probably ere long ascertain all the conditions of its being. Nay, the human mind can penetrate far beyond the sun. There is no relation therefore between the faculties of man and the scale in creation of the planet which he inhabits' (p. 394). His plea for human greatness reinvigorates Lothair who, in the field of religion at least, has previously only been assailed by doctrines of submission. Furthermore, Paraclete's critique of Phoebus enables Lothair to shed another influence which, while useful temporarily, is unable to provide Lothair with a sustainable creed. Lothair's definition of Phoebus's beliefs as pantheism is denounced by Paraclete: 'Pantheism, it is Atheism in domino. The belief in a creator who is unconscious of creating is more monstrous than any dogma of any of the Churches in this city' (p. 395).

Having made the case for humanity acting under the eyes of a watchful deity, Paraclete develops his position, arriving at a typical Disraelian conclusion: 'God works by races,' the two most privileged being, 'the

Hellenes and the Hebrews' (p. 397). This racial dualism was not Disraeli's invention. It features in Matthew Arnold's *Culture and Anarchy*, first published in 1869. Arnold, in turn, may have taken the two terms from Heinrich Heine. We know that Arnold sent a copy of *Culture and Anarchy* to Disraeli, so he was acquainted with Arnold's formula. However, Michael Ragussis has argued that Disraeli was working with these concepts as far back as 1851, in *Lord George Bentinck*. In the earlier biography, Disraeli had written that 'the Greek nevertheless appears exhausted. The creative genius of Israel on the contrary never shone so bright' (pp. 493–4).[24] For Arnold, Hebraism and Hellenism comprised two different modes of thought and action, exerting a deterministic effect on human societies: 'between these two points of influence moves our world'. While Hellenism is, for Arnold, characterised by 'spontaneity of consciousness,' Hebraism is governed by 'strictness of conscience'. However, while *Culture and Anarchy* is in accord with Disraeli's view that Christianity is an extension of Judaism, it differs markedly from Disraeli's philosophy, in the sense that Arnold places the Hellenic above the Hebraic. Disraeli's *Lothair* points out the limitations of Hellenic principles by having his hero abandon Phoebus for the more spiritually serious Paraclete, though the rest he gains under Phoebus's care suggests that the Hellenic still has its uses. *Culture and Anarchy* also demonstrates the fact that Disraeli's preoccupation with race was by no means an eccentricity of his own interest; rather it was a matter of considerable interest for his society as a whole. As Arnold wrote, 'science has now made visible to everybody the great and pregnant elements of difference which lie in race'.[25] *Lothair*, therefore, does not develop Disraeli's creed, nor is it a declaration of a maverick philosophy with regard to race. Instead, *Lothair* restates ideas voiced in *Tancred* and *Lord George Bentinck*, while also calling to mind an opinion voiced in both of the earlier works, 'all is race'. Disraeli recognises Arnold's argument, yet he absorbs it into his own position, on race generally and Judaism in particular, which he had held since the 1840s. Paraclete, despite his exotic appearance, draws the hero back to familiar terrain for readers of Disraeli's novels. He thus forms a part of Lothair's metaphorical homeward journey, before Lothair himself heads back to England.

Chapter eighty returns to fashionable London. Armed with a set of beliefs shaped by his foreign adventures, Lothair is able to rise above the triviality and gossip of high society. Both his own observations and those of the narrator are satirical, signifying that a level of knowledge beyond the superficial and the clichéd has been attained. For instance, Lothair says of marriage, 'among the lower orders, if we may judge from the newspapers, they are always killing their wives, and in our class we get rid of them in a more polished way, or they get rid of us,' while the narrator says of Lady Clanmore, 'she was content to talk and did not insist on conversational reciprocity. She was a pure freetrader in gossip' (p. 430). Lothair also manages a last encounter with Cardinal Grandison. During their conversation it becomes clear that the Cardinal's ideas do not differ markedly from those which Lothair has developed, nor are they at odds with Disraeli's beliefs. The Cardinal states: 'there is only one alternative for the human intellect: Rationalism or Faith'. He also asks, 'what does separation between Church and State mean? That society is no longer consecrated' (p. 436). These ideas echo notions put forward in *Tancred* – Grandison stresses the importance of religion retaining a social context. Furthermore, the Cardinal voices Disraeli's anxieties concerning the secret societies, who 'are hurrying the civil governments of the world, and mostly the governments who disbelieve in their existence, to the brink of a precipice, over which monarchies and law and civil order will ultimately fall and perish together' (p. 437). Alarmist though this rhetoric undoubtedly sounds, it may also be regarded as prescient in view of the fact the Paris Commune took place in 1871 in the wake of French defeat in the Franco-Prussian war. Furthermore, the European revolutions of 1848 were still fresh in the memory. The warning signals of *Lothair* are not paranoiac ravings, but reflections of a period in which there were real anxieties about the prospect of violent social upheaval. The fact that Disraeli presented these views through Grandison suggests that the differences he had developed with Catholicism had less to do with philosophy than strategy. Having been, from his own point of view, politically betrayed by the Catholic hierarchy in England in the second half of the 1860s he used *Lothair* to articulate his mistrust of the Catholic Church as an institution. Disraeli's presentation of Catholicism in *Lothair* anticipates as much as it exaggerates reality; within weeks of the novel's publication, the Catholic Church's declaration of papal infallibility reinforced the perception of an expansionist religion confidently establishing its territorial and theological rights. Alternatively, the conversation between Lothair and the Cardinal may be intended to illustrate the latter's sophistry, as he adopts new tactics in his ongoing quest to lure Lothair into the Church. In either case the secret societies in *Lothair* radiate a sinister aura, as they are seen in action as well as being alluded to by many of the characters. Where many of Disraeli's novels project confidence about the hero's potential to reinvigorate society, *Lothair* is far less buoyant, with the instability of contemporary international politics tempered only by the hero's reabsorption into a corner of English society resistant to the tremors caused by militant religious and political doctrines.

With Theodora dead and Clare Arundel withdrawing into a convent, the path is clear for Lothair to return to his first love, Lady Corisande. His proposal is validated by the surroundings, 'an ancient garden of the ancient house' (p. 464); the historical pedigree of the surroundings signifies a movement away from triviality and a reconnection with a sense of seriousness and purpose. Under the shade of an oak Lothair gives his betrothed a string of pearls and an accompanying note: 'the offering of Theodora to Lothair's bride' (p. 467). The gift approximates a divine sanction; Theodora has been the most influential of Lothair's guides and he, through his devotion, elevated her to the status of a deity. The marriage is thus imbued with the narrative approval of the book's powerful omniscient force, reflecting Disraeli's views on the aristocracy in the context of a widening power base in the House of Commons: according to Blake 'Disraeli saw that the aristocracy, having lost much of their political power but having preserved all their prestige and multiplied their wealth, were in danger of losing the sense of duty which alone prevented them from degenerating into a useless caste.'[26] Lothair fulfils his duty to his country by returning to England and an English woman, resisting the temptations of foreigners and foreign faiths. Furthermore, as noted by Daniel Schwarz, the hero has withdrawn from adventurism into a familiar and comfortable world: 'he now understands the necessity of a national Church as a political institution, because it is desirable for the people of a nation to believe in a controlling deity to which they are morally responsible'.[27] In a three-cornered battle for the hero's loyalty, the Church of England defeats the Church of Rome, with a little help from the revolutionary spirit of Theodora.

Lothair's travels in the novel generate more hazard than reward. In this sense *Lothair* is a departure from most of Disraeli's previous novels, with only *The Young Duke* having a similar narrative pattern (though a case can also be made for *Venetia*, in which the excesses of Romantic poets succumb eventually to the comforts of domesticity). Lothair's decision to chose safety and predictability over mystery and instability is a facet of the anxiety that pervades the novel as a whole. The vigour that Disraeli had exhibited a quarter of a century earlier in *Coningsby* and *Sybil* has been replaced by a nervous apprehension regarding a network of competing factions, some of which are rendered more sinister by virtue of their amorphous and furtive nature. Written from the vantage point of a senior statesman and, temporarily, ex-prime minister, *Lothair* captures an unstable Europe being moulded into new and warring states.

Disraeli, having survived internal party doubts about his leadership in the early part of 1872, re-established himself through his receipt of public adulation at ceremonies to celebrate the recovery of the Prince of Wales from serious illness, and through his speeches at Manchester and Crystal Palace. Subsequently, the death of his wife, Mary Anne, in December 1872 did not deflect him from his purpose. Gladstone's government faltered, and in March 1873 he offered his resignation to the Queen, who sent for Disraeli. However, Disraeli refused the office, not on the grounds of declining ambition but because he had made the strategic decision to allow Gladstone's administration to discredit itself further in the public's eye, thus increasing the likelihood of a Conservative victory in the upcoming General Election. Disraeli's judgement was borne out in the election of January 1874, which resulted in uninterrupted Conservative government until 1880. The election result gave the Conservatives 350 seats in the Commons, with Gladstone's Liberals the next biggest party on 245.

Disraeli's government set about passing acts which appeared to be the fruition of the principles he had been enunciating in his writing since the 1820s, and which had achieved concrete expression through the Young England trilogy. These principles were reinforced in explicitly political terms in the Manchester and Crystal Palace speeches of 1872, in which he claimed: 'pure air, pure water, the inspection of unhealthy habitations, the adulteration of food, these and many kindred matters may be legitimately dealt with by the legislature,' adding, 'the first consideration of a minister should be the health of the people'.[28] The Conservative government shortened factory working hours and extended the licensing hours in 1874, subsequently embarking on a major programme of social legislation in 1875, unrivalled until the Liberal administration of the early twentieth century, which introduced old-age pensions, national insurance and the payment of Members of Parliament. Indeed, the parliamentary session of 1875 was devoted, probably for the first time, to the pursuit of social reform.[29] Disraeli's government passed the Employers and Workmen Bill (replacing the Master and Servant Act, with the change in terminology being in itself significant[30]) and the Conspiracy and Protection of Property Bill, which increased the rights of workers to withdraw labour in industrial disputes.[31] The Artisans Dwelling Bill sought to improve housing conditions for working people. The Agricultural Holdings Act addressed tenants' grievances, a Factory Act protected women and children against exploitation, and a Friendly Societies Bill helped sustain the main organisation for working-class self-help. The year 1876 saw the Rivers Pollution Act, the Education Act and the Merchant Shipping Act, intended to improve safety at sea. In total, the legislation, identified by Blake as 'the biggest instalment of social reform passed by any one government in the nineteenth century,'[32] seemed to be an attempt to secure the One Nation for which Disraeli had long yearned. His foreign policy triumph at the Congress of Berlin in June 1878, which achieved a settlement in the Balkans and gave Cyprus to Britain, further cemented his reputation as a statesman of the first order.[33] Paul Smith has argued that 'his appearance at Berlin among the foremost European statesmen, settling the destiny of nations amid a blaze of high society, was indeed the summit not only of his life but of his conception of life. It was the concrete, public and personal manifestation of the power for which alone, Vivian Grey had concluded, "men, real men should strive."'[34]

However, it would be too simplistic to see the social reform legislation as the unadulterated application of Disraeli's political philosophy developed primarily through his novels. First, Disraeli was less instrumental in the passage of much of the legislation than his Home Secretary, R. A. Cross, while the detailed work of his premiership was left to his private secretary, Montague Corry. Secondly, some of the Bills were already waiting to be passed before Disraeli's administration took office, with a number of them being the legislative outcomes of Royal Commissions or Select Committees. Thirdly, some of the measures were quite frivolous and carried little or no opposition. They were easy Bills to pass and would have become law irrespective of which party held office. Moreover, the Treasury surplus left by the Liberal administration created the conditions in which social reform could be passed without undue pressure on central government expenditure. From a sceptical perspective, Paul Smith has suggested that the Conservative Party 'wanted working-class votes, and were prepared to pay for them in the hard currency of social reform'.[35] More recently, Edgar Feuchtwanger has written, 'all historians are now agreed that the social legislation was neither the result of a coherent programme nor of a distinctive ideological orientation different from the prevailing orthodoxy of economic liberalism. It filled the gap left by the absence of constitutional reform.'[36] Regardless of the altruism or cynicism that may have informed the actions of Disraeli and his government, it cannot be denied that 'breaks' and disparities exist between Disraeli's vision as established in the novels and his governments, but it would be no less reductive to remove Disraeli's influence from the picture altogether, or to suggest that he was just a cipher, without whom the same measures would have been taken up universally. Moreover, Disraeli was limited by his own power base; he could not have effected any further or more far-reaching reforms without alienating the very people upon whom he relied for support, as Paul Adelman has noted: 'it was only the mildness and limited nature of the Government's social reforms that made them palatable to the country gentry'.[37] Disraeli had been consistently voicing concerns about poverty and the social consequences of industrialisation from an early point in his career. Furthermore, he led a government which made life a little better for a lot of people. As Blake stated: 'the social measures passed in 1874–80 did something to make the lot of the urban masses less unhappy, less precarious and less unhealthy. Disraeli was at the head of the administration that brought this about, and he encouraged the policy even if he did not concern himself with its details. He deserves his share of the credit.'[38] Therefore, and replicating the pattern enacted through the passing of the 1867 Reform Act, Disraeli's actions were determined by electoral considerations and parliamentary opportunity. However, his overall strategy was consistent with the principles laid out in his literary works from the 1820s onwards: improving the welfare of the people was beneficial intrinsically, while at the same time being conducive to the maintenance of stable government.

The defeat of Disraeli's government in the General Election of 1880 was due primarily to economic factors beyond the administration's control. Rapid economic expansion by industrial competitors overseas challenged Britain's supremacy, and falling profits resulted in lower wages, alienating the workers towards whom much of the legislation of the mid-1870s had been targeted. Strikes increased, affecting the sympathies of the recently enfranchised working classes as noted by Richard Shannon: 'London masons, a great turn-out of Lancashire cotton operatives, with major disturbances in Blackburn and elsewhere, registered the cancellation of most of the trade unions' gratitude for the legislation of 1875.'[39] Successive bad harvests had damaged agriculture, a situation compounded by imported American wheat. In addition, a severe winter in 1878–9 caused further hardship and therefore worsened the government's position. It is now maintained by historians, among them K. Theodore Hoppen, that there was no 'homogeneous "Great Depression" in these years,' but, nonetheless, there was a perception of widespread economic gloom, undermining any feel-good factor (to use the modern term) that might have saved Disraeli's government, especially if he had gone to the country after the Berlin Congress.[40] However, colonial misadventures in Afghanistan and the Zulu War also contributed to the government's downfall, and in these matters the administration was more culpable. In the event, the election of 1880 saw 353 Liberals returned to the Commons, against 237 Conservatives, reversing almost exactly the Conservative majority of 1874. Despite this ignominious end to his second spell as Prime Minister, Disraeli did not disappear into the background. He continued to perform a political role in the House of Lords, to which he had been elected in August 1876, adopting the title Earl of Beaconsfield and, on the literary front, he completed *Endymion*.[41]

ENDYMION

'The affections of the heart are property, and sympathy of the right
person is often worth a good estate.'

At first glance, *Endymion* appears to be the most autobiographical of Disraeli's novels. The plot revolves around a young man with limited prospects, who rises to become Prime Minister. According to Daniel Schwarz, *Endymion* is: 'a bourgeois novel about succeeding in an aristocratic world'.[42] The hero's sister, Myra, resembles Disraeli's sister, Sarah (especially in the sense that she is devoted to her brother), and Endymion's eventual wife, Berengaria, Countess of Montfort and a widow, may be compared with Mary Anne Disraeli.[43] The politically militant character of Thornberry is probably based on an amalgam of the Radicals, Richard Cobden and John Bright, who led the Anti-Corn Law League. However, the Eglinton tournament of 1839, a celebration of Medieval culture marred by heavy rain, is reinvented in *Endymion* as the Montfort tournament, complete with glorious sunshine. Furthermore, the hero's celebrated maiden speech in the Commons differs markedly from Disraeli's (during which he was heckled relentlessly and eventually had to sit down), suggesting that the autobiographical elements of *Endymion* are optimistic reinventions of the truth, rather than actual replications. Moreover, the autobiographical nature of *Endymion* is complicated in more fundamental ways, not least by the fact that the hero, Endymion Ferrars, is a Whig. In addition, the treatment of political ideology in *Endymion* is surprisingly cursory. The novel, therefore, is more of an energetic, subjective overview of English society and party politics from 1827 to 1855. Focusing mainly on the period between the two major Reform Acts, *Endymion* occupies less volatile political territory than *Lothair*: the hero progresses to high office and, unlike Lothair, he is not beset by ambitious factions, partly as a result of his inconspicuous start in society, but also because the times in which Endymion Ferrars moves are presented by Disraeli as altogether less sinister.

Endymion had a lengthy gestation period; Disraeli probably commenced the work in 1870, writing the first fifty chapters. The next twenty-five or so were likely written in 1878. The novel was finished after the 1880 election defeat.[44] Given the diligence, therefore, with which Disraeli pursued his literary objective in *Endymion*, it was clearly a project which he regarded as important, to place on record his impressions of London during the years in which he rose from a youthful dandy to become Chancellor of the Exchequer. The verdict of Archbishop Tait,

171

who finished the book 'with a painful feeling that the writer considers all political life as mere play and gambling,'[45] neglects the investment of time and effort in the production of *Endymion*, and further misunderstands the brisk procedure of the novel which militates against the in-depth consideration of political *minutiae*. The Archbishop's judgement was more a reflection of ingrained prejudices against Disraeli than an objective verdict on the novel itself. Conversely, Robert Blake's comment that *Endymion* is a 'fascinating retrospective commentary on political history during Disraeli's formative years,' is both fair and persuasive.[46] *Endymion* is certainly, like its author – now retired from frontline politics – less ideologically obsessed; instead, it seeks to pursue a wider, artistic agenda. The faithful recreation of a period is its objective.

The novel opens in St James Street, the heart of fashionable London, following the end of military conflict with France. Endymion's father, William Pitt Ferrars, and a friend discuss the likely direction that British politics will take. The European question appears to have been settled, and 'the salvation of England should be rather the subject of our present thoughts'. The characters feel that they are on 'the eve of a great change,' and that the Duke of Wellington is unlikely to be able to provide the required level of statesmanship. Ferrars is comparatively sanguine: 'the country is employed and prosperous, and were it not so, the landed interest would always keep things straight,' yet his companion, Sidney, feels a sense of foreboding: 'it is the increase of population, and of a population not employed in the cultivation of the soil, and all the consequences of such circumstances that were passing over my mind' (pp. 2–4). The characters occupy a point in history when an expanding population, a demobilised military and the social consequences of emergent industrialisation combined to displace large numbers of people, thereby altering fundamentally the social fabric of the nation. While Ferrars clings on to the idea that the territorial aristocracy will provide a reliable point of stability and thus form a bulwark against disorder, his companion is more conscious of the possibility of serious social dislocation and rupture. Their conversation summarises the political dilemma which preoccupied English parliamentary life in the run-up to the Reform Act of 1832; how was the country to adjust to wealth creation within a rapidly developing, industrial and entrepreneurial capitalist economy?

Endymion offers qualified, nostalgic support for a period before the Industrial Revolution. It was a period of aristocratic rule, when 'the manufacturers, the railway kings, the colossal contractors, the discoverers of nuggets, had not yet found their place in society and the senate'. The provision of welfare, like the outlook of society's inhabitants, was parochial, 'the world attended to its poor in its country parishes, and subscribed and danced for the Spitalfields weavers when their normal distress had overflowed, but their knowledge of the people did not exceed these bounds, and the people knew very little more about themselves. They were only half born' (p. 22). These comments, which appear in chapter five, identify both the benefits and the limitations of early nineteenth-century government. Parliament and high society are not shown to have been blessed by the expansion of the franchise ('discoverers of nuggets' sound more like fortunate prospectors than the calculating, successful capitalists who would soon dominate society), yet the horizons of the people were narrow, their opportunities negligible at best. *Endymion* thus offers a more balanced and equivocal assessment of national development through industrialisation than had been the case in many of Disraeli's earlier novels; the nostalgia of *Coningsby* and *Sybil* is qualified here by a recognition that pre-industrial society militated against personal advancement.

By chapters six and seven, the action has moved through the end of the 1820s and into the early 1830s, presented as a period of immense instability, yet Disraeli does not attribute this solely to economic causes. There is a recognition of lower-class discontent, manifesting itself in destructive activity, 'blazing homesteads baffled the feeble police and the helpless magistrates,' but Disraeli identifies an exterior cause: 'the government had reason to believe that foreign agents were actively promoting these mysterious crimes' (p. 31). At the end of the previous chapter Disraeli had already alluded, through the character of Baron Sergius, to the secret societies. Disraeli was never satisfied fully with material explanations for societal ills; he constantly looked towards spiritual inspiration, vaguely grounded historical theories or, in the case of *Endymion* and *Lothair,* malign foreign influence. A seditious or revolutionary, indigenous underclass in England would not have fitted in with the Disraelian world-view. Individual trouble-makers, such as Stephen Morley in *Sybil,* were never representative of a class which, in Disraeli's fiction, was fundamentally decent and honourable. However, Disraeli's lower classes are also essentially passive and thus vulnerable to exploitation by either the thuggish Liberator of the People in *Sybil,* or foreign spies in *Endymion.*

One of the casualties of change is Endymion's father, who, thwarted of his ambitions for high office, is obliged to move his family away from London. The family rents a house in Berkshire which, in its appearance, encapsulates a number of Disraeli's chief values: 'in the front of the hall huge gates of iron, highly wrought, and bearing an ancient date as well as the shield of a noble house, opened on a village green, round which were clustered the cottages of the parish with only one exception, and that was the vicarage house, a modern building, not without taste, and surrounded by a small but brilliant garden' (p. 40). It is a location where aristocracy cohabited with the people around a common space, within which the only element of modernity signifies a rejuvenated clergy. The emptiness of the house, Hurstley, suggests aristocratic values are in a state of hibernation, yet it will prove to be a useful and reliable shelter and site of gestation for Endymion as he grows to adulthood. Hurstley's remoteness from a railway station enhances its ancient credentials, while also signifying William Pitt Ferrar's total removal from the seat of power. However, one of the most notable aspects of the move to Hurstley is the reaction of Myra, Endymion's twin sister, as she states to her brother, 'I feel as if we had fallen from some star' (p. 42). Yet again in Disraeli's novels, a female character is set to have an inspirational effect upon the hero, pushing him on to great achievement. Given that she is his twin she may also be read as an alter ego: the bold, driven and ambitious side to Endymion, suppressed beneath his sanguine persona. Her choice of simile reflects a loss of both hope and social status; henceforth, her energies will be channelled through her brother in order to effect the restoration of her prospects.

Pernicious modern values are present at Hurstley through Job Thornberry. An argument between Thornberry and Endymion's father exposes the conflicting economic and political discourses prevalent in the first half of the nineteenth century:

'The people in the large towns are miserable,' said Mr Ferrars.

'They cannot be more miserable than the people in the country,' said Job.

'Their wretchedness is notorious,' said Mr Ferrars, 'Look at their riots.'

'Well, we had Swing in the country only two or three years ago.'

Mr Ferrars looked sad. The reminiscence was too near and too fatal. After a pause he said with an air of decision, and as if imparting a state secret, 'If it were not for the agricultural districts, the King's army could not be recruited.'

'Well, that would not break my heart,' said Job.

'Why, my good fellow, you are a Radical!'

'They may call me what they like,' said Job; 'but it will not alter matters. However, I am going among the Radicals soon, and then I shall know what they are.'

'And can you leave your truly respectable parent?' said Mr Ferrars rather solemnly, for he remembered his promise to Farmer Thornberry to speak seriously to his son.

'Oh! My respectable parent will do very well without me, sir. Only let him be able to drive into Bamford on market day, and get two or three linen-drapers to take their hats off to him, and he will be happy enough, and always ready to die for our glorious Constitution.' (p. 51)

Ferrars cannot present the country as an idyll, yet he is able to point to its inhabitants as being possessed of a sense of patriotic duty. While Thornberry's argument is cogent it is also potentially dangerous in the sense that it spills over into a seditious perspective within which loyalty to state and even family is disregarded; the Thornberry family dramatises the changing face of agriculture in the nineteenth century as long-standing practices give way to a more dissatisfied, even militant perspective. In addition, Ferrar's defence of the agricultural population ties in with Disraeli's wider analysis concerning the inherent patriotism of the lower classes. Thornberry's commercial and utilitarian standpoint is aligned with a form of Radicalism which threatens to uproot society in the name of economic progress.

The year of the Reform Act, 1832, is described in chapter fourteen as 'the darkest and most distressing year in the life of Mr Ferrars' (p. 51). Endymion's father belongs to the pre-democratic age and thus has no place in the new settlement. Within a general climate of upheaval, religion promises a measure of stability, voiced through the character of Nigel Penruddock. His character is a gesture of peace and reconciliation from Disraeli to Cardinal Manning (who had returned to the Conservative fold), following his appearance as the scurrilous Grandison in *Lothair*. Endymion idolises and emulates Penruddock, while the young clergyman recommends the Church as the only appropriate profession of the age, and the Oxford Movement (which attacked perceived religious indifference in the early and mid-century) as the context within which to receive intellectual and spiritual guidance.

The humorous conclusion to the chapter sees Myra saying to her brother, 'if you are to be a clergyman, I should like you to be a Cardinal' (p. 55). Myra secularises the Church; her ambitious perspective converts religion into another arena within which Endymion can excel and thus restore the family's fortunes. Furthermore, at certain points in the text her function is that of a seer, telling her brother, 'you will find friends in life, and they will be women' (p. 75). This proves true for Endymion, as he enjoys the sustained patronage and eventually the hand in marriage of Lady Montfort, yet it is equally applicable to, for example, the Young Duke, Tancred or Lothair. The female muse is a constant source of inspiration for the Disraelian hero, as necessary in its own way as the enigmatic, guiding, patriarchal figure who also appears as a stock character in the novels. In this sense Myra has a particular level of importance in *Endymion*, transcending her role as twin sister and alter ego, and imbuing her with a significant function in respect of character and narrative. However, her naïvety, as expressed in her thoughts concerning Endymion's religious career, turns her into a fundamentally endearing rather than scheming character, presented as a bedrock for the hero as the novel progresses. The hero's twin, she also has twin roles to play within the novel.

Myra also exposes flaws in the character of her father, when she refuses Nigel Penruddock's proposal of marriage. Her father's reaction prompts comparisons with *Henrietta Temple*, as he intrudes aggressively on her personal feelings, maintaining that she is obliged to trade efficiently in marriage in order to restore the family's fortunes: 'you know not what you are talking about. It is a matter of life or death. Your decorous marriage would have saved us from absolute ruin' (p. 117). Comparisons with *Henrietta Temple* are further validated if we consider that Endymion's mother is similarly strident, telling the hero that 'your business in life is to build up again a family which was once honoured' (p. 75). Both parents see their children as compensatory mechanisms, tools with which to lever up the Ferrars family fortunes. The early death of Mrs Ferrars, and her husband's subsequent suicide, leaves Endymion and Myra as orphans, yet they had always received more pressure than succour from their parents. What Disraeli constructs effectively, however, is an increased sense of their achievements in life. Myra marries a nobleman and then a monarch; Endymion rises from lowly clerk to Prime Minister. *Endymion* is thus a tale of upward mobility in the context of an age in which it became possible for a limited number of people to transcend social boundaries and rise to prominence, not least Disraeli himself, establishing his role as leader of the party of the landed interest, despite his roots in the middle classes and Judaism.

Endymion deals with Peel's first cabinet, formed in December 1834. Disraeli, even from the vantage point of 1880 and an extraordinarily long and successful political career cannot resist a few jibes at his one-time opponent. William Ferrars says that Peel, 'is an honourable man, but he is cold'. The narrative also endorses subtle criticism, laced with grudging praise for Peel: 'Sir Robert never displayed more resource, more energy, and more skill, than he did in the spring of 1835. But knowledge of human nature was not Sir Robert Peel's strong point' (pp. 70–1). Following on from the methodology practised nearly thirty years earlier in *Lord George Bentinck*, Disraeli appropriates his genre for polemical purposes; in this instance, a novel allows the replaying of long buried parliamentary animosities. The Young England trilogy facilitated the presentation of a philosophy, but *Endymion* is more concerned with the combative nature of political and, to a lesser extent, literary life.

Disraeli's main excursion into literature as a subject matter in *Endymion* occurs through the character of St Barbe, widely held to be based upon William Makepeace Thackeray. There was evidently some residual animosity between Thackeray and Disraeli, even overshadowing the ill feeling between the latter and Peel. Thackeray had more directly insulted Disraeli in the form of his parody of *Coningsby*, 'Codlingsby,' which was published in *Punch*. St Barbe is part malcontent and part sycophant, his disdain for privilege and inherited wealth being matched only by his craven obsequiousness in the face of any person of high esteem. Nor does Dickens escape criticism, identified as Gushy: a novelist whose sentimentality is implicit in his name. A cynical view of literary life is propounded in *Endymion*, as St Barbe rails against his rival: 'I am as much robbed by that fellow Gushy as men are on the highway. He is appropriating my income, and the income of thousands of honest fellows. And then he pretends he is writing for the people! The people! What does he know about the people?' (p. 101). The novelist Benjamin Disraeli is conspicuously absent from this landscape of mutual artistic acrimony; *Endymion* allows him to have the last word against Thackeray and Dickens, who died in 1863 and 1870 respectively.

Endymion first encounters St Barbe at the age of sixteen, in his first job as a lowly clerk, yet Endymion's innate qualities, nurtured in the rural environs of Hurstley, are formidable: 'he had acquired some skill in scholarship and no inconsiderable fund of sound information; and the routine of religious thought had been superseded in his instance by an amount of knowledge and feeling on matters theological, unusual at his time of life. Though apparently not gifted with any dangerous vivacity, or fatal facility of acquisition, his mind seemed clear and painstaking, and distinguished by common sense. He was brave and accurate' (p. 76). Endymion's mixture of intelligence, seriousness and courage is to be expected of the Disraelian hero, yet this one has none of the privileged material advantages of, for example, the Young Duke, Coningsby, Egremont, Tancred or Lothair. He does not roam in society's high circles. Instead, Endymion must apply his qualities in order to gain social advancement. In doing so he enables his creator to undertake a panoramic sweep of class and culture as he moves briskly though a whole political generation. The office where Endymion first meets St Barbe contains a variety of characters, each of whom voices a distinct perspective which, in turn, dramatises aspects of political debate in the 1830s and '40s. For example, Jawett, a Radical, denounces churches: 'they are not productive institutions. There is no reason why they should exist. There is no use in them' (p. 81). Endymion's outrage at this proposal recalls Lothair's reaction to a similar pronouncement. Both texts defend the importance of faith while also suggesting implicitly that the intellectual interrogation of society can spill over into pernicious, anti-establishment policies. Disraeli's own philosophy, with its distinct spiritual underpinning, disdained unadulterated rationalism, linking it with utilitarianism, his long-time philosophical and political bugbear.

While *Endymion* facilitates the settling of old scores, it also allows for generous appraisals of former allies. The character of Waldershare is based on George Smythe, who had previously held centre stage as the model for the hero of *Coningsby*. In *Endymion,* Waldershare is charismatic but not pragmatic. However, within the scheme of the novel, he charms far more than he frustrates: 'Waldershare was one of those vivid and brilliant organisations which exercise a peculiarly attractive influence on youth.' He is further described as 'the child of whim, and the slave of an imagination so freakish and deceptive, that it was always impossible to foretell his course' (pp. 92–3). Having characterised him as a Romantic, the subsequent chapter notes Waldershare's infatuation with the past: 'the bubbling imagination of Waldershare clustered with a sort of wild fascination round a living link with the age of the cavaliers' (p. 100). Later he identifies the Tory party as 'a succession of heroic spirits', language which calls to mind Disraeli's celebration of Conservative principles in chapter fourteen of book four of *Sybil,* and which also reinforces the link between Waldershare and Smythe, as the latter uttered these words at a speech at Canterbury in 1847.[47]

However, Waldershare's character is undermined in the same chapter by another character who describes him as wonderful, 'but I fear not practical' (p. 169). Disraeli presents Waldershare, and by extension Smythe, as a mercurial figure, dashing yet inconstant. In so doing, Disraeli both salutes and dismisses the Young England movement, describing one of its leading figures as a brilliant but ephemeral character consisting of more style than substance. Chapter sixty replays the Eglinton tournament, a cultural expression of Young England, but it is significant that Endymion cuts himself off from the festivities. While this act is partly an expression of jealousy at the popularity of a rival, the Count Ferroll (purportedly modelled on Bismarck[48]), it is also a metaphorical movement away from Young England, the political limitations of which were more compelling than the brief period of prominence it offered for Disraeli in the1840s. Disraeli's worldly acceptance of the flaws in Young England in *Endymion* may be used to suggest that he had not sought to apply its principles in his government's social legislation of the mid-1870s. However, Disraeli's belief in socially ameliorative measures both pre- and post-dated his involvement in Young England, as evident in even a cursory inspection of his published writings from the 1820s onwards.

As it progresses, *Endymion* continues to switch its focus, ranging from the domestic to the international. On the one hand, the narrator comments on the impact of the French Revolution, which 'had introduced the cosmopolitan principle into human affairs instead of the national, and no public man could succeed who did not comprehend and acknowledge that truth' (p. 101). This dualistic tension lay at the centre of Disraeli's understanding of political engagement, predating the Young England trilogy and evolving into an important aspect of an explicit and fully developed political creed presented in person to the public in Disraeli's keynote public speeches of 1872. On the other hand, Endymion witnesses the intimate, personal deterioration of his emaciated mother: 'he embraced her, but he could not believe it was his mother. A visage at once haggard and bloated had supplanted that soft and rich countenance which had captivated so many. A robe concealed her attenuated frame; but the lustrous eyes were bleared and bloodshot, and the accents of the voice, which used to be at once melodious and a little drawling, hoarse, harsh, and hurried' (p. 106). Personal and political trauma in *Endymion* are fundamentally interwoven; the loss of the hero's domestic comfort propels him further into the realms of public life. He also connects with a surrogate family, the Neuchatels, based on the Rothschilds, and their financial influence facilitates Endymion's advancement. In both *Coningsby* and *Sybil* the personal and the political are connected, as the romantic union at the end of each novel symbolises the possibility of a new political harmony. However, in *Endymion* the two are intertwined throughout the text; personal and political plot lines run alongside each other, with none of the strenuous demarcation between the two which characterises, for example, *Sybil*, in which the brutality of the tommy-shop or the conspiracy of the trade unionists occurs a world away from Egremont and Sybil's stroll in a briefly pastoralised London. *Endymion*, surveying Disraeli's life in politics, deals equitably with both daily life and national government; the two are inseparable.

Endymion accompanies Waldershare to the House of Commons, where they are both spectators. The hero is thus allowed 'contact with those who are playing the great game' (p. 116). With Endymion gaining exposure to the environment within which he will ultimately prosper, it becomes the appropriate time for the Disraelian hero to acquire wisdom from a more experienced male guide. In chapter twenty-eight he meets a stranger, 'calm and high bred' (p. 118), who becomes known as the Count of Otranto, or Colonel Albert in chapter thirty-four; his initially enigmatic nature signifies his subsequent narrative importance, which emerges when he is later identified as Prince Florestan and, finally, Napoleon III. However, and unusually for a Disraeli novel, as the action moves forward again into the late 1830s, the Count is less immediately important to the hero than one of the Count's retinue, Baron Sergius. The reason for this lies in the fact that the Count will ultimately become the hero's brother-in-law and

the French Emperor. As the husband of Endymion's twin and a prominent European leader he would lose his enigmatic nature, which thus
passes to his nearest acquaintance. The Baron is Endymion's Sidonia:
'news is always interesting, whether it comes from home or not'. He
develops this principle by stating, 'the most successful man in life is the
man who has the best information,' and introduces the familiar Disraelian
idea of power being exercised by shadowy figures beyond the public gaze
when he states, 'the most powerful men are not public men' (pp. 151–2).
As Endymion prepares to advance in public life, he absorbs wisdoms like
these, aphorisms which suggest higher truths without being tied down to
specific instances; the unsatisfactory, ambiguous nature of Sergius's
pronouncements to the reader misses the point, as his words imbue the
hero with a philosophy which he acts upon to the extent that he continues
to gain knowledge and understanding from the broad range of experiences
he undergoes at different levels of society. Endymion's exchange with
Sergius is a precursor to his first public speech at the Union Society, a
debating club which mimics the rituals of the House of Commons and
thus forms another part of Endymion's apprenticeship for Parliament. He
is undergoing a broad indoctrination in philosophy and politics which will
inform his character hereafter.

The introduction of the Earl of Roehampton in chapter thirty-nine, 'the
strongest member of the government, except, of course, the premier
himself' (p. 164) accelerates the political aspects of *Endymion*, not least
because the character (who becomes the first husband of Endymion's
twin) is based on Henry Palmerston. However, the hero by this stage is
equal to the demands that will be placed upon him. Despite being 'only
on the verge of his twentieth year' his qualities are increasingly impressive: 'no doubt his good looks, his mien – which was both cheerful and
pensive – his graceful and quiet manners, all told in his favour, and gave
him a good start, but further acquaintance always sustained the first
impression' (p. 181). The character grows alongside the narrative,
emerging from his shell to become a resourceful politician. The development of the plot along political lines also allows Disraeli to conduct
political and social debates through his characters. In chapter forty-four
Roehampton draws attention to some of the cultural effects of imperialism, 'what is colonial necessarily lacks originality. A country that
borrows its language, its laws, and its religion, cannot have its inventive
powers much developed', prompting a reply from Colonel Albert which
defends both national identity and a national voice: 'a nation has a fixed
quantity of invention, and it will make itself felt' (p. 190). The clarity of
these positions is subsequently undercut by Roehampton's advocacy of
Disraeli's own belief in furtive influences working behind the scenes; 'half

Europe is in a state of chronic conspiracy' (p. 191) he states, yet there is a general sense of rational debate surrounding the issues preoccupying politicians at the time.

A threat to the political establishment is personified through the character of Jorrocks, a Radical member of the Commons: 'he was a pretentious, underbred, half-educated man, fluent with all the commonplaces of middle-class ambition, which are humorously called democratic opinions, but at heart a sycophant of the aristocracy' (p. 206). Not only does this description ignore the fact that Disraeli himself had stood for Parliament as a Radical before adopting Conservative colours (unless the author is parodying his own youthful experiences), it also degrades the Radicals, turning them into ignorant opportunists. Disraeli's cynicism in this passage subsequently spills beyond Parliament into an assessment of Endymion's hopes and future:

> It did not yet occur to Endymion that his garden could not always be sunshiny; that cares crop up in villas, even semi-detached, as well as joys; that he would have children, and perhaps too many; that they would be sick, and that doctors' bills would soon put a stop to romantic excursions; that his wife would become exhausted with nursing and clothing and teaching them; that she herself would become an invalid, and moped to death; that his resources would every day bear a less proportion to his expenditure; and that wanting money, he would return too often from town a harassed husband to a jaded wife! (p. 211)

Disraeli's cynicism veers into misanthropy at this point. The mode of living he castigates here became increasingly common as industrialisation embedded itself as the dominant economic and political principle of the nineteenth century. An improved standard of living, with the specific reward of the occupancy of private space, was the incentive to work arduously for an employer over long hours, yet Disraeli draws attention to the unsavoury consequences of over-exertion. Such a critique seems anomalous when it is voiced by one of the nineteenth century's most prominent politicians, yet it should be remembered that Disraeli was, at heart, no industrialist. While, as both Chancellor of the Exchequer and Prime Minister, he posed no fundamental challenge to the dominant system, he was instinctively more drawn to the anti-industrialism of the Romantics, or the hierarchical social stability yearned for by the Young Englanders. The melding of his political instinct with the practical considerations of government produced a political programme targeted at the welfare of the masses, constructed within the confines of a parliament apprehensive about admitting the working class as voters, never mind representatives.

Chapter fifty-four of *Endymion* brings the narrative up to 1839. By this stage we have met Lord Montfort (Monmouth in *Coningsby* and, in common with the earlier novel, based on the Third Marquis of Hertford) who personifies a neglectful, indifferent aristocracy: 'there was no subject, divine or human, in which he took the slightest interest' (p. 225). One of the few characters to demonstrate seriousness at this point is Penruddock, whose beliefs all stem from his religious commitment. He advocates Theocracy: 'there is but one Church, and it is Catholic and apostolic; and if we act on its principles, there will be no need, and there ought to be no need, for any other form of government' (p. 237). Despite *Lothair*'s condemnation of the Catholic Church and its machinations, there is a trace of Disraeli's former attraction to Catholicism in *Endymion*. Penruddock's desire to apply religious principles in government is the very issue for which Tancred travelled to the East in Disraeli's novel of 1847. Religion further insists upon the importance of principle and continuity in opposition to expediency; to form judgements on the basis of imme-diate convenience was, for Disraeli, an aspect of the utilitarianism which he had despised since the 1820s. Conversely, long-embedded, spiritual beliefs transcended the boundaries of the historical moment and offered, for Disraeli, the possibility of a truth which privileged an individual or even national spirit above the narrow priorities of a newly powerful indus-trial and entrepreneurial class. Young England had long since ceased to exist by the time Disraeli came to write *Endymion*, but the idealism of its author had not diminished.

The familiar theme of race is considered in chapter fifty-six. At a dinner party of titled individuals, also attended by Endymion, pertinent comments are made by the character who exists as a virtual sage within the text, Baron Sergius: 'no man will treat with indifference the principle of race'. Prompted for specific instances, he unsurprisingly holds partic-ular approbation for Jews: 'there is no race gifted with such tenacity, and such skill in organisation' (pp. 245–6). A belief in Judaic superiority never left Disraeli, one that he never ceased to voice in his writings. Despite his father's conversion of his children to Christianity in 1817, Disraeli's sense of his own Jewishness never left him, as he advocated the strengths of his lineage through a disquisition on race in all of his major writings from the 1840s onwards. Prior to the publication of *Coningsby* in 1844, Disraeli had not voted in favour of Jewish emancipation, despite having had the opportunity to do so in 1837 and 1841, the latter being a bill enabling Jews to hold municipal office. It therefore appears as though *Coningsby* marks his emergence as a pro-Jewish writer and politician, although he strangely remained silent during the passage of an emancipation bill in 1845. He only finally spoke in favour of Jewish emancipation in 1847. When race is considered in Disraeli's literary works, however, he returns time and again to the idea of Jewish people having made a unique contribution to economic, political, cultural and spiritual life for the world in general. *Punch* magazine had made repeated anti-Semitic jibes against Disraeli; the insults were never forgotten, and Disraeli's final completed novel gave him to a chance to lambast, in turn, one of its major contributors, Thackeray.

In chapter sixty-three of *Endymion*, a set-piece argument takes place between the hero and Job Thornberry. The setting is significant in itself: 'turning from the high road, a walk of half a mile brought them to a little world of villas; varying in style and size, but all pretty, and each in its garden'. The characters step out of the mainstream and, while the buildings bear testimony to changing living patterns in the nineteenth century, the houses are characterised by individuality rather than uniformity. This is Thornberry's home, where the food matches the pride and care of the house, while also calling to mind the first meeting between Coningsby and Sidonia, when a plain, wholesome meal is similarly used to signify decency and honesty. Disraeli notes, of the meal at Thornberry's house, 'the repast was simple, but plenteous, and nothing could be neater than the manner in which it was served' (p. 275). The teetotal habits of the family only underline their diligence and seriousness.

The debate that ensues between Endymion and Thornberry is not acrimonious, nor does one party try to score points gratuitously off the other. Instead, the case for agriculture and industry respectively is presented in a synoptic and lucid form. Endymion states, 'you cannot deny that the home market is a most important element in the consideration of our public wealth, and it mainly rests upon the agriculture of the country'. Conversely, Thornberry argues, 'a man with a large estate is said to have a great stake in the country because some hundreds of people or so are more or less dependent on him. How has he a greater interest in the country than a manufacturer who has sunk £100,000 in machinery, and has a thousand people, as I had, receiving from him weekly wages?' (pp. 277–8). Sidestepping further argument with Thornberry, whose views have altered somewhat since his first appearance in the text as an aspiring Radical, Endymion next encounters Enoch Craggs, who articulates a more distinctly working-class perspective, less favourable to the merits of industrialists. Craggs argues that 'the real producers become mere hirelings, and really are little better than slaves,' before declaring himself against capitalists. From this potentially seditious position, Craggs then steers back temporarily into an argument that concurs substantially with Disraeli's long-held point of view, before re-establishing his militant credentials.

'So I sometimes think, if we are to be ruled by capitalists, I would sooner, perhaps, be ruled by gentlemen of estate, who have been long among us, than by persons who build big mills, who come from God knows where, and, when they have worked their millions out of our flesh and bone, go God knows where. But perhaps we shall get rid of them all some day – land-lords and mill-lords.'

'And whom will you substitute for them?'

'The producers,' said Enoch, with a glance half savage, half triumphant.

'What can workmen do without capital?'

'Why, they make the capital,' said Enoch; 'and if they make the capital, is it not strange that they should not be able to contrive some means to keep the capital?' (p. 280)

Whereas the Young England trilogy proposed an alliance of landowners and workers, *Endymion* imbues this imagined, harmonious state of reciprocity with a less savoury, broad historical analysis: Craggs's socialist teleology envisages the workers taking power. It appears as though Disraeli was reassessing his political philosophy in the light of the late-nineteenth century, when the organised working class was formulating both a political creed and, by the turn of the century, a political party to forward its aspirations. The working class could no longer be conceived of as the grateful recipients of aristocratic patronage; the social harmony envisaged by Young England must have seemed further away than ever. By connecting the words 'savage' and 'triumphant' with Craggs, Disraeli implies both working-class ambition and ruthlessness, a fearful combination with which to confront mainstream politicians. Craggs concludes the chapter by calling for co-operation, but this cannot be read simply as a return to familiar Disraeli territory and a call for social symbiosis, as the co-operative movement, having emerged in the mid-nineteenth century, had subsequently expanded and stood as an example of how autonomous working-class systems of mutual support, without aristocratic patronage, could succeed.

As the action of *Endymion* moves forward into the 1840s, the narrative voice asserts the value of property by presenting it in emotional terms. That is, subjective experience is articulated as a territory with boundaries, and a marketable value: 'the affections of the heart are property, and the sympathy of the right person is often worth a good estate' (p. 291). As a firm believer in the merits of a territorial aristocracy, it is not surprising that Disraeli imagined property as a pervading principle exerting a deterministic effect on the expression of personal feeling. On a reciprocal level, to understand personal feelings in territorial terms is to give wide-ranging validity to a system constructed by societies: the division of property is a social, though not necessarily equitable, process, yet to adopt the language of property ownership in a substantially different context suggests that territory is as much instinct as habit. Disraeli's adherence to property, its rights and obligations, was arguably his most fundamental political belief which he saw as the ultimate guarantee of stability and harmony.

In chapter seventy-one Endymion is elected to Parliament, a path previously undertaken by his creator, though Endymion becomes an MP four years later than Disraeli. Endymion's good fortune is, typically for a Disraelian hero, brought about by female influence in the form of the Countess of Beaumaris and Adriana Neuchatel; though their assistance is secular rather than spiritual, they are no less helpful to the hero than Theodora is to Lothair. Thereafter Disraeli describes Endymion's maiden speech in the House. If we are to read autobiographical elements into Endymion's career, and the fundamental structure of the narrative invites such a comparison, then on this occasion *Endymion* is not so much the assessment of a career as the complete rewriting of it. In the same way that Disraeli reconstructs the Eglinton tournament of 1839 (a cultural and sporting celebration of Medievalism, ruined by bad weather) by setting it on a glorious day, he also totally reinvents his maiden speech as a resounding success. Like Aubrey Bohun in *A Year at Hartlebury*, Endymion makes a stunning impact: 'he had a kind audience, and an interested one. When he opened his mouth he forgot his first sentence, which he had long prepared. In trying to recall it and failing, he was for a moment confused. But it was only for a moment; the unpremeditated came to his aid, and his voice, at first tremulous, was recognised as distinct and rich. There was a murmur of sympathy, and not merely from his own side.' The success of his speech may be measured by the fact that 'he sat down amid general applause' (p. 361). The liberties taken with the known facts are considerable in *Endymion*. Some of them yield plausible explanations: the fact of the literary hero's being a Whig may be understood in view of Disraeli's senior position in the Conservative Party. A dissection of the weaknesses and faction-fighting within the party would have only undermined the Tories' public image. However, and in spite of the fact that the narrative becomes increasingly concerned with parliamentary life, *Endymion* is startlingly apolitical. The content of Endymion's maiden speech is not dealt with, nor is his political philosophy presented in any detail. *Endymion* records more of a personal journey than a political one; while the two themes are linked in the novel, the balance between them suggests a competing hierarchy, the personal taking priority over political interests. The reinvention of the Eglinton tournament and the hero's maiden speech contribute to the exuberant tone of a novel which relegates political ideology beneath an individual's journey to the top of 'the greasy pole'.[49]

Chapter eighty sees the reintroduction of Nigel Penruddock, whose

Catholic sympathies have now resulted in his being both a convert to the Church and, moreover, 'the representative of the papacy' (p. 365) in England. Furthermore, he has benefited from the change: 'instead of that anxious and moody look which formerly marred the refined beauty of his countenance, his glance was calm and yet radiant. He was thinner, it might almost be said emaciated, which seemed to add height to his tall figure' (p. 368). His appearance signifies ascetic habits, yet there is an overall feeling of serenity. The beneficent transformation in his character and its cause is echoed by Waldershare, who states, 'there is more true democracy in the Roman Catholic Church than in all the secret societies of Europe' (p. 370). While again, the observation is only weighing the Church's merits in relation to the oppressive, conniving secret societies, it retains some respect for Catholicism. Disraeli was reluctant to jettison entirely his attraction to aspects of Catholicism. An experience perceived by Disraeli as a betrayal, when the Catholic hierarchy switched its political allegiance away from him in 1868, had certainly soured his disposition towards the faith, yet something of his former admiration remained.

For Endymion, the rejection of Catholicism is a rational decision, informed by both the conversion of his sister to Catholicism as a consequence of her second marriage to Prince Florestan, and the political consequences of religious faith. Far from advocating a theocracy at this point, *Endymion* perceives clerical influence as pernicious. He states his objections to Penruddock (now an archbishop):

'I must tell you now frankly, the secession of my sister from the Church of her fathers was to me by no means a matter of unmixed satisfaction.'

'The time will come when you will recognise it as the consummation of a Divine plan,' said the archbishop.

'I feel great confidence that my sister will never be the slave of superstition,' said Endymion. 'Her mind is too masculine for that; she will remember that the throne she fills has already once been lost by the fatal influence of the Jesuits.'

'The influence of the Jesuits is the influence of Divine truth,' said his companion. 'And how is it possible for such influence not to prevail? What you treat as defeats, discomfitures, are events which you do not comprehend. They are incidents all leading to one great end – the triumph of the Church – that is, the triumph of God.'

'I will not decide what are great ends; I am content to ascertain what is wise conduct. And it would not be wise conduct, in my opinion, for the King to rest upon the Jesuits.' (p. 426)

The certainty of Penruddock in this specific conversation calls to mind the pomposity of Grandison, Catesby and Coleman in *Lothair*, though

Endymion's objections are far more strident than Lothair's passivity. Penruddock prophesises the recognition of the Catholic hierarchy within two years, creating the impression that the Church has an expansionist agenda. Therefore, the overall presentation of Catholicism in *Endymion* is partly a continuation of the anxieties registered in *Lothair*; a distinction is drawn between the spiritual richness of the Church on the one hand, and its failings and avaricious ambitions as an institution on the other. However, Catholicism does not pose a direct threat to the hero in *Endymion*, as it certainly did in *Lothair*, suggesting that Disraeli's discomfort with the Church had lessened to some extent. Endymion avoids an ideological argument and opts for prudence.

Myra's rise in society is no less spectacular than her brother's. She continues to invest extraordinary hope and expectation in Endymion, confirming her designated role as the primary female muse for the hero. She tells her brother: 'power, and power alone, should be your absorbing object, and all the accidents and incidents of life should only be considered with reference to that main result' (p. 378). Given Endymion's subsequent rise to the Prime Ministership, Myra is a more accurate prophet than Penruddock. Access to higher wisdom in *Endymion* is an act of individual inspiration rather than a privilege attainable only through religious affiliation. Furthermore, the privileging of the individual over the institution in this respect is a feature of Disraeli's literary work. As far back as *Contarini Fleming*, an unnamed stranger advised the hero to 'trust not overmuch in the blessed Magdalen,' in chapter thirteen of book one. Myra is not angelic. At one point she upbraids Endymion for his refusal to marry Adriana Neuchatel: 'all the devotion of Myra will end in your destroying her' (p. 434). Myra picks up the role abandoned by her parents, while also imbuing her protestations with emotional blackmail. By doing so she underlines the extent to which marriage within Disraeli's culture was an act of trade as well as an emotional investment. His own marriage to an older widow had enabled him to placate his creditors at a time when financial difficulties threatened to derail his political career.

As *Endymion* enters the 1850s, the hero becomes Foreign Secretary, and later Prime Minister. His progress in the political establishment is often smooth, occurring without sharp ideological conflict. In certain respects this is unavoidable as, given the wide temporal and social range of the novel, it becomes difficult to treat any specific area in anything other than a synoptic manner; the conclusion to the novel, in which Myra (now Queen of France) and Endymion (now Prime Minister) physically embrace represents imagistically the full restoration of the Ferrars family and the undiluted triumph of the Ferrars children. However, a more telling reason for the thin treatment of the detailed realities of political life in *Endymion* lies in the fact that Disraeli's quest is to record the personal odyssey of a character who rises above mediocrity through good human qualities and good fortune. It is noticeable, however, that Endymion does not dominate the narrative. He is unlike the self-absorbed heroes of Disraeli's early works, or the politically preoccupied central characters in the Young England trilogy. The only Disraelian hero to whom Endymion does bear a significant resemblance is Lothair, as both are frequently the passive recipients of forces beyond their immediate control. However, Lothair has an overriding mission in his story, an objective that consumes him, making him more akin to Tancred. In this sense *Endymion* is a departure from all of Disraeli's previous novels, as it is more descriptive, location-based work than a pure character study. While this claim may also be made of *Coningsby* and *Sybil*, *Endymion* is unique in the sense that it does not limit itself to politics as it sweeps through the social and cultural milieu Disraeli had known at first-hand, as he enacted his own bold sweep through an establishment minded to resist him.

Disraeli's final literary project was a novel unfinished at his death, *Falconet*. The surviving chapters, first published in *The Times* in 1905, are an attack by Disraeli on William Gladstone, the Liberal politician with whom he had been engaged in a state of unremitting and bitter rivalry for many years, with the only truce between them occurring round the death of Disraeli's wife in December 1872. The central figure in *Falconet*, though his character has little time to develop, is self-satisfied and sanctimonious. For example, he has 'a complete deficiency in the sense of humour,' and 'he wished to believe that he was the man ordained to vindicate the sublime cause of religious truth'. Disraeli's central characters often undergo a sustained period of spiritual discovery and self-discovery, yet for Falconet it is taken as read, signifying pomposity above religious seriousness. Furthermore, 'it was as the lay champion of the church that he desired to act, and believed that in such a position his influence would be infinitely greater than in that of a clergyman, whatever his repute' (pp. 474–5). Falconet thus emerges as an instinctive churchman whose ambitions exceed those offered by religion as a profession. This militates against his being seen as a statesman, as he is set to appropriate parliamentary life, rather than consciously move towards it with explicitly governmental aims.

However, Falconet is presented in chapter two as a splendid orator; this was one respect in which Gladstone had a clear advantage over Disraeli throughout the course of their political rivalry. One of the factors contributing to the defeat of Disraeli's government in 1880 was Gladstone's 'Midlothian campaign,' an oratorical attack on what he termed 'Beaconsfieldism'. Gladstone also attacked successfully Disraeli's

Eastern policies, as atrocities committed by Turkish forces in the Balkans raised fears of an assault upon Christianity; it has been suggested by Michael Ragussis that this anxiety forged a subliminal connection in the popular imagination with Disraeli's own origins and the enthusiasms he had expressed for the East in his novels, especially *Tancred*.[50] Furthermore, the historian E. A. Freeman had argued in 1877 that Turks and Jews had united against Christians.[51] Conversely, Disraeli, while a skilled parliamentarian, was not a well-renowned public orator; his speeches of 1872 are an anomaly in the context of his career as a whole, and he rarely used public occasions as the means of presenting his political philosophy. George Watson remarked that, 'Disraeli floated upwards on oratory,'[52] but his skills were applied in literature and in Parliament. In the post-1867 context of a broadly mass electorate, mass meetings were an increasingly important means of reaching out to the voters. In this sense, therefore, *Falconet* draws substantially from a defining feature of Gladstone's political methods, aiming to project a widespread message to an expanding electorate. Given that the author of *Falconet* was an ex-Prime Minster and a leading public figure of his day, a large audience was guaranteed.

While the central character of *Falconet* promised to be very different from Disraeli's customary heroes, there are respects in which *Falconet* is clearly a Disraelian novel. For example, the text opens with a description of a pastoral idyll within an urban context, Clapham Common: 'an unenclosed park of 200 acres, well turfed and timbered, and, though free to all and without a paling, so well managed that a domain in a distant country could scarcely be more orderly and refined' (p. 471). The location is not without its ambiguities; Clapham Common was a distinctly suburban environment, and by placing the Falconet family here Disraeli removes them from the natural terrain of leaders, namely, the large, aristocratic houses. However, in general terms, Disraeli clearly does use rural settings to signify benignity with regard to narrative, character, or both. In *Sybil*, a rural enclave is found by the heroine and Egremont (Book IV, ch. 6); in *Lothair* a natural landscape forms the context for the hero's proposal to Lady Corisande; and as far back as *Vivian Grey* the final place of respite found by the hero is essentially feudal. Disraeli's use of natural settings is consistent with his wider historical and political analysis and his promotion of the principles of pre-industrial society and therefore rural contexts facilitated the expression of a character's true essence, unencumbered by the pressures of modern, industrial society. Disraeli's use of nature is also typically romantic, in the sense that the rural environment is restorative and free from corruption and, on a wider level, the influence of Romanticism on Disraeli was considerable. He took Byron and Shelley as the inspiration for his central characters in *Venetia* and, more generally, his central characters have visionary imaginations and a sense of the extraordinary capacities of the individual.

Falconet develops Disraeli's existing preoccupations, as it presents religious analyses of society. For example, in chapter three, a Buddhist, Kusinara, states: 'I have heard much of late of the decay of faith in England,' before adding near the end of the chapter, 'death is only happiness, if understood' (p. 481), a statement reflecting both a highly reductive understanding of Buddhism and Disraeli's ceaseless attraction to enigmatic aphorisms. In the same chapter the typical Disraelian structural device of the mysterious, impressive and wise figure is also featured, announcing, 'I have no name' (p. 481). In chapter nine, an anxious tone is generated by a stranger saying, 'everything is changing, and changing rapidly. Creeds disappear in a night. As for political institutions, they are all challenged, and statesmen, conscious of what is at hand, are changing nations into armies' (p. 500). Disraeli had lived and worked through wide-ranging parliamentary reform and the intellectual tumult brought about by evolutionism. Prussia's crushing military defeat of France had happened only a decade earlier, succeeded by the Paris Commune. Consequently, it is not hard to see the author's fears making themselves known in this passage. In addition, in *Falconet* Disraeli continues to imply the presence of shadowy figures and organisations wielding tremendous power, as the stranger states, 'those who know the whole truth are the lords of the world'. The conclusion he comes to is that, 'there are thinkers, I know many, not unequal to the times in which we move, but they are all of opinion that what we require now is not so much further thought as a transcendent type of that thought alike to guide and inspire us' (p. 500). *Falconet* thus presents society at a pivotal point in its development; a new philosophy is sought, capable of engaging with nation states and the competing economic and political interests emerging between them. Furthermore, the new belief is articulated in broadly spiritual terms, not as an intellectual template designed to render society intelligible, but as something incontestable, beyond the realms of debate, more talisman than template.

The brevity of *Falconet*, which ends during the opening paragraph of chapter ten, means that strangers remain unidentified and the central character's fate is unknown. This is a pity, as the text promises an interesting development of the Disraelian novel, in the sense that the 'hero' is poised to engage in an antagonistic relationship to the narrator, a clear departure from any of Disraeli's previous novels. Running alongside this tension are the familiar Disraelian themes of power and faith, reflecting in this instance many of the anxieties of the last quarter of the nineteenth century. A new distribution of power in Europe was set to pose a challenge to Disraeli's philosophy, which had always emphasised the local and the importance of stability, in the sense that he perceived genuine authority as residing in continuity which generated a consciousness of the responsibilities as well as the rights of power. In chapter eight of *Falconet* the stranger introduced in chapter three states, 'the local influences are the strongest' (p. 496), a belief which also summarises aptly the principles of his creator.

Daniel Schwarz claimed that Disraeli's final novels 'rediscover the imagination, playfulness and fantasy that had become increasingly submerged during his political odyssey,'[53] a claim which can certainly be sustained. The narrative twists and turns of *Lothair* intrigue the reader because they are not tethered to a strict ideological line, as had been the case in *Coningsby* and *Sybil*. However, fantasy is an integral part of *Tancred*, thus suggesting a more organic connection between the two separate phases of Disraeli's literary career. The thematic connections between *Tancred* and *Lothair*, implicit in the consideration of the latter novel in this chapter, are reinforced by an observation made by Thom Braun: 'at one point in chapter thirty [of *Lothair*] Disraeli wrote "Tancred" in his manuscript when he meant "Lothair"'.[54] While this may have been merely an accident, it may also have been a subconscious recognition of the fundamental similarities between the two characters, who seek relief from the complexities of their own societies by voyaging to the East, and who both privilege spiritual inspiration above material advancement. More generally, Disraeli's final, completed works move from anxiety to equanimity, as the paranoia and unease that pervades *Lothair* is replaced by the evaluative and elegiac atmosphere of *Endymion*. *Falconet* promised a further departure and a renewal of political venom within Disraeli's literary work, but the intended resolution of the text remains unknown. In the last decade of an extraordinary lifetime, Disraeli still had sufficient faith both in the novel as a form and his own talents as a writer to use the genre as a means of presenting his thoughts on faith, patriotism and politics to the public.

Conclusion | 'Gradation is the Spell of Nature's Sway'

The *Revolutionary Epick*, Benjamin Disraeli's early long poem, never achieved its desired objective: to capture the spirit of an age. It was abandoned by Disraeli following a lukewarm response to the publication of its early sections. However, the *Epick* has left us with a one-line synopsis of Disraeli's core political belief: 'Gradation is the spell of nature's sway'. Government by a territorial aristocracy, the highest tier in the strata of nature, was, for Disraeli, the ideal. Their credibility validated by history and the soil, the aristocracy offered, for Disraeli, a guarantee of stability and continuity in the context of an age of economic and social upheaval. For Disraeli, change should still occur, but only in successive, subtle, graded stages, so as not to rupture the careful fabric of pre-industrial existence. Disraeli was responding conservatively to his own revolutionary epoch, wondering how the violent lurches across Europe in the late-eighteenth and the nineteenth century might be avoided in Britain. Disraeli's belief in the aristocracy was not an eccentric position. Despite the Reform acts of the nineteenth century, the aristocracy remained powerful politically, and indeed the landed gentry formed a majority of every cabinet until 1906: Disraeli himself was the first Prime Minister who did not come from a landed family.[1] In addition, Disraeli's belief in the aristocracy was intertwined with a robust insistence on the importance of social responsibility. True leaders had an ameliorative and self-effacing agenda. Again, this was a mainstream position in the nineteenth century. Even Disraeli's most formidable political foe, William Gladstone, agreed that 'the possession of landed property' was 'so closely associated with definite duty'.[2] Some of Disraeli's best-remembered fictional heroes, for example Egremont or Lothair, embody these qualities. Moreover, when an aristocrat rebels against his responsibilities, such as the Young Duke, the narrator compels him to see the error of his ways and brings him around to Disraeli's position.

A simple, direct link does not exist between Disraeli's politics and his novels. Both arenas are governed by their own rules and conventions, and the two areas of Disraeli's life exist in a complex relationship, sometimes complementary, often startlingly contradictory. However, it is clear that Disraeli *did* use literature to serve political ends. His early works identify political malaise in England: the malleable and decrepit aristocrat in *Vivian Grey,* the satirical indictment of utilitarianism in *Popanilla,* the lacklustre parliamentarians in *The Young Duke*: all point towards a nation in need of corrective political treatment. Thereafter, Disraeli pushed the whole genre of the political novel to the foreground through the Young England trilogy, a set of texts concerned with sociological analysis and a formula for political renewal. Even in his final novels Disraeli remained interested in exploring and evaluating politics. While it would be improper to treat Disraeli's novels as a simplistic template for his political career, we cannot ignore the clear and substantial connections between his life and work.

Disraeli's novels made him a comparatively well-known figure prior to his entry into Parliament. On a practical level this was an asset as, given that members of parliament were unpaid and elections were costly, Disraeli was able to achieve a public profile, despite not having the finances to underwrite his ambition. However, fame is a double-edged sword, and Disraeli's early novels and public persona drew more notoriety than acclaim, though he was able to establish his name and his views through his literary works to an extent which would otherwise have been impossible for somebody with comparatively modest advantages in life.

Once Disraeli had become a parliamentarian, literature again proved useful to him in the 1840s as it provided him with a platform from which he could voice his vision of the Conservative Party and the state of the nation. The Young England trilogy raised his political profile; the novels' symbiotic relationship with the Young England faction in Parliament served Disraeli on two fronts. First, it established him as a significant commentator on the plight of society; secondly it raised him to a position of parliamentary prominence, a position which he surpassed in the 1840s only through his parliamentary assaults on Peel. *Coningsby* and *Sybil* are both the work of a political careerist (though not necessarily an unprincipled one), as they identify problems before proposing solutions based on the potency of a central character whose views concur with the author's; the oratorical flourish of the final three paragraphs of *Sybil* raises the narrative voice to the level of a would-be statesman, assessing, in a grand sweep, the fundamental problem at the heart of English society. However, *Tancred* challenges the reading of the Young England trilogy as a sustained opportunistic manoeuvre. The novel's move beyond a consideration of modes of government and into a more fundamental and introspective speculation on political rule and its spiritual legitimacy signifies an intense philosophical interest. The journey eastwards acts as a conceit for an investigation into both the potential and the limitations of a self committed to a higher purpose, to be attained through political engagement.

When reading Disraeli's novels, the reader will commonly find the author's socially ameliorative agenda appealing. The sense of compassion for the poor and anger at their maltreatment is palpable; the description of the tommy-shop in *Sybil* is shocking in its callousness and brutality. Moreover, Disraeli's analysis is especially persuasive in view of the fact that he identifies structural as well as individual failings in society (an approach implicit in the very use of 'two nations'); his analysis is considered and developed, rather than a reactionary tirade against injustice. However, aspects of Disraeli's philosophy which appear in his writings are not appealing. Foremost amongst these is the issue of race. Disraeli is vulnerable to the accusation of racism; it is one thing for him to advocate Jewish abilities and virtues in the context of a society in which anti-Jewish prejudice was rife and therefore Disraeli's observations address an imbalance. But it is quite another for him, through his literary characters, to insist in both *Tancred* and *Lord George Bentinck*: 'all is race'. In a primitive, early version of eugenics, Disraeli errs in associating human characteristics with the biological and racial make-ups of their characters. To insist that the final question is race is a crass act of atavism, wholly at odds with the systematic, modern analysis of society presented at various points elsewhere in Disraeli's novels. At their worst, Disraeli's views on race can be viewed as a prototype of the violent nationalism which subsequently bedevilled Europe in the twentieth century. However, Disraeli's thoughts on race need to be seen in the context of the age and society in which they were produced. As Michael Ragussis has pointed out, 'Disraeli's trilogy was a direct response to a kind of discourse about race and culture already in place by the early 1840s.' Ragussis further cites Robert Knox's *The Races of Men* (1850), in which the author refers directly to *Coningsby*: 'that the real Jew has no ear for music as a race, no love of science or literature; that he invents nothing, pursues no enquiry; that the theory of "Coningsby" is not merely a fable as applied to the real and undoubted Jew, but is absolutely refuted by all history'.[3] Disraeli was not perceived as an isolated, extremist voice; his own thoughts and feelings were in large measure determined by the standards of the society and age in which he lived. However, while Disraeli's views on race are an interesting reflection of the prejudices of an age, they are also unquestionably moribund.

A further problem with Disraeli's novels is his presentation of women, who act solely as muses for the central, male character. Far from being fully rounded characters, Disraeli's fictional women are, at their worst, mere springboards to assist the ascent of the male hero. In *Sybil*, commonly adjudged to be Disraeli's major literary achievement and one of only three Disraeli novels named after a female character, the heroine is the embodiment of an idealised former era. She brings aid to the poor and she inspires Egremont, yet the brutality intended upon her reduces her role to that of a mere damsel in distress to be rescued. When an important female character does engage in action in Disraeli's novels, notably Theodora Campian spearheading a military campaign in *Lothair*, she is killed and thereby returned to the safer status of guide, protector and inspiration. Disraeli's novels also feature male characters stereotyped as gurus. Wise, male characters often pass on wisdom to the Disraelian hero: from a stranger in *Vivian Grey* through to Sidonia in the Young England trilogy, Baron Sergius in *Endymion* and a final stranger in *Falconet*, the enigmatic man furnishes the hero with principles for living. On one level, the instructive male and inspirational female characters in Disraeli's novels enact paternal and maternal roles respectively. Many Disraelian heroes are orphans or lack satisfactory parents; these roles are occupied by other characters within the text. In *Coningsby*, for example, Sidonia teaches the hero while Edith inspires him, while the closest thing he has to a parent, Lord Monmouth, is a figure who must be rejected on the grounds of his irresponsibility. In *The Young Duke*, father and daughter perform the parental roles from within the Dacre family. Much later, Lothair passes through three female figures of inspiration and a series of men who seek to teach him: his return to England and domesticity with Lady Corisande is his arrival in full, autonomous adulthood, in which he will no longer look upwards for guidance. Therefore, Disraeli's presentation of female figures cannot be seen simply as inadequate characterisation on his part. Instead, female characters, in common with male characters, enact a process of surrogate parenthood, in which their importance rests not so much on the composition of their individual personalities as the service they provide to the hero. They determine his learning curve and their status as characters is secondary to their basic narrative function.

With the notable exception of *Lothair*, sympathetic representations of Catholicism abound in Disraeli's novels. What appealed to Disraeli was the ritual of the Catholic Church, its historical longevity and its status as an outsider (Catholic Emancipation was only passed by Parliament in 1829). Disraeli, himself an outsider without a public school education or a university degree and (in his youth) a dandified, extravagant personality, championed Catholicism. Disraeli used the Church to signify a reliable and honourable past in opposition to a corrupt and unstable present. However, in the 1840s Catholicism was superseded in Disraeli's imagination by Judaism. He had already constructed a Jewish literary hero in the 1830s, Alroy, who had been brought down through losing his spiritual foundation. In the 1840s, Disraeli drew together a personal spiritual foundation rooted in Judaism. The victim of anti-Semitic jibes in *Punch*, Disraeli could not have escaped his Jewish ancestry even if he had wanted to. Instead, he employed and then empowered his Jewish heritage to claim superiority over his opponents. With the use of his fictional creations, most notably the character of Sidonia, Disraeli constructed an image of Judaism as a spiritually, intellectually and culturally fertile ethnicity which had survived exclusion from mainstream power structures. As Disraeli had projected aspects of his self-conception onto his perception of Catholicism, so, from the 1840s onwards, his own tenacity and ingenuity in the face of hostility (even his own party was reluctant to accept him as its leader in the House of Commons despite a lack of clear alternatives), was articulated imaginatively through his fictional representations of Jewish characters and the Jewish faith.

At various points in his life Disraeli presented his political ideas explicitly. In 1833 he produced his first political pamphlet, *What is He?*, in order to clarify a political position which had been muddied by his apparent electoral opportunism and the fame and subsequent infamy brought upon his reputation as a result of *Vivian Grey*. Almost forty years later he pledged the Conservative Party to a series of domestic and imperial principles, over the course of two important speeches at Manchester and Crystal Palace. However, these texts are not the unqualified expression of a personal philosophy, as they are tied inextricably to electoral politics and the pursuit of power. Disraeli was canvassing votes, and he used language to justify himself in the former instance, and his party's claim to government in the latter. Even his most comprehensive statement of political principles, *Vindication of the English Constitution* (1835), is the work of an aspiring politician, coloured by parliamentary ambition and the pursuit of public prominence. Disraeli's political prose, therefore, is more accurately read as part of what his character, Endymion, calls 'the great game'.

Paradoxically, Disraeli's literary works provide a more thorough record of his thoughts, beliefs and anxieties, and while some of these are purely personal, many relate to political principle or governmental practice. Thus it is in Disraeli's novels that we are best placed to evaluate Disraeli's political philosophy. His disdain for utilitarianism is evident in his early satires, and his appropriation of One Nation and the development thereof into a party political aspiration is expressed comprehensively through the Young England trilogy. His political novels are clearly linked to his political career and, like his non-fiction, the pursuit of power exerts a deterministic effect on his novels' content. However, the stranglehold on his material is noticeably less tight in Disraeli's fiction; central characters explore the world around them and have their beliefs shaped by experience and the guidance of significant others. Egremont's philosophical, spiritual and political position evolves, as does the Young Duke's, Coningsby's and Lothair's. Unlike his political prose, Disraeli's novels embrace uncertainty and engage with it. Moreover, Disraeli's writings, taken as a whole, enable us to trace and identify developments, changes and continuities in his thinking. The boisterous romantic heroes of his early novels give way to the more thoughtful and inquisitive central characters of the Young England trilogy, leading on finally to the passive and evaluative Lothair and Endymion. The adventurous wanderings of Vivian Grey, considered alongside the more deliberate (if ultimately no less adventurous) voyage of Tancred and the circular journey of Lothair, reveals the clear message that the England left behind is the most satisfactory resting place. In contrast, the exotic – represented by foreign spirituality and continental strife and war – is dangerous and ultimately jettisoned.

Disraeli's achievement as a novelist is difficult to assess. The novel became the dominant literary form of the nineteenth century yet, despite his substantial output as a writer, Disraeli is not considered amongst the foremost novelists of the Victorian age. Moreover, his books were not best-sellers in his own time until the publication of *Lothair*. Disraeli did not capture the plight of the poor as vividly as Dickens, he has left no novel with the visual detail and psychological accuracy of George Eliot's *Middlemarch*, he did not describe a waning rural existence with the rustic exactitude of Thomas Hardy. Nevertheless, his achievements as a novelist were considerable. In the 1820s, he found success within the popular genre of the novel of high society. His early novels were also confessional and Romantic, suggestive of the influence of Goethe and Byron. In the 1840s, he made a move which was as bold on a literary level as it was on a political one. The Young England trilogy advanced the political novel as a genre, bringing the machinations of government and the political parties to a new audience; the parliamentary prominence of their author enhanced their sense of verisimilitude. Furthermore, *Tancred* takes even greater risks, using foreign adventures and exotic landscapes to signify a character's pursuit of a truth which is as internal and psychological as it is political. More than twenty years later Disraeli demonstrated considerable skill in *Lothair* which has the appeal of a thriller or an espionage novel as the hero weaves his way through a plethora of influences, both benign and threatening. Following the evaluative *Endymion,* Disraeli was in the process of utilising the novel for polemic purposes once again in *Falconet*; sadly, it never moved beyond the early stages. Therefore, while Disraeli may not rank with the highest of nineteenth-century English novelists, he deserves a substantial place in the canon. The flaws in his writing are compensated for by the innovations he presents in his texts. *Sybil*, for example, blends empirical data with dramatized individual cases in a manner which both illuminates parliamentary findings and persuades through its close alignment with reality (this despite occasional weaknesses in the character portrayals). His ability to write successfully in different genres is remarkable, and *Tancred* shows a willingness to push at generic boundaries when it suited his purpose. Traces of Disraeli's influence can be found in Anthony Trollope's novels of parliamentary life, and in George Eliot's advocacy of the Jewish faith in *Daniel Deronda*. Disraeli is commonly and quite properly remembered for his impact on politics, but his achievements in literature should also merit close attention.

When Disraeli was an active politician, politics became more adversarial and Disraeli himself undoubtedly played a part in this. By turning on his own parliamentary leader in the House of Commons in the 1840s, Disraeli contributed to a change in the tone and substance of political life in Britain: during Disraeli's lifetime, it became the role of the opposition to oppose the government. Disraeli also realised how a single idea, patriotism, could serve party political ends. Indeed, the level of faith he invested in patriotism explains his extension of the electoral franchise in 1867 far more persuasively than any claim that Disraeli was a natural democrat. Disraeli thought that the population was instinctively patriotic, and he used this belief to align the Conservatives with faith in the monarchy and in the nation.

The perception of an alliance between conservatism and patriotism, forged by Disraeli, sustained the Conservative Party for many years after the 1870s. No other political party was able to rally to the Union Jack with such ease. Only now, with New Labour's unexpected and successful claims to the British middle classes in the late 1990s, has the Conservative Party lost some of its patriotic gloss. The England they purported to represent no longer existed. Disraeli's government of the mid-1870s also showed how politics and Parliament could be used to improve, however marginally, the welfare of the vast majority of the population, and not only those who were enfranchised, but also those who were, in terms of the ballot box, politically voiceless. In contrast, today's Tories cannot resort to such efforts. The vast majority of English people are not impoverished; children do not work in factories; there is not a large white working-class mass to appeal to.

Immigration, the effects of increased personal wealth, and living conditions, have all shifted the debate. Yet Disraeli's beliefs, born out of an era of imperialism and industrialisation, might still offer some significance and solutions to the problems posed by post-imperial, post-industrial Britain in the twenty-first century.

Indeed, Disraeli has never strayed far from the Conservative consciousness, given the extent to which his politicised concept of patriotism has influenced a number of the Conservative Party's subsequent leaders as noted by John Ramsden: 'some part of Salisburyite Conservatism's Second Jubilee jingoism, Bonar Law's exploiting of the Loyalist card in the 1910s, Churchill's playing to the imperial gallery in the 1930s and 1940s, and Margaret Thatcher's "Iron Lady" identity in the 1980s were all rooted in the character that Disraeli claimed for the Conservatives'.[4] More obviously, the One Nation group of Conservative MPs, formed in the 1950s, declared their indebtedness to Disraeli in their choice of name, and, in 2004, the prominent Shadow Cabinet member, Oliver Letwin is spearheading the Renewing One Nation campaign, demonstrating that the spirit of Disraeli is alive and well within Conservative ranks. With the numbers of people voting at elections declining at an alarming rate, a broad perception now exists that politicians are disconnected from the rest of us, encouraged perhaps by the celebrity approach to any sort of public pre-eminence the media affords. With these factors in mind it may be pertinent to recall the author of *Sybil* and his illustrations of the social consequences of economic policies, or the author of *The Young Duke*, who pointed out the ruinous implications of socially irresponsible living within the ruling classes, or the author of *Lothair* who sought to capture both the inspirational and violent aspects of revolutions. A number of Disraeli's ideas, espoused in his novels, have been overtaken by history, yet his emphasis on the importance of reciprocal social obligations may yet help to steer Conservative politics away from small-government individualism and into a more electorally viable position.

Glossary

There follows a list of a number of individuals named in the text with whom the reader may not be familiar. The primary source for the information is the *Dictionary of National Biography*.

Jeremy Bentham (1748–1832)   Bentham came from a Tory family. He is best known for his advocacy of utilitarianism, 'the greatest happiness of the greatest number.' In his writings he sought to encompass the disparate fields of ethics, jurisprudence, logic and political economy. He was active in prison reform and was opposed to the colonies. In 1823 he helped to establish the *Westminster Review*, parodied by Disraeli in *The Young Duke* as the *Screw and Lever Review*. A proponent of utility to the very last, he left his body to be dissected.

Francis Burdett (1770–1844)   A frequent correspondent of Bentham, Burdett held a seat in the House of Commons from 1796 to 1806, gradually moving towards the Tories. He was wounded in a duel in 1807, the year in which he also regained a seat in Parliament. In 1809 he was briefly incarcerated in the Tower of London for a breach of parliamentary privilege. He was again imprisoned briefly in 1820 after criticising the authorities, consequent upon the Peterloo massacre.

George Canning (1770–1827)   Canning was a Whig in his youth but converted to the Tories after the French Revolution of 1789. He entered the House of Commons in 1794, and from 1796 to 1809 held a variety of government posts, culminating in Foreign Minister. He was obliged to leave government after fighting a duel with Lord Castlereagh. Canning returned to the Foreign Office in 1822, and in 1827 became Prime Minister. However, his advocacy of Catholic Emancipation caused Tory defections, resulting in Canning forging an alliance with the Whigs. Moreover, his spell as Prime Minister was short lived, as he died on 8 August.

Thomas Carlyle (1795–1881)   Carlyle welcomed the Reform Bill as the first movement towards the destruction of the old order. A prolific writer and essayist, Carlyle published a number of hugely influential works in the 1830s and '40s, such as *Sartor Resartus* (1833–4), *The French Revolution* (1837), *Chartism* (1839) and *Past and Present* (1843). In December 1874 Disraeli offered him the Grand Order of the Bath and a pension: Carlyle declined.

William Cobbett (1762–1835)   Cobbett emigrated to America in 1792, having served with distinction in the British army. He became a factor in American politics as a pamphleteer, before returning to England in 1800 where his journalistic activities continued. In 1810 he was imprisoned for two years after writing an article on military flogging. He became the leading journalist for the movement for parliamentary reform, and subsequently obtained a seat for Oldham in the post-Reform Act House of Commons.

John Wilson Croker (1780–1857)   Disraeli and Croker met only three times, but there was no love lost between them. In his early twenties Croker published satires on Dublin and its literary life. Between 1809 and 1845 he was a regular contributor to the *Quarterly Review*. He sat intermittently in the House of Commons from 1806 to 1832. Initially a friend and supporter of Canning, he went on to become a close ally of Peel, until they fell out over reform of the Corn Laws. Croker was quite probably the first person to use the word Conservatives, instead of Tories, in a *Quarterly Review* article of January 1830. He was Disraeli's model for the character of Rigby in *Coningsby*.

Frederick William Faber (1814–1863)   While at Oxford, Faber became a devotee of Rev. John Henry (later Cardinal) Newman. In November 1845 Faber abjured Protestantism and was received into the Roman Catholic church. Faber published poems, hymns and spiritual works.

Felicia Hemans (1793–1835)   Hemans was a prolific writer who began publishing poetry in 1808. In 1812 she met Captain Alfred Hemans. They married and had five children before separating in 1818, never to meet again. In addition to poetry, Hemans wrote plays and contributed to magazines. Her reputation extended to America, where a collected edition of her poems was published in 1825.

Laetitia Elizabeth Landon (1802–1838)   Landon published poetry

201

under the name, 'L. E. L.' First published in 1820, she gained widespread attention with 'The Improvisatrice' (1824). Her writing supported her family, and scandal frequently surrounded her personal life. In 1838 she married George Maclean, governor of Cape Coast Castle. She arrived in Cape Coast in August 1838, but died in October, having taken prussic acid. It is not known whether her death arose from an overdose (accidental or deliberate) or foul play.

Chandos Leigh (1791–1850) A friend of Byron in his youth, Leigh was raised to the peerage in 1839 as Lord Leigh of Stoneleigh. His first published poem was 'The Island of Love' in 1812. He kept publishing poems until 1832.

Lord Melbourne (1779–1848) First returned to the House of Commons in 1806, Melbourne lost his seat in 1812 over his support for Catholic emancipation. He sat in the Commons again over the periods 1816–25, and from 1827–29. A supporter of Canning, he was against parliamentary reform. In 1829 he took his seat in the Lords. Appointed Home Secretary in 1830, he supported the Reform Bill because he thought it was an inevitability. He was Prime Minister in 1834 and again from 1835–41. He was personally opposed to Corn Law reform, yet advised peers not to oppose abolition of the Corn Laws in 1846.

Richard Monckton Milnes (1809–1885) In 1837 Milnes was elected Conservative M.P. for Pontefract. Like Disraeli, he expected but did not receive ministerial office from Peel in 1841. Milnes subsequently joined the Liberals over the issue of free trade. In 1863 he was created Baron Houghton of Great Houghton. In the Lords he supported reform of the franchise.

John Murray (1778–1843) Murray began running his own publishing firm in 1803. He met Byron in 1811; their business relationship persisted until the publication of *Don Juan*, when Murray's Tory sympathies brought about a separation. He was involved with Disraeli in *The Representative* fiasco. He went on to publish Disraeli's *Contarini Fleming* and *England and France; or, a cure for the ministerial Gallomania*.

Daniel O'Connell (1775–1847) Known as 'The Liberator,' having founded the Order of Liberators in 1826, O'Connell was one of the first Irish Catholics to practise at the bar, following the Catholic Relief Act of 1793. He took no part in the United Irishman uprising of 1798. He agitated for Catholic emancipation and was opposed to the Act of Union. However, he also opposed trades unionism. He was elected as an M.P. in 1828. Having mortally wounded an opponent in a duel in 1815, he was subsequently involved in challenges with both Peel and Disraeli, though duels were not fought on the latter two occasions. In 1844 he was convicted of conspiracy following a series of large-scale public meetings on repeal of the union with Britain. He served three months of a twelve-month sentence, after which his health declined.

Robert Peel (1788–1850)   Peel was elected to the House of Commons in 1809, becoming under-secretary for war and the colonies in 1810, and chief secretary for Ireland in 1811. While holding this office he challenged Daniel O'Connell to a duel in 1815, though it was never fought (Disraeli underwent a similar experience with O'Connell in 1835). In 1822 Peel joined the Home Office; in 1827 he left Canning's government over the issue of Catholic Emancipation. He was reinstated as Home Secretary in 1828, and went on to introduce the Catholic Emancipation Bill in 1829, the year in which he also created the Metropolitan Police. He spoke against the 1832 Reform Bill. He was Prime Minister from 1834–35, and again from 1841–46. Disraeli dedicated his 'Letters of Runnymede' to Peel, a collection of letters on current affairs which had been originally published in *The Times*. However, Disraeli opposed Peel on Corn Law reform in 1846 and was instrumental in his downfall.

Lionel De Rothschild (1808–1879)   The model for Sidonia in *Coningsby*, Lionel De Rothschild became chief manager of the Rothschild banking house in England in 1836. In 1847 he was elected as a Whig for the City of London but refused to take the parliamentary oath. He was not permitted to swear an allegiance in the Jewish form (i.e. on the Old Testament) until 1858. In 1876 he advanced money to Disraeli's government for the purchase of Suez Canal shares.

Robert Plumer Ward (1765–1846)   Between 1802 and 1823 Ward held a seat in Parliament. He was broadly loyal to Pitt. In 1825 he published *Tremaine,* a hugely successful portrait of the lives of the rich and famous which undoubtedly influenced Disraeli's first novel, *Vivian Grey*. He continued to publish, but never replicated the success of his first novel. His last work of any significance was *De Clifford; or, the Constant Man* (1841).

 *Notes*

Chapter One   The Young Man

1   *Benjamin Disraeli Letters Volume I: 1815–1834* (hereafter *Letters I*), ed. by J. A. W. Gunn and others (Toronto:University of Toronto Press, 1982), p. 447.
2   Disraeli Papers, Box 231, E/V/A/9/216.
3   Benjamin Disraeli, *Popanilla and Other Tales* (London: Peter Davies, 1927), p. v. Robert Blake describes 'A True Story' as 'a magazine article published in 1820, sometimes attributed to Disraeli'. See Robert Blake, *Disraeli* (London: Methuen, 1966, repr. 1969), p. 778.
4   Benjamin Disraeli and William George Meredith, *Rumpel Stiltskin* (Glasgow: Robert Maclehose and Co., 1952).
5   Disraeli Papers, Box 309/1, fols. 1–44.
6   Disraeli Papers, Box 231, E/V/A/1.
7   Benjamin Disraeli, *The Present State of Mexico: as detailed in a report presented to the General Congress, by the Secretary of State for the Home Department and Foreign Affairs, at the opening of the session in 1825* (London: John Murray, 1825). According to the editors of *Letters I*, *The Present State of Mexico* was only partly written by Disraeli. See *Letters I*, p. 29ff.
8   *Letters I*, p. 39.
9   Thom Braun, *Disraeli the Novelist* (London: George Allen and Unwin, 1981), p. 27.
10 See Jane Ridley, *The Young Disraeli* (London: Sinclair-Stevenson, 1995), pp. 38–9.
11 *Letters I*, p. 39.
12 *Benjamin Disraeli Letters: Volume Six, 1852–1856*, ed. by M. G. Wiebe and others (Toronto: University of Toronto Press, 1997), p. 342.
13 Benjamin Disraeli, *Vivian Grey* (London: Peter Davies, 1927).
14 Blake, *Disraeli*, p. 35.
15 See W. F. Monypenny and G. E. Buckle, *The Life of Benjamin Disraeli, Earl of Beaconsfield*, 6 vols (London: John Murray, 1910–20), 1: 83; see also B.

R. Jerman, *The Young Disraeli* (Princeton: Princeton University Press, 1960), p. 49.

16 Braun, *Disraeli the Novelist*, p. 31; Matthew Whiting Rosa, *The Silver-Fork School: Novels of Fashion Preceding* Vanity Fair (Port Washington, NY: Kennikat Press, 1964), p. 103.

17 See Ridley, *The Young Disraeli*, p. 45.

18 Ibid., p. 44.

19 Daniel Schwarz, *Disraeli's Fiction* (London: Macmillan, 1979), p. 11.

20 The *Blackwood's* reference is cited in, Rosa, *The Silver-Fork School*, p. 101; both are featured in Jerman, *The Young Disraeli*, p. 66.

21 Benjamin Disraeli, *The Dunciad of Today, a Satire and The Modern Aesop*, intro. By Michael Sadleir (London: Ingpen and Grant, 1928).

22 Benjamin Disraeli, *The Young Duke* (London: Peter Davies, 1927).

23 Disraeli contributed a further article to *The Court Journal* in 1831. See, *Letters I*, p. 114ff; p. 172ff.

24 *Letters I*, p. 113.

25 C. L. Cline, 'Unfinished Diary of Disraeli's Journey to Flanders and the Rhineland,' *University of Texas Studies in English (Austin)*, 23: 1943, p. 100; cited in, Ridley, *The Young Disraeli*, p. 29.

26 Blake, *Disraeli*, p. 58.

27 Benjamin Disraeli (with Baron de Haber), *England and France; or, a cure for the Ministerial Gallomania* (London: John Murray, 1832).

28 Disraeli published a number of non-fiction articles in the *New Monthly Magazine* in 1832 and 1833. See, *Letters I*, p. 208ff; p. 320ff.

29 Robert O'Kell, '*The Revolutionary Epick*: Tory Democracy or Radical Gallomania?', *Disraeli Newsletter* (2: Spring 1977), 24–42 (p. 25).

30 Monypenny and Buckle, *The Life of Benjamin Disraeli*, I: 218.

31 See Blake, *Disraeli*, p. 90.

32 Paul Smith, *Disraeli* (Cambridge: Cambridge University Press, 1996), p. 28.

33 Jerman states that, in *Contarini Fleming*, 'Disraeli wears no mask,' although, strictly speaking, there are some significant differences in the life circumstances of Disraeli and his fictional alter-ego: Contarini is Italian, upper class and well-connected politically. See Jerman, *The Young Disraeli*, p. 136.

34 Paul Smith, 'Disraeli's Politics,' in, *The Self-Fashioning of Disraeli* (Cambridge: Cambridge University Press, 1998), pp. 152–73 (p. 155).

35 O'Kell, '*The Revolutionary Epick*: Tory Democracy or Radical Gallomania?', p. 25.

36 *Letters I*, p. 447.

37 Smith, *Disraeli*, p. 15.

38 *Letters I*, p. 323.

39 Benjamin Disraeli, *Alroy* (London: Peter Davies, 1927).

40 Schwarz, *Disraeli's Fiction*, p. 42.

41 *Letters I*, p. 447.

42 Schwarz, *Disraeli's Fiction*, p. 47.

43 *Letters I*, p. 445.

44   Monypenny and Buckle, *The Life of Benjamin Disraeli*, I: 200.

45   Benjamin Disraeli, 'What is He?', in, *Whigs and Whiggism: Political Writings by Benjamin Disraeli*, ed. By William Hutcheon (London: John Murray, 1913), pp. 16–22.

46   Disraeli also published a non-fiction article in the *Court Magazine* in January 1834. See *Letters I*, p. 250ff. In addition, Disraeli published twice more in 1833, producing 'Pilgrimage to the Holy Sepulchre' for *The Amulet*, and *Velvet Lawn: A Sketch Written for the Benefit of the Buckinghamshire Infirmary*. See, *Letters I*, p. 214,ff; p. 365,ff.

47   Benjamin and Sarah Disraeli, *A Year at Hartlebury: Or, The Election* (London: John Murray, 1983).

48   John Matthews, 'Appendix I: Cherry and Fair Star,' in, Benjamin and Sarah Disraeli, *A Year at Hartlebury*, p. 203.

49   Ibid., pp. 206–7.

50   *Letters I*, p. 446.

51   John Matthews, 'Appendix II: New light on Disraeli's early politics,' in, Benjamin and Sarah Disraeli, *A Year at Hartlebury*, p. 214.

52   See Jerman, *The Young Disraeli*, pp. 251–2.

53   Sections of the review in question are quoted in Matthews, 'Cherry and Fair Star,' p. 207–8.

54   Benjamin Disraeli, *The Revolutionary Epick* (London: Edward Moxon, 1834).

55   *Letters I*, p. 380.

56   Henry Layard, cited in, Jerman, *The Young Disraeli*, p. 220.

57   *Letters I*, p. 380.

58   See, Blake, *Disraeli*, p. 114; see also, Jerman, *The Young Disraeli*, p. 231.

59   Benjamin Disraeli, 'The Crisis Examined,' in, *Whigs and Whiggism*, 23–41 (p. 32).

60   Benjamin Disraeli, 'Vindication of the English Constitution,' in, *Whigs and Whiggism*, pp. 111–232.

61   Philip Davis, *The Oxford English Literary History, Volume 8, 1830–1880: The Victorians* (Oxford: Oxford University Press, 2002), p. 273.

62   Benjamin Disraeli, *Henrietta Temple: A Love Story* (London: Peter Davies, 1927).

63   Blake, *Disraeli*, p. 143.

64   Jerman, *The Young Disraeli*, p. 287; Smith, *Disraeli*, p. 35.

65   Benjamin Disraeli, *Venetia* (London: Peter Davies, 1927).

66   *Letters I*, p. 447.

67   Benjamin Disraeli, *The Tragedy of Count Alarcos* (London: Henry Colburn, 1839).

68   Monypenny and Buckle, *The Life of Benjamin Disraeli*, II: 38.

69   Ibid., II: 66.

70   John K. Walton, *Disraeli* (London: Routledge, 1990, repr. 1999), p. 18; see also Schwarz, *Disraeli's Fiction*, p. 13.

71   *Letters I*, p. 447.

Chapter Two   The Young Englander

1   See Benjamin Disraeli, *Vivian Grey* (London: Peter Davies, 1927), pp. ix–xx.

2   Benjamin Disraeli, *Coningsby: or, the New Generation* (London: Peter Davies, 1927).

3   Robert Blake, *Disraeli* (London: Methuen, 1966, repr. 1969), p. 190. Isaiah Berlin also refers to Disraeli as, 'the inventor of the political novel,' see Isaiah Berlin, 'Benjamin Disraeli, Karl Marx and the Search for Identity,' in, *Against the Grain: Essays in the History of Ideas* (London: Pimlico, 1997), pp. 252–86 (pp. 263–4). Stanley Weintraub refers to *Coningsby* as 'the first significant political novel in England'. Stanley Weintraub, *Disraeli* (London: Hamish Hamilton, 1993), p. 219.

4   See, Christopher Harvie, *The Centre of Things: Political Fiction in Britain from Disraeli to the Present* (London: Unwin Hyman, 1991), p. 33.

5   Kathleen Tillotson, *Novels of the Eighteen-Forties* (London: Oxford University Press, 1961), p. 73.

6   Philip Davis, *The Oxford English Literary History, Volume 8, 1830–1880: The Victorians* (Oxford: Oxford University Press, 2002), p. 276.

7   Cited in, Blake, *Disraeli*, p. 193.

8   Weintraub, *Disraeli*, p. 219.

9   See, ibid., pp. 233–4.

10   The Oxford Movement was formed around 1833 by a group of Oxford scholars and clergymen. They attacked religious indifference: 'they believed that a revival of the doctrine of apostolical succession would reawaken the clergy to the significance of their church'. They also believed in the importance of ceremony. Their leading figure, Newman, joined the Catholic church in 1845. See Sir Llewellyn Woodward, *The Oxford History of England: The Age of Reform 1815–1870*, 2nd edn (Oxford: Oxford University Press, 1962, repr. 1997), pp. 512–20 (p. 515).

11   See, Blake, *Disraeli*, p. 172.

12   Weintraub suggests that Coningsby resembles John Evelyn (a Young England supporter and a future Conservative MP) morally and politically, and Lord John Manners physically, but this is not the majority opinion. He also describes Coningsby as, 'a daydream Disraeli in Smythe's clothes'. See Weintraub, *Disraeli*, pp. 211–12. The claim for Oswald Millbank being based upon Walters is made by Alice Chandler, *A Dream of Order: The Medieval Ideal in Nineteenth-Century English Literature* (London: Routledge and Kegan Paul, 1971), p. 169.

13   See Harvie, *The Centre of Things*, p. 40.

14   Weintraub, *Disraeli*, pp. 232–3.

15   *Benjamin Disraeli Letters Volume IV, 1842–1847* (hereafter *Letters IV*), ed. by Mel Wiebe and others (Toronto: University of Toronto Press, 1989), p. 27.

16   Louis J. Jennings, *Memories of John Wilson Croker*, 3 vols (1884), cited in Blake, *Disraeli*, p. 177.

17   Blake, *Disraeli*, p. 171.

18 Karl Marx and Friedrich Engels, *The Communist Manifesto*, trans. By Samuel Moore (London: Penguin, 1967, repr. 1985), p. 107.

19 Cited in Richard Faber, *Young England* (London: Faber and Faber, 1987), p. 80.

20 Cited in Kevin L. Morris, *The Image of the Middle Ages in Romantic and Victorian Literature* (London: Croom Helm, 1984), p. 121.

21 Faber, *Young England*, p. 97 & 184.

22 See ibid., p. 121.

23 *Letters IV*, p. 31.

24 Norman Gash, *The Life of Sir Robert Peel after 1830* (London: Longman, 1986), pp. 93–9.

25 Blake, *Disraeli*, p. 202. Baron Lionel de Rothschild was almost certainly part of the inspiration for Sidonia. See, *Letters IV*, p. 123 & ff.

26 Blake, *Disraeli*, p. 203.

27 Disraeli Papers, Box 30, B/II/1.

28 William Makepeace Thackeray, 'Codlingsby,' *in Burlesques from Cornhill to Grand Cairo and Juvenalia* (London: Macmillan, 1903), p. 163.

29 Blake, *Disraeli*, p. 203.

30 Faber, *Young England*, p. 192.

31 Benjamin Disraeli, *Sybil: or, the Two Nations* (London: Peter Davies, 1927).

32 The figures are taken from Sheila M. Smith, *The Other Nation: The Poor in English Novels of the 1840s* (Oxford: Clarendon Press, 1980), p. 5. See also p. 7.

33 Cited in Tillotson, *Novels of the Eighteen Forties*, p. 82.

34 Cited in Weintraub, *Disraeli*, p. 221.

35 See Blake, *Disraeli*, pp. 191–2, 194.

36 Cited in Chandler, *A Dream of Order*, p. 178.

37 The idea that *Sybil* begins as a fashionable novel is mentioned in, Richard Cronin, *Romantic Victorians: English Literature, 1824–1840* (Basingstoke: Palgrave, 2002), p. 130.

38 Blake, *Disraeli*, p. 201.

39 Cited in ibid., p. 556.

40 Tillotson, *Novels of the Eighteen-Forties*, p. 81.

41 Arthur Pollard, 'Disraeli: Politician as Novelist,' *Disraeli Newsletter* (3: Spring, 1978), pp. 5–18 (p. 13).

42 See Faber, *Young England*, p. 88.

43 See Smith, *The Other Nation*, p. 230.

44 *Hansard*, 3rd series, lxxix, 562.

45 Smith, *The Other Nation*, p. 184.

46 Ibid., p. 81.

47 *Hansard*, 3rd series, lxxxiii, 1347.

48 Frederick Engels, *The Condition of the Working Class in England* (London: Grafton, 1969, repr. 1986), pp. 55, 58, 109, 287 & 290.

49 Marx and Engels, *The Communist Manifesto*, pp. 80–2, 106–7.

50 Benjamin Disraeli, *Tancred* (London: Peter Davies, 1927).

51 Daniel R. Schwarz argues that a number of contemporaneous texts share significant features with *Tancred*, stating that Disraeli's novel, 'is a fictional version of the Victorian spiritual autobiography, epitomized by Newman's *Apologia*, Carlyle's *Sartor Resartus* and Tennyson's *In Memoriam*. Along with *Tancred*, several examples of the genre were published within a few years, including Charles Kingsley's *Yeast* (1848), James Anthony Froude's *Shadows of the Clouds* (1847), and Newman's *Loss and Gain* (1848)'. See Daniel R. Schwarz, 'Disraeli's romanticism: self-fashioning in the novels,' in, Charles Richmond and Paul Smith, ed., *The Self-Fashioning of Disraeli 1818–1851* (Cambridge: Cambridge University Press, 1998), pp. 42–65 (pp. 60–1).

52 Clyde J. Lewis, 'Theory and Expediency in the Policy of Disraeli,' *Victorian Studies* (4: 1961), pp. 237–58 (p. 244).

53 See J. M. Golby and A. W. Purdue, *The Civilisation of the Crowd: Popular Culture in England 1750–1900* (London: Batsford, 1984). See also, Peter Bailey, *Leisure and Class in Victorian England: Rational Recreation and the Contest for Control, 1830–1885* (London: Routledge and Kegan Paul, 1978).

54 *Hansard*, 3rd series, xcv, 1330.

55 *Benjamin Disraeli Letters, Volume III, 1838–1841*, ed. By M. G. Wiebe and others (Toronto: University of Toronto Press, 1987), p. 356.

56 Faber, *Young England*, p. 201.

57 Weintraub, *Disraeli*: 'Disraeli used *Syrian* almost interchangeably with *Hebrew*' (p. 231).

58 See for example Blake, *Disraeli*, p. 191.

59 Blake, *Disraeli*, p. 455.

60 It took Disraeli some time to get accepted as a member of Crockford's, probably owing to his Jewish origins. See Michael Flavin, *Gambling in the Nineteenth-Century English Novel: 'A Leprosy is o'er the Land'* (Brighton and Portland: Sussex Academic Press, 2003), p. 73.

61 Blake, *Disraeli*, p. 210.

62 Smith, *The Other Nation*, p. 6.

63 Tillotson, *Novels of the Eighteen-Forties*, p. 88.

64 Benjamin Disraeli, *Lord George Bentinck* (London: Colburn, 1852).

65 *Hansard*, 3rd series, lxxxiii, 1341: 'the 'Territorial Constitution . . . will always secure the investment of capital in the soil of England'.

66 *Benjamin Disraeli Letters, Volume V, 1848–1851*, ed. By Mel Wiebe and others (Toronto: University of Toronto Press, 1993), p. 118.

67 *Hansard*, 3rd series, lxxviii, 1028.

68 *Hansard*, 3rd series, lxxix, 565.

69 See Christine Bolt, *Victorian Attitudes to Race* (London: Routledge and Kegan Paul, 1971), p. 9.

70 Cited in Paul Smith, *Transactions of the Royal Historical Society*, fifth series (37: 1987), pp. 65–85 (p. 83ff). See also George Watson, *The English Ideology: Studies in the Language of Victorian Politics* (London: Allen Lane, 1973), p. 130.

71 Cited in Ann Pottinger Saab, 'Disraeli, Judaism and the Eastern Question,' *The International History Review* (10: 1988), pp. 559–78 (p. 565).

72 The commentary on Milnes's article is taken from, Morris, *The Image of the Middle Ages in Romantic and Victorian Literature*, p. 126. See also *Edinburgh Review* (86: 1847), pp. 138–55.

73 Lewis, 'Theory and Expediency in the Policy of Disraeli,' p. 242.

74 On the subject of Disraeli's political manoeuvrings, Charles Richmond has written, 'Disraeli revered historical examples and traditions; but he did not scruple to commit any act which broke with precept and ensured survival in the future'. See 'Disraeli's Education,' in, Richmond and Smith, ed., *The Self-Fashioning of Disraeli*, pp. 16–41 (p. 30).

75 Robert Blake argues that *Tancred* has more in common with *Lord George Bentinck* than with the first two books of the trilogy, largely because *Tancred* and *Lord George Bentinck* both present at length Disraeli's views on race and religion. However, *Lord George Bentinck* also considers (in far less detail, admittedly) the kind of ideal modes of commerce illustrated by Millbank in *Coningsby* and Trafford in *Sybil*.

76 Cited in Flavin, *Gambling in the Nineteenth-Century English Novel*, p. 73.

77 Paul Smith, 'Disraeli's Politics,' in *The Self-Fashioning of Disraeli*, p. 167.

Chapter Three **The Elder Statesman**

 1 The legislation is summarised in section 3 of chapter 22 of, Robert Blake, *Disraeli* (London: Methuen, 1966, repr. 1969), pp. 494–503.

 2 See Ian Gilmour, *Inside Right: A Study of Conservatism* (London: Hutchinson, 1977), p. 82.

 3 Edgar Feuchtwanger, *Disraeli* (London: Arnold, 2000), p. 143.

 4 Catherine Hall, Keith McClelland and Jane Rendall, *Defining the Victorian Nation: Class, Race, Gender and the Reform Act of 1867* (Cambridge: Cambridge University Press, 2000), p. 4.

 5 *Hansard*, 3rd series, clxxxiii, 99.

 6 Paul Adelman, *Gladstone, Disraeli and Later Victorian Politics* (London: Longman, 1970, repr. 1976), p. 12.

 7 Cited in Donald Read, *England 1868–1914: The Age of Urban Democracy* (London: Longman, 1979), p. 150.

 8 Benjamin Disraeli, *Lothair* (London: Peter Davies, 1927).

 9 Blake, *Disraeli*, p. 519.

10 Daniel R. Schwarz, *Disraeli's Fiction* (London: Macmillan, 1979), p. 128.

11 W. F. Monypenny and G. E. Buckle, *The Life of Benjamin Disraeli, Earl of Beaconsfield: Volume V, 1868–1876* (London: John Murray, 1920), p. 155. See also Stanley Weintraub, *Disraeli* (London: Hamish Hamilton, 1993), p. 481.

12 Buckle believed that the character of Grandison may have owed something to Bishop Wiseman, who also provided the inspiration for the eponymous religious hypocrite in Robert Browning's dramatic monologue, 'Bishop Blougram's Apology' (1855). See Buckle, *The Life of Benjamin Disraeli, Earl of Beaconsfield: Volume V*, p. 152.

13 Weintraub contends that Phoebus is based on the society painter, Frederic Leighton. See Weintraub, *Disraeli*, p. 486.

14 See Blake, *Disraeli*, p. 517.

15 See ibid., p. 602.

16 See ibid., pp. 505–6.

17 Ibid., p. 524.

18 T. E. Kebbel (ed.), *Selected Speeches of the Late Right Honourable the Earl of Beaconsfield,* 2 vols. (London: Longmans, Green, and Co., 1882), II: 494, 525.

19 Paul Smith, *Disraeli: A Brief Life* (Cambridge: Cambridge University Press, 1996), p. 164.

20 It has recently been argued that the pressure to bestow an imperial title upon Victoria came from the Queen herself. See Feuchtwanger, *Disraeli*, p. 177. This point has also been made by Bruce Coleman, *Conservatism and the Conservative Party in Nineteenth-Century Britain* (London: Edward Arnold, 1988), p. 151.

21 Sarah Bradford, *Disraeli* (London: Wiedenfeld and Nicolson, 1982), p. 287.

22 Schwarz explains Disraeli's naming of the Mary-Anne societies in *Lothair* thus: 'Lothair's devotion to the person who inspired the Mary Anne societies is a touching tribute that Disraeli pays to his wife, Mary Anne, and to their mutual romantic love which he believed had sustained him throughout his political career'. See *Disraeli's Fiction*, p. 129.

23 Thom Braun, *Disraeli the Novelist* (London: George Allen and Unwin, 1981), p. 135.

24 See Michael Ragussis, *Figures of Conversion: 'The Jewish Question' & English National Identity* (Durham, CT: Duke University Press, 1995), pp. 214, 225. The influence of Matthew Arnold on *Lothair* has also been considered by Patrick Brantlinger in 'Disraeli and orientalism,' in, Paul Smith and Charles Richmond, ed., *The Self-Fashioning of Disraeli, 1818–1851* (Cambridge: Cambridge University Press, 1998, pp. 90–105 (p. 102).

25 Matthew Arnold, *Culture and Anarchy* (Cambridge: Cambridge University Press, 1932, repr. 1988), pp. 130, 132, 141.

26 Blake, *Disraeli*, pp. 518–9.

27 Schwarz, *Disraeli's Fiction*, p. 134.

28 Kebbel, *Selected Speeches of the Late Right Honourable the Earl of Beaconsfield,* II: 51–2.

29 See Smith, *Disraeli*, p. 178.

30 Paul Smith, *Disraelian Conservatism and Social Reform* (London: Routledge and Kegan Paul, 1967), p. 215.

31 Robert Gildea argues that Disraeli's government undertook industrial relations legislation, 'to ensure that organized labour did not capitulate to extreme views'. See Robert Gildea, *Barricades and Borders: Europe 1800–1914* (Oxford: Oxford University Press, 1987, repr. 1991), p. 231.

32 Blake, *Disraeli*, p. 553.

33 E. J. Feuchtwanger has argued that Disraeli would have won a further term

in office, had he gone to the country immediately after Berlin. See E. J. Feuchtwanger, *Disraeli, Democracy and the Tory Party* (Oxford: Clarendon Press, 1968), p. 23.

34 Smith, *Disraeli*, p. 196.
35 Smith, *Disraelian Conservatism and Social Reform*, p. 265.
36 Feuchtwanger, *Disraeli*, p. 172.
37 Adelman, *Gladstone, Disraeli and Later Victorian Politics*, p. 18.
38 Blake, *Disraeli*, p. 556.
39 Richard Shannon, *The Age of Disraeli, 1868–1881: the Rise of Tory Democracy* (London: Longman, 1992), p. 333.
40 See K. Theodore Hoppen, *The Mid-Victorian Generation, 1846–1886* (Oxford: Clarendon Press, 1998), p. 635.
41 Benjamin Disraeli, *Endymion and Falconet* (London: Peter Davies, 1927).
42 Schwarz, *Disraeli's Fiction*, p. 146.
43 According to Bradford, 'Disraeli himself told the Queen that he had drawn upon features of Lady Palmerston in her youth "for his character of Berengaria, & some traits of devotion drawn from someone else", by which he intended Mary Anne'. *Disraeli*, p. 380.
44 See Braun, *Disraeli the Novelist*, pp. 141–2.
45 Blake, *Disraeli*, p. 766.
46 Ibid., p. 190.
47 W. F. Monypenny and G. E. Buckle, *The Life of Benjamin Disraeli, Earl of Beaconsfield: Volume VI, 1876–1881* (London: John Murray, 1920), p. 562.
48 Feuchtwanger, *Disraeli*, p. 206.
49 See Blake, *Disraeli*, p. 487.
50 See Ragussis, *Figures of Conversion*, pp. 205–11. Paul Smith has noted 'the appearance of so-called modern political anti-semitism across Europe at the end of the 1870s'. See Smith, *Disraeli*, p. 202.
51 See Smith, *Disraeli*, p. 189.
52 George Watson, *The English Ideology: Studies in the Language of Victorian Politics* (London: Allen Lane, 1973), p. 129.
53 Schwarz, *Disraeli's Fiction*, p. 126.
54 See Braun, *Disraeli the Novelist*, p. 137.

Conclusion 'Gradation is the Spell of Nature's Sway'

1 F. M. L. Thompson, *English Landed Society in the Nineteenth Century* (London: Routledge and Kegan Paul, 1962), p. 295.
2 Cited in, David Cannadine, *The Decline and Fall of the British Aristocracy* (London: Macmillan, 1992), p. 386.
3 Michael Ragussis, *Figures of Conversion: 'The Jewish Question' and English National Identity* (Durham, CT: Duke University Press, 1995), pp. 211–12.
4 John Ramsden, *An Appetite for Power: A History of the Conservative Party since 1830* (London: HarperCollins, 1998), p. 117.

Bibliography

Primary Texts

Disraeli, Benjamin, *An Inquiry into the Plans, Progress, and Policy of the American Mining Companies* (London: John Murray, 1825).

____, *Lawyers and Legislators: or, Notes on the American Mining Companies* (London: John Murray, 1825).

____, *The Present State of Mexico: as detailed in a report presented to the General Congress, by the Secretary of State for the Home Department and Foreign Affairs, at the opening of the session in 1825* (London: John Murray, 1825).

____, (with Baron de Haber), *England and France; or, a cure for the ministerial Gallomania* (London: John Murray, 1832).

____, *The Revolutionary Epick* (London: Edward Moxon, 1834).

____, *The Tragedy of Count Alarcos* (London: Henry Colburn, 1839).

____, *Lord George Bentinck: A Political Biography* (London: Colburn and Co., 1852).

____, *Selected Speeches of the Late Right Honourable the Earl of Beaconsfield*, ed. by T. E. Kebbel, 2 vols (London: Longmans, Green and Co.), 1882.

____, *Whigs and Whiggism: Political Writings*, ed. by William Hutcheon (London: John Murray, 1913).

____, *The Bradenham Edition of the Novels and Tales of Benjamin Disraeli, 1st Earl of Beaconsfield*, 12 vols. (London: Peter Davies, 1926–7).

____, *The Dunciad of Today and The Modern Aesop*, int. by Michael Sadleir (London: Ingpen and Grant, 1928).

____, and William George Meredith, *Rumpel Stiltskin* (Glasgow: Robert Maclehose, 1952).

____, and Disraeli, Sarah, *A Year at Hartlebury: or, The Election* (London: John Murray, 1983).

Secondary Texts

Berlin, Isaiah, 'Benjamin Disraeli, Karl Marx and the Search for Identity', in, *Against the Current: Essays in the History of Ideas* (London: Pimlico, 1997), pp. 252–86.

Blake, Robert, *Disraeli* (London: Methuen, 1969, repr. 1978).

____, *Disraeli's Grand Tour: Benjamin Disraeli and the Holy Land 1830–31* (London: Weidenfeld and Nicolson, 1982).

Bloomfield, Paul, *Disraeli* (London: Longman, Green and Co., 1961).

Bradford, Sarah, *Disraeli* (London: Weidenfeld and Nicolson, 1982).

Braun, Thom, *Disraeli the Novelist* (London: George Allen and Unwin, 1981).

Burton, Wendy E., 'The Composition of Vivian Grey', *Disraeli Newsletter* (2: Fall 1977, 30–46).

Eldridge, C. C., *Disraeli and the Rise of a New Imperialism* (Cardiff: University of Wales Press, 1996).

Endelman, Todd M., 'Disraeli's Jewishness Reconsidered', *Modern Judaism* (5: 1985), pp. 109–23.

____, and Tony Kushner (ed.), *Disraeli's Jewishness* (London: Vallentine Mitchell, 2002).

Feuchtwanger, E. J., *Disraeli, Democracy and the Tory Party* (Oxford: Clarendon Press, 1968).

____, *Disraeli* (London: Arnold, 2000).

Froude, J. A., *Lord Beaconsfield* (London: Sampson Low, Marston, Searle and Rivington, 1890).

Ghosh, P. R., 'Disraelian Conservatism: a financial approach', *English Historical Review*, (99: 1984), 268–96.

Gilham, Abraham, 'Benjamin Disraeli and the Emancipation of the Jews', *Disraeli Newsletter* (5: Spring 1980, 26–46).

Gunn, J. A. W., and others, eds, *Benjamin Disraeli Letters*, 6 vols (Toronto: Toronto University Press, 1982–1997).

Jenkins, T. A., *Disraeli and Victorian Conservatism* (Basingstoke: Macmillan, 1996).

Jerman, B. R., *The Young Disraeli* (Princeton: Princeton University Press, 1960).

Keveson Hertz, B., '"Clubs": A Discussion of Chapter XIII expurgated from Second and Subsequent editions of *The Voyage of Captain Popanilla*, by Benjamin Disraeli', *Disraeli Newsletter* (3: Fall 1978), 3–7.

Lewis, Clyde J., 'Theory and Expediency in the Policy of Disraeli', *Victorian Studies* (4: 1961), 237–58.

Machin, Ian, *Disraeli* (London: Longman, 1995).

Merritt, James D., 'The Novelist St Barbe in Disraeli's *Endymion*: Revenge on Whom?', *Nineteenth-Century Fiction* (23: 1968), pp. 85–7.

Monypenny, W. F. and G. E. Buckle, *The Life of Benjamin Disraeli, Earl of Beaconsfield*, 6 vols. (London: John Murray, 1910–20).

O'Kell, Robert, 'Ixion in Heaven: The Representative Hero', *Disraeli Newsletter* (1: Spring 1976), 14–26.

____, 'The Revolutionary Epick: Tory Democracy or Radical Gallomania?', *Disraeli Newsletter* (2: Spring 1977), 24–42.

Pearson, Hesketh, *Dizzy: The Life And Nature of Benjamin Disraeli, Earl of Beaconsfield* (London: Methuen, 1951).

Pollard, Arthur, 'Disraeli: Politician as Novelist', *Disraeli Newsletter* (3: Spring 1978), 5–18.

Bibliography

Richmond, Charles and Paul Smith, Ed., *The Self-Fashioning of Disraeli 1818–1851* (Cambridge: Cambridge University Press, 1998).

Ridley, Jane, *The Young Disraeli* (London: Sinclair-Stevenson, 1995).

Saab, Ann Pottinger, 'Disraeli, Judaism and the Eastern Question', *The International History Review* (10: 1988), 559–78.

Schwarz, Daniel R., *Disraeli's Fiction* (London: Macmillan, 1979).

Selzer, Michael, 'Benjamin Disraeli's Knowledge of his Ancestry', *Disraeli Newsletter* (1: Fall 1976), 8–17.

Smith, Paul, *Disraelian Conservatism and Social Reform* (London: Routledge and Kegan Paul, 1967).

___, 'Disraeli's Politics', *Transactions of the Royal Historical Society* (37:1987), 65–85.

___, *Disraeli: A Brief Life* (Cambridge: Cambridge University Press, 1996).

Vincent, John, *Disraeli* (Oxford: Oxford University Press, 1990).

Walton, John K., *Disraeli* (London: Routledge, 1990).

Weintraub, Stanley, *Disraeli* (London: Hamish Hamilton, 1993).

Wohl, Anthony S., '"Dizzi-Ben-Dizzi": Disraeli as Alien', *Journal of British Studies* (34: 1995), 375–411.

Background Material

Adelman, Paul, *Gladstone, Disraeli and Later Victorian Politics* (London: Longman, 1970).

Arnold, Matthew, *Culture and Anarchy* (Cambridge: Cambridge University Press, 1932, repr. 1988).

Bailey, Peter, *Leisure and Class in Victorian England: Rational Recreation and the Contest for Control, 1830–1885* (London: Routledge and Kegan Paul, 1978).

Beales, H. L., *The Early English Socialists* (London: Hamish Hamilton, 1933).

Belchem, John, *Industrialization and the Working Class: The English Experience, 1750–1900* (Aldershot: Scolar, 1991).

Blake, Robert, *The Conservative Party from Peel to Major* (London: Heinemann, 1997).

Bolt, Christine, *Victorian Attitudes to Race* (London: Routledge and Kegan Paul, 1971).

Brantlinger, Patrick, *The Spirit of Reform: British Literature and Politics, 1832–1867* (Cambridge, MA: Harvard University Press, 1977).

___, 'Nations and Novels: Disraeli, George Eliot, and Orientalism', *Victorian Studies* (35: 1992), 255–76.

Butler, Lord, ed., *The Conservatives: A History from their Origins to 1965* (London: George Allen and Unwin, 1977).

Cannadine, David, *The Decline and Fall of the British Aristocracy* (London: Macmillan, 1996).

Cazamian, Louis, *The Social Novel in England 1830–1850*, trans. Martin Fido (London: Routledge and Kegan Paul, 1973).

215

Chandler, Alice, *A Dream of Order: The Medieval Ideal in Nineteenth-Century English Literature* (London: Routledge and Kegan Paul, 1971).

Coleman, Bruce, *Conservatism and the Conservative Party in Nineteenth-Century Britain* (London: Edward Arnold, 1988).

Collini, Stefan, *Public Moralists: Political Thought and Intellectual Life in Britain, 1850–1930* (Oxford: Clarendon Press, 1991, repr. 1993).

Cronin, Richard, *Romantic Victorians: English Literature, 1824–1840* (Basingstoke: Palgrave, 2002).

Davis, Philip, *The Oxford English Literary History, Volume 8, 1830–1880: The Victorians* (Oxford: Oxford University Press, 2002).

Engels, Friedrich, *The Condition of the Working Class in England* (Oxford: Oxford University Press, 1993).

Ensor, Sir Robert, *The Oxford History of England 1870–1914* (Oxford: Oxford University Press, 1936, repr. 1992).

Faber, Richard, *Young England* (London: Faber and Faber, 1987).

Ford, Boris, ed., *The New Pelican Guide to English Literature Volume 6: From Dickens to Hardy*, rev edn (London: Penguin, 1982, repr. 1996).

Fulford, Roger, ed., *The Greville Memoirs*, rev. edn (London: Batsford, 1963).

Gash, Norman, *Sir Robert Peel; The Life of Sir Robert Peel after 1830* (London: Longman, 1972, rev edn, 1986).

Gildea, Robert, *Barricades and Borders: Europe 1800–1914* (Oxford: Oxford University Press, 1987, repr. 1991).

Gilmore, Robin, *The Novel in the Victorian Age* (London: Edward Arnold, 1986).

Gilmour, Ian, *Inside Right* (London: Hutchinson, 1977).

Golby, J. M. and A. W. Purdue, *The Civilisation of the Crowd: Popular Culture in England 1750–1900* (London: Batsford, 1984).

Golby, J. M., ed., *Culture and Society in Britain 1850–1890* (Oxford: Oxford University Press, 1986).

Guy, Josephine M., *The Victorian Social-Problem Novel* (Basingtoke: Macmillan, 1996).

_____, ed., *The Victorian Age: An Anthology of Sources and Documents* (London: Routledge, 1998).

Hall, Catherine et al., *Defining the Victorian Nation: Class, Race, Gender and the British Reform Act of 1867* (Cambridge: Cambridge University Press, 2000).

Harvie, Christopher, *The Centre of Things: Political Fiction in Britain from Disraeli to the Present* (London: Unwin Hyman, 1991).

Hewitt, Martin, ed., *An Age of Equipoise?: Reassessing Mid-Victorian Britain* (Aldershot: Ashgate, 2000).

Himmelfarb, Gertrude, *Poverty and Compassion: The Moral Imagination of the Late Victorians* (New York: Alfred A. Knopf, 1991).

Hobsbawm, E. J., *Industry and Empire: from 1750 to the Present Day* (Harmondsworth: Penguin, 1968, repr. 1981).

Hoppen, K. Theodore, *The Mid-Victorian Generation: 1846–1886* (Oxford: Clarendon Press, 1998).

Kitson Clark, G., *The Making of Victorian England* (London: Methuen, 1962, repr. 1965).

Bibliography

Lee, Stephen J., *Aspects of British Political History, 1815–1914* (London: Routledge, 1994, repr. 1996).

Lerner, Laurence, ed., *The Context of English Literature: The Victorians* (London: Methuen, 1978).

Marx, Karl and Friedrich Engels, *The Communist Manifesto*, trans. By Samuel Moore (London: Penguin, 1967, repr. 1985).

Mayer, Annette, *The Growth of Democracy in Britain* (London: Hodder and Stoughton, 1999).

Morris, Kevin L., *The Image of the Middle Ages in Romantic and Victorian Literature* (London: Croom Helm, 1984).

Plamenatz, John, *The English Utilitarians* (Oxford: Blackwell, 1966).

Quinlan, Maurice J., *Victorian Prelude: A History of English Manners 1700–1830* (Hamden, CT: Archon, 1965).

Ragussis, Michael, *Figures of Conversion: 'The Jewish Question' and English National Identity* (Durham: Duke University Press, 1995).

Ramsden, John, *An Appetite for Power: A History of the Conservative Party since 1830* (London: Harper Collins, 1999).

Read, Donald, *England 1868–1914: The Age of Urban Democracy* (London: Longman, 1979).

Roberts, David, *Victorian Origins of the British Welfare State* (New Haven: Yale University Press), 1960.

Rosa, Matthew Whiting, *The Silver-Fork School: Novels of Fashion Preceding Vanity Fair* (Port Washington, NY: Kennikat, 1964).

Said, Edward W., *Orientalism* (London: Penguin, 1978, repr. 1995).

Shannon, Richard, *The Age of Disraeli, 1868–1881: the Rise of Tory Democracy* (London: Longman, 1992).

Smith, Sheila M., *The Other Nation: The Poor in English Novels of the 1840s and 1850s* (Oxford: Clarendon Press, 1980).

Thackeray, William Makepeace, 'Codlingsby, By B. De Shrewsbury, Esq.', in *Burlesques from Cornhill to Grand Cairo and Juvenilia* (London: Macmillan, 1903), pp. 159–73.

Thompson, F. M. L., *English Landed Society in the Nineteenth Century* (London: Routledge and Kegan Paul, 1963).

Tillotson, Kathleen, *Novels of the Eighteen-Forties* (London: Oxford University Press, 1954, repr. 1961).

Watson, George, *The English Ideology: Studies in the Language of Victorian Politics* (London: Allen Lane, 1973).

Wheeler, Michael, *English Fiction of the Victorian Period 1830–1890* (London: Longman, 1985).

Williams, Raymond, *The English Novel from Dickens to Lawrence* (London: Hogarth, 1984).

____, *Culture and Society* (London: Hogarth, 1987).

Wilson, A. N., *The Victorians* (London: Hutchinson, 2002).

Woodward, Sir Llewellyn, *The Oxford History of England: The Age of Reform, 1815–1870*, 2nd edn (Oxford: Oxford University Press, 1962, repr. 1997).

Index

Index

Disraeli, Benjamin: converts to Christianity, 2, 79; buys shares in South American mining companies, 5–6; debts, 6, 17, 31, 51, 57; first novel written, 5; *An Inquiry . . .* written, 5; *The Representative* founded, 7–8; authorship of *Vivian Grey* discovered, 15; *The Representative* folds, 8; involved in *Star Chamber*, 15–16; illness, 18, 36; lengthy travels abroad, 5, 18, 118, 145; contests High Wycombe, 24, 40, 46; contests Bucks, 40; contests Marylebone, 39, 40; contests Taunton, 47; introduced to Lord Melbourne, 46; challenged to a duel by O'Connell, 28; elected as M.P. for Maidstone, 65; maiden speech, 171, 185; marriage, 51, 54, 187; letter to Peel seeking office, 126; Manchester Free Trade Hall speech, 91; Leader of Young England, 72; gathers material for *Sybil* in North, 102, 145; first 'two nations' speech, 98; attacks Peel, 72–3, 85, 88, 99–100, 137, 138, 139–40, 144; support for Jewish Emancipation, 125, 182; becomes leading opposition figure in Commons, 145; Peel dies, 140; appointed Chancellor, 145; returned to power as Chancellor, 147; role in second Reform Act, 147–8; appointed Prime Minister (1868), 147; Disraeli's government falls, 147; wife dies, 168; attains public popularity, 167–8; Manchester and Crystal Palace speeches, 157–8, 168, 179, 189, 196; survives internal party dissent, 167; refuses Queen's request to form a government, 168; returned to power (1874), 168 ; passage of major social legislation, 168–70; Victoria proclaimed Empress of India, 129, 158; ennobled as Earl of Beaconsfield, 170; Balkan problems, 189; Congress of Berlin meets, 169; economic difficulties, 170; foreign policy difficulties, 170; government falls, 170

Novels: *A Year at Hartlebury*, 40–4, 65, 156, 185; *Alroy*, 2, 4, 17, 31–8, 126, 130; *Aylmer Papillon*, 5; *Coningsby*, 2, 24, 47, 50–1, 67–90, 91, 96, 115, 116, 123, 125, 126, 132, 135, 136, 145–6, 164, 167, 173, 178, 188, 191, 193, 195, 201, 203; *Contarini Fleming*, 4, 5, 25–30, 39,

65, 126, 187; *Endymion*, 1, 2, 3, 58, 70, 171–88, 191, 195, 197; *Falconet*, 3, 188–91, 195; *Henrietta Temple*, 19, 49–58, 62, 64, 176; *Lothair*, 2, 21, 33, 148–67, 173, 187, 189, 191, 195, 197; *Sybil*, 2, 32–3, 37–8, 43, 47, 50–1, 53, 54, 61, 67, 68, 70, 71, 73, 76, 84, 87, 90–118, 123, 124, 126, 132, 135, 136, 146, 158, 164, 167, 173, 178, 179, 188, 189, 191, 193, 194, 195, 198, 199, 208n; *Tancred*, 2, 18, 33, 67, 68, 97, 98, 117, 118, 118–136, 146, 148, 152–3, 156, 161, 163, 165, 166, 191, 193–4, 198; *The Young Duke*, 2, 17–23, 55, 65, 109, 117, 145–6, 151, 167, 193, 195; *Venetia*, 2, 19, 58–64, 66, 167, 190; *Vivian Grey*, 1, 2, 4, 7, 8–16, 27–8, 55, 65, 84, 126, 132, 145, 189, 193, 195, 196, 197, 203

Other Works: 'A True Story', 4; *A Vindication . . .* , 24, 47–9, 196; *An Inquiry . . .* , 5–7; 'England and France', 23, 100; 'Ixion in Heaven', 23–4, 75; *Lawyers and Legislators . . .* , 7; *Lord George Bentinck*, 3, 34, 137–45, 165, 176; *Revolutionary Epick*, 41, 45–6, 192; *Rumpel Stiltskin*, 5; 'The Carrier Pigeon', 49; 'The Consul's Daughter', 49; *The Crisis Examined, by Disraeli the Younger*, 47; *The Dunciad of Today*, 16; 'The Infernal Marriage', 24; 'The Mutilated Diary', 1, 4, 27, 32, 38, 41, 63, 65, 164; *The Present State of Mexico*, 7; 'The Rise of Iskander', 38–9; *The Tragedy of Count Alarcos*, 64–5; *The Voyage of Captain Popanilla*, 5, 16–17, 193; 'Walstein, or, A Cure for Melancholy', 40; *What is He?* 39–40, 196

Pseudonyms: Cherry and Fair Star, 40–1; Mivartinos,17

His views on: Aristocracy, 3, 18, 19, 23, 46, 48, 52–3, 56, 58, 62, 65, 78, 85, 100, 118, 120, 138, 140, 141, 167, 184, 192; Byron, 11, 24; Catholicism, 2, 21, 23, 26–7, 49, 55, 59, 77, 102, 112, 123, 149–50, 151–3, 155, 157, 160–2, 166, 182, 186–7; Chartism, 43, 68–9, 81, 106–7, 110–12, 113; Church of England, 121–2, 167; Commercialism, 14, 15, 17, 41, 44, 65, 66; Conservatism, 39, 47, 72–3, 80, 85, 88, 109, 138, 138–9, 158,